PRAISE FOR
WINNING THE MERGER ENDGAME

The strategies behind industry consolidation and corporate growth are easy to understand in principle, but difficult to achieve in practice. This book offers valuable insights into strategic decision making on portfolio selections and value creation, and provides the means to look across different industries with a common yardstick.

> —Dr. Santhan V. Krishnan,
> Vice President of Innovation and
> Chief Scientific Officer, Johnson Diversey Inc.

Endgames is a breakthrough new concept that centers top executives and shareholders on the final strategic battlefield: Industry consolidation. Companies of all industries will benefit from this ultimate new insight.

> —Dr. A. Stefan Kirsten,
> Chief Financial Officer, Metro AG

A fascinating study! It will change our understanding of strategic behavior in an era of innovation and globalization. The analytical discussion is crisp and the data analysis is highly illuminating. This book is must reading for anyone interested in understanding how the future will look like. I predict that the "Endgames Curve" will quickly become one of managers' favorite strategic tools.

> —Sebastian Edwards
> Henry Ford II Professor of International Management
> Anderson Graduate School of Management, UCLA

What's powerful about the Endgames model is that it synthesizes a very complex set of relationships in the life cycle of an industry into a diagram that's easy to understand, flexible in its application, and useful for planning. This conceptual tool provides a unifying principle on which growth strategies can be based.

> —Dr. Andrew Brod
> Director of Business and Economic Research
> Bryan School of Business and Economics,
> The University of North Carolina at Greensboro

Winning the Merger Endgame

A Playbook for Profiting from Industry Consolidation

Graeme K. Deans
Fritz Kroeger
Stefan Zeisel

McGraw-Hill

New York Chicago San Francisco Lisbon London
Madrid Mexico City Milan New Delhi San Juan
Seoul Singapore Sydney Toronto

658.16
D28w

The **McGraw·Hill** Companies

1 2 3 4 5 6 7 8 9 0 AGM/AGM 0 9 8 7 6 5 4 3 2

ISBN 0-07-140998-X

Editorial and production services provided by CWL Publishing Enterprises, Inc., Madison, WI , www.cwlpub.com.

This publication is designed to provide accurate and authoritative information in regard to the subject matter covered. It is sold with the understanding that neither the author nor the publisher is engaged in rendering legal, accounting, or other professional service. If legal advice or other expert assistance is required, the services of a competent professional person should be sought.

JK

—From a Declaration of Principles jointly adopted by a Committee of the American Bar Association and a Committee of Publishers

McGraw-Hill books are available at special quantity discounts to use as premiums and sales promotions, or for use in corporate training programs. For more information, please write to the Director of Special Sales, McGraw-Hill, 2 Penn Plaza, New York, NY 10121. Or contact your local bookstore.

 This book is printed on recycled, acid-free paper containing a minimum of 50% recycled de-inked fiber.

To my three ladies: Almuth, Carolin, and Isabel

■ ■ ■

For my wife, Julia, and my children, Benjamin and
Penelope, with all my love

Contents

Part One. Introduction

Part Two. The Four Stages of the Endgame

companies establish market dominance.

|Foreword

Viewed up close, business—like war, football, or childhood—is chaos. But step back a bit and patterns emerge across space and time. Identifying those patterns, sorting the significant from the random, is an excruciating process of number-crunching, experience, and intuition. The task is especially difficult in a global economy, with tens of thousands of large companies employing hundreds of millions of workers and serving billions of customers over decades.

But in the book you now hold in your hands, the three authors—veteran executives with global experience with A.T. Kearney, the management consulting subsidiary of EDS—have done the trick. Yes, they draw order from chaos, but they also provide practical, profitable advice for managers and shareholders. And they are bracingly confident—with good reason—about their conclusions and projections.

What Graeme Deans, Fritz Kroeger, and Stefan Zeisel have written is nothing less than a natural history of mergers and acquisitions. They explore not merely why such consolidations happen and succeed (or, more often, fail)—with copious real-life examples from around the world—but, more important, they show *how* they happen, their life

cycles, their anatomy. In the course of this surprising and powerful
analysis, the authors debunk myths, show CEOs the best times to
merge and the best partners to seek, and direct private-equity investors
and conventional shareholders to the most lucrative companies and
sectors.

As a journalist constantly battling the constraints of expensive
newsprint, I'm impressed with authors who don't hem and haw but get
straight to the point:

- "There is no optimal or maximum company size. To survive,
  companies must continuously grow. Period."
- "Mergers are inevitable if a company is to outgrow the competition."
- "There are no protectable niche markets.... Niche players will
  be consolidated."
- "The auto industry will see the emergence of more significant
  global players, such as Volkswagen, GM, and Ford."
- "Banking will continue to consolidate in North America and
  Europe, and then across the globe."
- "There will be a one-trillion-dollar merger creating a de facto
  global industry monopoly within the next five years. About that
  we are sure."

The thesis here is that mergers determine profitability, market
share, and stock prices. Mergers aren't a sideshow. They are the main
event—or, as the authors put it, "the Endgame."

I'll admit I was drawn to *Winning the Merger Endgame* at first
because it has a perspective on the stock market that is similar to my
own. The authors' predictive model looks 20 years into the future. It
projects increased merger activity, and abundant mergers are directly
correlated—they find—with a rising stock market. The market capitalization for all listed stocks tripled between 1980 and 1990, and
tripled again between 1990 and 2000. Deans, Kroeger, and Zeisel figure that it will triple once more by 2010.

I was also dazzled by their contrarian conclusions. Everything I
thought I knew about mergers turned out to be wrong. The authors'

research—based on an in-depth analysis of 1,345 large mergers by 945 acquiring companies from a database of more than 25,000 global firms—determined that more mergers destroy value than create it; that merger activity, nonetheless, is logical rather than emotional or ego-driven; that an internal growth strategy is not superior to a merger strategy (in fact, many of the best companies use both); and that every industry is driven by the same forces of consolidation and deconsolidation—of merging and un-merging.

In fact, this powerful generalization is the core of *Winning the Merger Endgame*. The book presents an elegantly simple theory—that all industries consolidate in a similar way all over the world. And they state flatly that "merger actions and consolidation trends can be predicted with some certainty." This process, which the authors call the Endgames curve, has four distinct stages stretched over an average of about 25 years (though it's now speeding up).

1. *Every* industry starts at Stage 1. The authors call the stage a "Wild West" for commerce. The activity begins with start-ups in completely new sectors like biotechnology or online retailing, in spin-offs that follow the complete consolidation of industries, or in sectors that have just been deregulated or privatized, like energy, water, railroads, and telecommunications and, in many countries, banking and insurance. During this stage, businesses try to build up barriers to entry like patents, they move quickly to boost revenues and expand market share, and they begin—just begin—to consolidate.

2. In the second stage, firms within a sector move to scale. The best and brightest CEOs start buying up competitors, staking out the choicest claims. Deans, Kroeger, and Zeisel describe how Hugh McColl took a small North Carolina bank, NCNB, and, through mergers, built the fourth-largest bank in the nation. (Unfortunately, McColl ran into trouble in Stage 3.) By the end of Stage 2, concentration rates (that is, the market share of the top three companies) rise to 45% in some sectors. While there are stock-market winners in every Endgames stage, the sweet spot for private-equity investors falls in Stage 1 and the beginning of

Stage 2, with an exit early in Stage 3, when acquisition premiums are high.

3. The third stage involves sharpening focus. After aggressive consolidation, successful companies find their most productive role in a sector and shuck off non-essential or secondary business units—then move to build even more market share. In this stage and the next, about two-thirds of total growth has to come from acquisitions. Firms can't do it organically any more and, as in Stage 2, mergers of near-equals occur (Morgan Stanley and Dean Witter in Stage 2; Exxon and Mobil in Stage 3).

4. In the final stage, industries boost their concentration rates as high as 90% and gain equilibrium. Here, as the authors put it, "titans of industry reign" in sectors like tobacco, aluminum, and soft drinks. Profits, however, can be hard to come by, and Stage 4 companies often adopt the strategy of spinning off growth businesses from their core, in an attempt to start new sectors or subsectors. The authors cite PepsiCo, which, "faced with the prospects of low growth in their core (Stage 4) soft-drink business...identified two new spin-off industries": sports drinks (Gatorade, which was purchased from Quaker Oats) and bottled water (where they grew their own).

It's refreshing to read a book that develops and confidently extends a convincing, self-contained thesis—one that's not contaminated by speculation on terrorism or tech bubbles or accounting scandals. The authors predict that the Dow will "grow fourfold by 2010." My own projection is a tad more modest—Dow 36,000. But I would love to be wrong on the low side.

—James K. Glassman

James K. Glassman is the financial columnist of The Washington Post and the International Herald Tribune. A resident fellow at the American Enterprise Institute in Washington, he is co-author of Dow 36,000 (1999) and author of The Secret Code of the Superior Investor (2002).

|Preface

In January 2001, Fritz Kroeger unveiled the Endgames curve at a meeting of A.T. Kearney's global strategy consulting practice. The room fell silent while these senior consultants absorbed the power and implications of Fritz's analysis. After a few minutes, the group exploded into a volley of questions and ideas that lasted for a couple of hours.

At that moment, we began to realize the importance of this discovery. We spent the next 12 months refining the analysis and speaking with clients and academics about it, and now we are pleased to share the results more broadly in the form of this book. We believe our research and the implications of merger endgames are so compelling that the story should be broadcast to the largest possible audience.

Our thinking is based on a massive database that covers the globe and represents 98% of corporate market capitalization over the last 13 years. We combine this data with selected cases representing a wide range of industries from the global arena. (For those who might wish to review even more data, you will find a database of 12 years of the largest M&A deals in the Appendix.)

A few words about content and definitions. We use the word "mergers" throughout the book as synonymous with mergers and acquisitions—recognizing that there are very few true mergers. In almost all cases, one entity consumes another. In fact, one of the incidental lessons of this book is that there's no such thing as a merger.

And of course, a few words from our attorneys, who want to be sure we tell you that this book is not intended as professional advice with respect to any particular investment situation. Readers who feel they need professional advice with respect to any particular investment should consult the appropriate professional advisers. We also note that the views expressed here represent the views of the authors and not those of our employer, A.T. Kearney, or its parent company, EDS.

ACKNOWLEDGMENTS

Throughout this project, the authors have benefited from the wisdom and expertise of many other people. We are most grateful to our colleagues and experts on M&A and merger integration at A.T. Kearney—especially Art Bert, Joseph Crepaldi, Andrew Green, Tom Herd, Tim MacDonald, Jim McDonnell, and Rajesh Shah.

Our research team kept us up to date on the constantly changing world of M&A deals and other arcane corporate data. We had the benefit of excellent input from Micah Chamberlain, Dirk Pfannenschmidt, Nancy Shepherd, and Marc Tiemeyer, who spent countless hours on fact finding and fact checking.

The A.T. Kearney marketing and editorial team contributed huge amounts of time and expertise to this project. We thank Lee Anne Petry, who spent yeoman days and nights (and weekends) polishing our prose to perfection and adding much-needed creative touches. We also thank the editorial team of Tony Vlamis, Bethany Crawford, and Paul Solans for ensuring that our manuscript met the editorial standards of A.T. Kearney as well as of our publisher. Nancy S. Bishop, our project manager, kept us organized, tended to strategic details, and made sure we were aware of the calendar. Finally, we thank Mary Glenn, senior editor at McGraw-Hill, for her patience and diligence in shepherding this book to print.

Chapter One | The Consolidation Landscape

The history of the world, my sweet, is who gets eaten and who gets to eat.

—Sweeney Todd to Mrs. Lovett,
from *Sweeney Todd: The Demon Barber of Fleet Street.* Book by Hugh Wheeler; music and lyrics by Stephen Sondheim, 1979.

After watching and participating in the growth of mergers, acquisitions, and divestitures across the globe for years, one thing is certain: the pace of corporate combinations may ebb (as it did in 2001) or flow (as it did throughout the 1990s), but consolidation is unstoppable. Its progress is continuous and inevitable. And its impact on individual industries is profound.

As one industry slows down, another wave of consolidations is touched off in a different sector. In turn, this triggers still another industry into restructuring mode to increase shareholder value. Over time, we see that these trends are not local, regional, or even national. The merger and consolidation "Endgame" has moved to the ultimate level of play: the global arena.

Our findings about Endgames can be summarized in five maxims, around which we weave the story of this book, which we discuss in

1

greater detail later in this chapter:

1. All industries consolidate and follow a similar course.
2. Merger actions and consolidation trends can be predicted.
3. The Endgames curve can be used as a tool to strengthen consolidation strategies and facilitate merger integration.
4. Every major strategic and operational move should be evaluated with regard to its Endgames impact.
5. Endgames positioning offers a guide for portfolio optimization.

Thus, despite the plethora of books published on various stages of mergers and acquisitions, we believe this book is different—and particularly important for three groups of readers:

- CEOs of companies in any industry
- Senior executives and directors of companies whose business strategies include acquisitions or divestitures
- Private equity investors who profit by consolidating or "rolling up" businesses

We might also offer a roadmap for reading our book. Chapters 1, 2, and 9 will provide good background for all readers. CEOs who want a good overall view of the implications of an Endgames strategy should also read Chapters 7 and 8. Corporate strategists and other senior executives should pay particular attention to the details in Chapters 3 though 6. CFOs will be most interested in Chapter 8 and will find valuable information in Chapters 3 through 6.

In this introductory chapter, we briefly describe our research, introduce the Endgames curve and its four stages, and expand upon the five maxims. Finally, we discuss the broader implications of Endgames for all prospective readers.

Endgames Research

Our long-term research on mergers and industry consolidation has verified many of our hypotheses and persuaded us to abandon others. In particular, the similarities across industries, and common traits and links among them, exhibit a pattern that enables us to explain and predict changes across industries. This pattern and the predictive lessons that emerge from it are the foundation for the Merger Endgames Theory.

To carry out the Endgames analysis, we drew from two databases. The first database contains information from the Securities Data Corporation (Thomson Financial's SDC Platinum Worldwide M&A), which tracked more than 135,000 mergers and acquisitions from 1990 to 1999. From this, we selected only those with a transaction value greater than US$500 million. Less than that would not be significant in a global context. In addition, we looked only at publicly traded companies that are quoted on a national exchange and examined only transactions in which the acquirer held at least a 51% interest at the close of the deal. We focused on 1,345 mergers and acquisitions by 945 acquiring companies.

With the screening complete, we broadened the scope of the analysis by comparing the Endgames data with information gathered from our second database, A.T. Kearney's proprietary Value-Building Growth database. This originated in 1988 with a survey of value growers—those companies that know how to maintain a specific balance between growth and profit to bring added shareholder value in the long run. Today, this constantly updated database includes analysis on more than 25,000 firms globally and represents 98% of world market capitalization, making it possible to analyze the buildup of industry concentration over time. Given the scope and depth of these parameters, this is the first time this type of data on the global industrial economy is available in a single body of work. Although the time period covered by both databases coincides with the stock market boom, we believe that the conclusions derived and explained in this book will apply universally, regardless of future market cycles.

One of the most popular metrics used to measure concentration is the so-called CR3, which is defined as the market share of the three largest players within an industry. We also calculated the Hirschman-Herfindahl Index, which is a measure of industry concentration using the sum of the squares of the market shares of all firms in an industry. Importantly, this index also brings the influence of smaller companies into the fold. In measuring the concentration rate in two ways, we found a 90% correlation rate between the two measures.

The Endgames Curve and Its Characteristics

The direction companies take on the Endgames curve is not uniform or linear. Some industries advance along the curve, while others may fall back, particularly at a later stage when industry concentration increases. When we plotted the major industries using two pieces of information—degree and speed of concentration—and put the results into a matrix, a pattern began to emerge that builds into an Endgames curve that spans roughly 25 years for any industry.

As industries move up the Endgames curve, market concentration of the top-tier players—measured by both the Hirschman-Herfindahl Index and the CR3—increases toward a theoretical maximum of 100%. The standard deviation of this speed is plus or minus five years. This means that from today's perspective, it takes less than 25 years for an industry to commence, deconsolidate, consolidate, and balance out. When correlated with the merger activities over the past 10 years, a strong correlation emerges for all industries between merger activity and the position on the Endgames curve. The industries on the low part of the Endgames curve have a higher level of merger activity, and those on the high end have a lower level of activity.

THE FIVE MAXIMS OF THE ENDGAMES CURVE

1. All industries consolidate and follow a similar course. Much like stepping onto an escalator, once an industry is formed it begins to ride up the Endgames curve and doesn't stop until it reaches the end.

Today it takes an industry roughly 20 to 25 years

> Merger competence becomes the core competence of winners.

to run through the consolidation process from the Opening Stage through the Scale and Focus Stages to the final Balance and Alliance Stage. Industries are transformed during consolidation; thus the pattern inevitably forms an S curve that divides into four stages.

Each stage implies specific strategic and operational imperatives (see sidebar: "Stages of the Endgame"). Knowing and following these imperatives will bring new benefits and position the firm to follow the Endgame for its industry. (Beware: Ignoring these imperatives can destroy the firm.)

Our findings about industry consolidation made us abandon some of our former assumptions about corporate strategy. For example, we believe:

- There is no optimal or maximum company size. To survive, companies must continuously grow.
- Organic growth is not the route to successful growth. Mergers are inevitable if a company is to outgrow the competition.
- There are no protectable niche markets. As all industries are, or become, global, niche players will be consolidated during the Focus Stage (Stage 3) and the Balance and Alliance Stage (Stage 4).

2. Merger actions and consolidation trends can be predicted. Our Endgames research enables prediction of upcoming consolidations and even future mergers and industry departures. In the long run, we predict that industry consolidations will correlate nearly 80% with the rise in global stock indices—which we predict will run at about 300% over the next 10 years. So the coming wave of mergers will continue to have a strong impact on global stock prices (*see Chapter 8, The Stock Market Connection*).

Examples affecting specific industries:

- The auto industry will see the dominance of more significant global players, such as Volkswagen, GM, Ford, or Daimler-Chrysler.
- Banking will continue to consolidate in North America and Europe, and then across the globe. It's not clear now where the eye of this merger hurricane will be. Will Deutsche Bank or Citigroup, for example, gain a leading global role? Which Japanese bank will survive as a leader?

3. The Endgames curve can be used as a tool to strengthen consolidation strategies and facilitate merger integration. As we mentioned, each Endgames stage implies specific strategic and operational imperatives. Being able to analyze the position of an industry on the Endgames S curve can help a company and its leadership develop a strategic viewpoint and a core competence in managing mergers.

STAGES OF THE ENDGAME

- **Opening Stage:** There is little or no market concentration and the first consolidators may appear. Newly deregulated, start-up, and spin-off subindustries occupy this space.
- **Scale Stage:** Size begins to matter. Major players begin to emerge and take the lead in consolidation. Concentration rates can be as high as 45% in some industries.
- **Focus Stage:** Successful players extend their core businesses, exchange or eliminate secondary units, and continue to aggressively outgrow the competition.
- **Balance and Alliance Stage:** A few players will dominate industries, with consolidation rates as high as 90%. Titans of industry reign, from tobacco to automotive companies and engine producers. Large companies may form alliances with other giants because growth at this stage is more challenging.

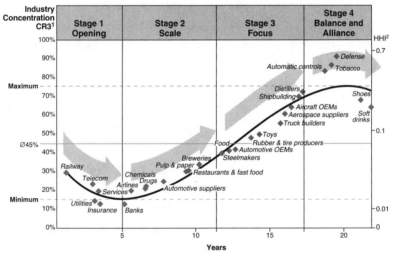

[1]CR3 = Market share of the three largest companies of the total market based on Value-Building Growth database (25,000 companies).
[2]HHI = Hirschman-Herfindahl Index corresponds to the sum of the squared market shares of all companies and is greater than 90%; the axis logarithmically plotted.
Sources: Value-Building Growth database; A.T. Kearney analysis

Figure 1-1. The merger Endgames S-curve

Learning how to successfully integrate an acquisition or merger partner is fast becoming a core competence of winners. Over the years, we have seen an improvement in merger success. Our original research, completed in 1999, showed that near-ly 60% of all mergers or acquisitions failed to increase shareholder value. Today that failure statistic has been reduced significantly—but still stands near 50%.

> *Much like stepping on an escalator, once an industry is formed it begins to ride up the Endgames curve and doesn't stop until it reaches the end.*

In addition, we analyzed the impact of the Endgames stages on merger success and found a remarkable correlation. Figure 1-2 shows the pattern of merger success.

In the past, large companies bought smaller ones, national companies bought in their home countries, and mergers were completed to build the core business. These are not the foolproof recipes for stardom they once were. Today, the strongest correlation is between the Endgames stage and merger success.

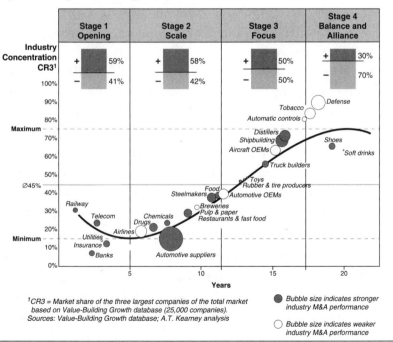

Figure 1-2. Merger and acquisition performance by industry

4. Every major strategic and operational move should be evaluated with regard to its Endgames impact. The value of a merger or acquisition will be found in the increased competitiveness of the combined entity, the resulting increase in shareholder value, and the move up the Endgames curve. The value of a merger should not be measured by the size of investment bankers' fees or CEO reward fees. In fact, shareholders should be suspicious of acquisitions that enrich the CEO with multi-million dollar bonuses.

> *The value of a merger or acquisition will be found in the increased competitiveness of the combined entity, the resulting increase in shareholder value, and the move up the Endgames curve.*

And strategic moves supporting a growth strategy, such as entering into operational alliances or financial partnerships or expanding into new global markets, should be measured with the same gauge. How do they affect the company's competitiveness and its Endgames position?

The case of the 150-year-old German construction company, Philipp Holzmann, is instructive. Through the 1970s and 1980s, Holzmann went on a worldwide expansion spree, acquiring local companies in many countries. Minus a strong underlying strategy, the company never progressed beyond Stage 2.

In the late 1990s, with Holzmann approaching insolvency, Chancellor Gerhard Schroeder came to the rescue. He offered Holzmann's creditor banks 250 million marks (US$130 million) of state money and persuaded banks to put up more than 200 million marks in additional funds to save the company. Later, the company's major bank shareholder sold off large portions of Holzmann stock to competitors.

Insolvent again, Holzmann filed for bankruptcy in 2002. The seemingly herculean effort to save this grand old company was futile because the Endgames impact of its restructuring was not taken into account.

5. Endgames positioning offers a guide for portfolio optimization. Companies should strive to optimize their aggregate portfolio of subsidiaries and business units across the different Endgames stages. It is important for the senior management team and Board of Directors of each company to continuously assess their portfolio of industries and subindustries to ensure that they are positioned for future growth along the Endgames curve.

This concept is being played out today in the global health care products industry. The industry as a whole is in transition from Stage 2 to Stage 3, with the industry experiencing heavy consolidation and difficult challenges to growth. Bristol-Myers Squibb and Schering-Plough, as typical examples, have both positioned their Endgames portfolio of businesses toward the pharmaceutical subindustry and the over-the-counter (OTC) and consumer products subindustry; both are also in the transition from Stage 2 to Stage 3. In so doing, each company is experiencing the brunt of this difficult transition—slow growth, difficulty with patent expirations, plummeting share prices, margin pressures from larger competitors, and the constant threat of being an acquisition target.

> *Companies should strive to optimize their aggregate portfolio of subsidiaries and business units across the different Endgames stages.*

By comparison, Johnson & Johnson has actively managed its portfolio of businesses and continues to have excellent growth prospects and a stable share price, despite the challenges facing its core pharmaceutical business. In addition to the pharmaceutical, OTC, and consumer products businesses, J&J has aggressively diversified its portfolio by acquiring and growing businesses in the medical equipment industry (Stage 2) and the biotechnology industry (Stage 1), to position its overall portfolio of businesses at a much earlier point in the Endgames curve. This offers J&J significant growth opportunities when its core business turns down, and offers a compelling and attractive story to its investors.

BEYOND CONSOLIDATION: IMPLICATIONS OF THE ENDGAMES CURVE

In brief, the Endgames curve also leads to the following broader implications, which we explore throughout this book.

A merger or acquisition should create a new entity that reaches a new position in the Endgames for its industry. The marriage of two lame ducks will not give birth to a racehorse. The position of the two players on our value-building growth matrix enables an acquirer to analyze the merits of a potential combination.

A case in point is the 1998 merger of Compaq and Digital Equipment. While company executives still say the combination has been a success, industry experts rate it a failure. Compaq lost its leadership in the PC market to Dell; the change left customers in confusion about the future of products they were using. Compaq's value plummeted 52% and earnings dropped from US$1.27 per share to 27 cents in the past three years, prior to the completion of its merger with Hewlett-Packard.

Analysts point out that very few mergers between major IT companies have resulted in increased shareholder value and improved customer relationships. The list of failures includes combinations such as Univac and RCA, Sperry Univac and Burroughs, Silicon Graphics and Cray, AT&T and NCR, Siemens and Nixdorf, Compaq and Tandem, and Fujitsu and Amdahl.

The value-building growth matrix, a concept pioneered in the book *The Value Growers*, is a good starting point for assessing which companies in an industry might be the best acquisition candidates to form a winning Endgames strategy (see Figure 1-3).[1] Acquiring a competitor in the "Underperformer" segment means that you are in for a turnaround, because the acquisition target has both revenue growth and value growth at less than the industry average rate. This type of acquisition usually brings much higher risks—unless the targeted company can instill a high growth culture and contain the downside risks. "Simple Growers" and "Profit Seekers" are more reasonable acquisition targets, because they already have a basis for growth, can often be acquired for a reasonable price, and won't consume inordinate amounts of management attention. Finally, "Value Growers" are often the best targets strategically—but they will be much more expensive buys.

Private equity investors—who profit by consolidating or rolling up smaller businesses—should acquire companies at the lower part of the curve and sell them at the beginning of the Focus Stage. Private equity investors can use the Endgames curve to help identify good—and shaky—investment decisions. In addition, the logic of the Endgames curve can be used to analyze and evaluate the positions of cities,

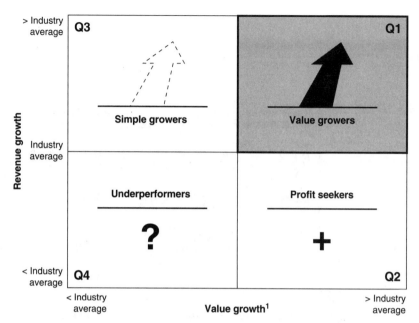

Figure 1-3. The A.T. Kearney growth matrix

regions, and countries with regard to growth and competitiveness. Plotting companies in a metropolitan area or national economy against the Endgames curve, for example, will reveal whether the economy is strong in young industries and can project strong future growth—or whether its strength is in old industries and thus its only recourse is to preserve the past.

But that's a long story and part of our Endgames vision for 2010, the concluding chapter. Let's start at the beginning: with the Rules and Logic of the Endgame.

Note

1. James McGrath, Fritz Kroeger, Michael Traem, and Joerg Rockenhaeuser, *The Value Growers* (New York: McGraw-Hill, 2001).

Chapter Two | Finding Order in Chaos: Rules and Logic of the Endgame

Nature itself, even in chaos, cannot proceed except in an orderly and regular manner.

—Immanuel Kant

Few elements of business are as chaotic—and seemingly unpredictable—as mergers and acquisitions. With thousands taking place every year in most geographic spheres, who can determine where the next merger headline will come from? What industry is on the verge of consolidation, or deconsolidation? What companies are in strong positions to target, or be targeted?

As we discussed in Chapter 1, our analysis has, in fact, uncovered the pattern behind the chaos. There is a clear and logical order to the process of industry consolidation. But discovering this pattern—the Endgames S curve—is only the beginning. The more important discovery is that the pattern, once exposed, can be used as a predictive tool. In other words, lacking a crystal ball, the Endgames curve serves as the next best thing.

In Chapter 1, we presented the five maxims; now it's time for the five fundamental truths. The difference? The maxims addressed the overarching implications of the Endgames curve, while the truths set the foundation for the in-depth discussion of the individual stages that follows in the next section. Knowing and understanding the implications of these truths is the first step in predicting the winners in tomorrow's Endgame—and using it to your competitive advantage.

1. Consolidation is inevitable, unavoidable, and inescapable. In analyzing the consolidation strategies of 25,000 companies across industries, it became clear that—without exception—the Endgames curve accounted for all movement. Whether they advanced or fell back on the curve, all industries moved between and among the different stages of our model. In other words, their actions were

> Lacking a crystal ball, the Endgames curve serves as the next-best thing.

not random, but followed the clear, predictable pattern of the Endgames curve.

The model also reveals other important characteristics of consolidation. For example, the curve shows how an industry's corporate population (the number of companies in an industry) expands and contracts as it moves through the four stages. In Stage 1, an industry will experience considerable deconsolidation due to market deregulation or high fragmentation in a start-up industry. The result is that by the end of the stage, the population quickly reaches its maximum capacity. In Stage 2, however, as consolidation begins to play out, the industry population contracts nearly 70%. In the final two stages, the number of companies is reduced by more than half again, only to experience a slight increase at the end of Stage 4, as companies that reposition their business portfolios cannot maintain their position against new market entries and sell or trade off units (see Figure 2-1).

Not only do we know how many companies there will be, we also know how long those companies will last. In fact, industry consolidation can be predicted annually. The overall time frame for an industry to move through the four stages currently stands at about 20 to 25 years, but this is subject to change. Consider that the old smokestack industries in the earlier days of industrialization took roughly 40 to 60 years to run a cycle of consolidation. Back then, it would be almost impossible to manage companies the size we have today. The commerce and information technology platforms simply didn't exist; neither did the

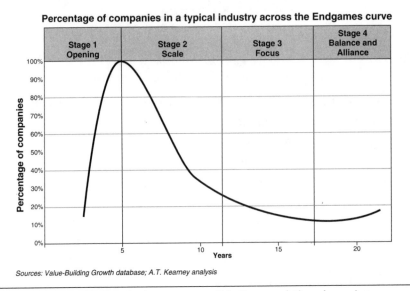

Percentage of companies in a typical industry across the Endgames curve

Sources: Value-Building Growth database; A.T. Kearney analysis

Figure 2-1. Predicting industry consolidation and the changing corporate population

telecommunications, nor did they have the financial resources to fund such capital-intensive investments.

Thus, the Endgames cycle that we see at work now is a more recent development—reaching back to the late 1980s and the start of the current merger and acquisition boom. Since that time, the number of mergers has been growing at a compound rate of nearly 21% per year, and the shift toward the "super deals" continues to grow. The trend is clear: as the speed of business continues to increase, so too will the pace of consolidation. In fact, we believe that eventually a full consolidation life cycle could run its course in just 10 to 15 years.

Even in these times of corporate scandal and falling stock prices, the Endgames dynamics are still at work: WorldCom's bankruptcy may induce an asset sale that will implicitly encourage further consolidation and Enron's demise might prod similar consolidation in the energy industry. The headline stories, whatever they may be, do not challenge the immutable long-term trends of the Endgames theory.

Knowing this, we can create long-term forecasts of merger movements and, more specifically, we should be able to predict which target companies might be part of the forecast. Eventually, calculations could be performed around what other companies are likely to be involved in and in what time frame.

2. All industries are global. The days of regional differentiation are over. All industries—small or large, local or global—begin on the same footing and are treated equally by the rules of Endgame consolidation. Old strategies that professed, "small is beautiful" or offered lessons on how companies could "survive in a niche" are no longer viable in the context of the universal Endgames curve.

Yes, it's true that there are still microcosms that thrive at the small business level, and there is a new generation of savvy entrepreneurs who develop and will continue to fuel healthy businesses in the shadow of corporate juggernauts well into the future. However, even these organizations are held to the rules of the Endgames. And one of the most important rules they will eventually face is key to their survival: acquire or be acquired. In other words, the only optimal size is bigger—bigger than last year, big-

> *The only optimal size is bigger—bigger than last year, bigger than the competitors, with a strategy to get even bigger tomorrow.*

ger than the competitors, with a strategy to get even bigger tomorrow. Stagnation or a slow-moving consolidation plan will prove disastrous.

Furthermore, as trade barriers continue to fall and the World Trade Organization becomes stronger and extends its influence into a growing number of countries, the trend toward total industry globalization will only accelerate. More and more, companies are expanding their global presence, but to consumers, this incursion remains transparent (see sidebar: "Ahold's Global Presence").

Globalization is a strong force that enables industry consolidation. During the Asian economic crisis in 1997 and 1998, global organizations such as the International Monetary Fund (IMF), the World Bank, and the World Trade Organization assisted and encouraged countries including Thailand, South Korea, and Indonesia to restructure their financial institutions and open up their economies by reducing trade barriers. A direct result of these restructuring policies was that global financial services companies began to acquire and buy equity stakes in the financial services players in each of these economies. From 1998 to 2000, Thailand experienced a wave of acquisition activity:

AHOLD'S GLOBAL PRESENCE

The decades-old mantra of "go global" sometimes belies how geographically unrestricted the marketplace already is. And, as Royal Ahold, the Netherlands-based food retail and foodservice company, demonstrates, even the local store isn't as local as it may appear. With operations in the United States, Europe, Latin America, and Asia, the company marked more than US$66 billion in consolidated sales in 2001. Its U.S. subsidiary, Ahold, generates roughly 60% of its worldwide sales.

Starting with its first acquisition (BI-LO) in 1971, it now owns and operates six regional supermarket companies under the brand names of Stop & Shop, Giant (Landover), Giant (Carlisle), Tops, BI-LO, and Bruno's. In 2001, Ahold's combined 1,600 stores generated consolidated retail sales of approximately US$23 billion.

In addition, Ahold owns and operates five U.S. foodservice companies with annual sales of approximately US$19 billion. The foodservice operations provide Ahold with a rapidly growing national presence in the still fragmented out-of-home markets. And Ahold has leading positions in various specialized foodservice fields, including healthcare, hospitality, restaurant, company cafeterias, and government. Ahold's success lies partly in its ability to build close cooperative relationships among units while maintaining local brand identity and culture. For example, two years ago Ahold purchased the once-struggling online grocer Peapod, giving it a strong foothold in both Internet commerce and the local markets that Peapod serves. Yet few consumers in these markets have ever heard of Ahold or are aware of its ownership when they click on Peapod's Web site.

- GE Capital bought auto finance firm GS Capital and credit card issuer Central Card in Thailand.
- The Development Bank of Singapore purchased the Thai Danu Bank.
- ABN-Amro acquired Bank of Asia, Thailand's 10th largest bank.

Similar acquisition patterns unfolded in South Korea and across the rest of Asia in the wake of the Asian crisis.

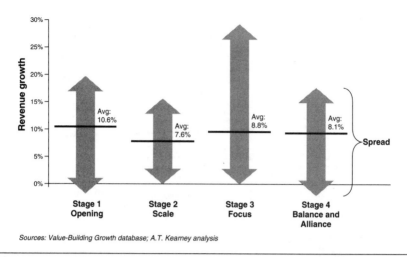

Sources: Value-Building Growth database; A.T. Kearney analysis

Figure 2-2. Stable revenue growth across the Endgames stages

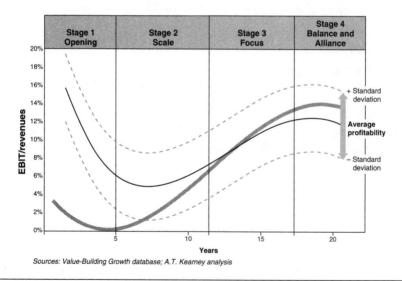

Sources: Value-Building Growth database; A.T. Kearney analysis

Figure 2-3. Profitability and the Endgames curve

3. Revenue is stable, but profitability changes according to the Endgames curve position. As Figure 2-2 illustrates, revenue growth over the Endgames curve is relatively stable. In the Opening Stage, as companies make their territorial claims, revenue growth averages 10.6%, falls to 7.6% in the Scale Stage as companies consolidate, and then stabilizes at 8.8% and 8.1% in the final two stages.

Corporate profits, however, follow the Endgames curve, albeit with a slight time lag (see Figure 2-3). In the Opening Stage, profitability is high as new industries grow quickly. For example, companies in the biotech and nanotechnology industries are currently enjoying an open field of players and solid profits. But the news isn't all good. The exception to high profitability in Stage 1 is with companies in older state-run industries that have been recently privatized, such as railroads. Often, these companies use monopolistic prices to fund fat organizational structures that suffer from built-in redundancy.

As companies move through the Scale Stage, profitability decreases dramatically. In fact, it drops to its lowest point of the curve, because consolidation reaches maximum speed. The reason? Many companies respond to the increased competition with severe cost-cutting measures, but there is an embedded danger in this approach: It often drives companies into a profitability trap that does not allow for future growth. Eventually key employees begin leaving and the organization adopts a conservative, risk-averse, profit-first culture.

In the last two stages—Focus, and Balance and Alliance—an oligopolistic competitive model emerges and allows the surviving players to set prices for healthy profits. Companies reach their highest margin of profitability in the Balance and Alliance Stage, simply because these market titans have eliminated many of their competitors. Yet they must keep in mind that resting on their laurels, no matter how expertly won, can lead to corporate inertia that will attract new, more cost-efficient and innovative competitors.

The bottom line? CEOs must move their companies as quickly as possible through Stage 2, both to improve profit margins and to gain a favorable final Endgames position.

4. Long-term success depends on riding up the Endgames curve. As the previous point touched on, speed is everything: Companies that move up the Endgames curve the fastest are the most successful. They capture critical ground early on and are destined to be first in the consolidation race. Slower companies eventually become acquisition targets and disappear from the curve. In other words, there is no niche position that serves as a consolation prize. Companies simply will not survive the Endgames curve by trying to stay out of it or, worse, by ignoring it. Niche players are aggressively challenged in the Balance and Alliance Stage—and are invariably too weak to seriously defend their positions (see sidebar, "Finding Their Endgames Pace: Commerzbank and MedQuist").

> There is no niche position that serves as a consolation prize. Companies simply will not survive the Endgames curve by trying to stay out of it, or worse, by ignoring it.

Being the first to embark on key strategies is also critical. For example, companies in deconsolidating industries must time when (or if) they should divest business units to reap the most

---

FINDING THEIR ENDGAMES PACE: COMMERZBANK AND MEDQUIST

Knowing when to acquire—or be acquired—is critical as companies move into late Stage 1 and Stage 2. Consider the diverse experience of two companies—Commerzbank, a German-based financial institution, and MedQuist, a U.S.-based transcription and information management service for the healthcare industry—both of which are in Stage 1 industries.

In riding up the Endgames curve, Commerzbank of Germany serves as an example of a healthy competitor that should have merged, but did not, and is now paying the price. With share prices at half their all-time high reached in August 2000 and market capitalization shrinking to US$9 billion from more than US$17 billion in 1999, the company continues to tread in dangerous waters.

Commerzbank, the smallest of the large blue-chip German private banks, has long held to a strategy based on internal growth. Although it was often at risk of being taken over by a much larger local rival, such as Deutsche Bank and Dresdner Bank, it consistently employed strategies to avoid such a takeover. In the end, Commerzbank did not grow fast enough to stay safe.

After the failed merger between Deutsche Bank and Dresdner Bank, Commerzbank had a chance to jump into the game but talks with Deutsche Bank were short-lived and ultimately proved unsuccessful. Having missed the opportunity to adjust its strategic direction, today the only question is how and when Commerzbank will join in on the financial sector's consolidation stage. It may occur through Münchner Rück, a German-based reinsurance company that now holds about 10% of Commerzbank shares. Or consolidation may begin with an acquisition in the United States. It is well known that Commerzbank is seeking a partner for its U.S. investment banking operations.

In contrast to Commerzbank, MedQuist has set a strong example for rapid consolidation in its industry. Although it holds only 5% market share in the medical transcription field, MedQuist has become the industry's chief consolidator through a string of acquisitions that began in 2001.

In effect, MedQuist has never met a local competitor that it didn't buy. When the company encounters a larger local rival, it usually fights and wins a war of attrition. For example, when Lernout & Hauspie, a speech recognition firm, tried but failed to extend its business to medical transcription, MedQuist was there to buy up its market share. According to the financial firm Grunthal & Co., this strategy has paid off: MedQuist is nearly five times larger than its nearest competitor.

However, there is more to the MedQuist success story than meets the eye. In 2000, Dutch electronics giant Royal Philips Electronics acquired 60% of MedQuist for US$1.2 billion. Philips manufactures voice recognition technology (VRT) and has the deep pockets to supply MedQuist with whatever new equipment it needs. For its part, Philips took a prime stake in a high-growth industry—MedQuist's revenue growth is running at more than 10% per year—and a chance to recover from a previous failed attempt to enter the VRT market. (Philips entered the market with equipment that was not up to market needs and standards.) David A. Cohen, Chairman and CEO of MedQuist, underscored the synergies of the deal: "As a result of this partnership we expect to introduce Philips' speech and other technologies to our 2,400 U.S. health care accounts, and Philips anticipates accelerating our existing plans to expand into Europe." MedQuist's solid Endgames strategy has put it into a strong growth position and will go far in propelling it to the Scale Stage.

attractive returns. Waiting too long or being reactive can lead to fire sale prices, leveraged buyouts, or managed buyouts by financial investors, all at less attractive prices.

Long-term success is the reward for those with a long-term plan. Predicting industry—and individual corporate—movement on the Endgames curve over a 10- to 15-year period is critical. All short-term focused tactics become ineffective or obsolete in the Endgames landscape.

5. The future belongs to the maestros of external growth. If long-term strategic success is achieved by outgrowing the competition, the question is, how should it be done? Internally, through organic growth? Or externally, through acquisitions? The majority of managers with whom we discussed this still hold to the traditional view—that organic growth is generally the most opportune way of growing. Yet our research reveals a much different story: By itself, organic growth does *not* have enough force to propel a company up the Endgames curve at the necessary speed.

Even so, the necessity to grow externally will vary depending on the stage. For example, at the beginning of the race, organic growth is vital as a way to form the cultural nucleus of a company, but it must be quickly supplemented with acquisitions. Over time, the importance of acquisitions increases tremendously: they almost totally fuel growth at the end of the curve. So the sooner management masters the acquisition game, the better the outlook for long-term strategic success.

USE THE PAST TO PREDICT THE FUTURE

These five lessons are immutable. They are, in essence, a combined history lesson of 25,000 companies, representing the sum total of successes and failures of industry consolidation over the past 10 years. And although history teaches us well, it only goes so far. The key is to use these lessons as a foundation for each of the individual stages.

In the next section, as we delve into the four stages along the Endgames curve, these guideposts will prove invaluable. For each stage, we discuss key players, explore the defining characteristics, and offer strategic imperatives to help guide companies onward and upward.

Chapter Three | The Opening Stage

"Once you have missed the first buttonhole you'll never manage to button up."
—Johann Wolfgang von Goethe

The Opening Stage is the frontier of industry consolidation: an expanse of limitless innovation, opportunity, and risk. There are very few companies in the beginning of the stage, and fewer still with substantial revenue or market share; there may not even be many publicly held companies. Consequently, entry barriers are low. As opportunities begin to pan out and it looks as though the next big opportunity is right next door, word gets out quickly. Before long, companies face heated competition in what quickly turns into a race to gain—and then secure—market footholds.

Overall, this is a period of unparalleled new activity, and the smell of opportunity whets the appetites of venture capitalists and entrepreneurs alike (see Figure 3-1). The temptation to enter the fray can be overwhelming, but as the industry and company profiles in the next section reveal, mastering the first stretch of the Endgames curve with an eye to the final stage is critical from day one.

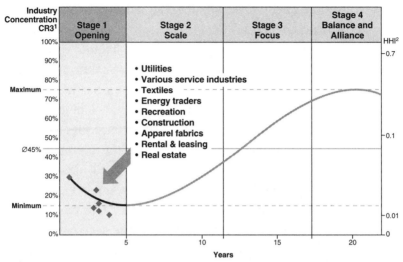

Figure 3-1. Industry concentration rate in the Opening Stage

STAGE 1 SNAPSHOTS: WHO'S WHO

The Opening Stage of the Endgames curve consists of industries that are newly created, spin-offs, and older industries that have been recently deregulated.

Newly Created Industries

These industries are often highly localized and include unregulated businesses such as e-traders, Internet banks, e-business portals, and professional services firms. No single company owns any measurable percentage of market share, and the rapidly changing landscape makes establishing a strong foothold difficult at best. Consider the following examples:

> No single company owns any measurable percentage of market share, and the rapidly changing landscape makes establishing a strong foothold difficult at best.

Biotechnology. A cross-section of medicine, healthcare, industrial applications, nutrition, and environmental issues, the biotechnology industry dates back to the identification of DNA in 1868 by a Swiss biologist, Friedrich Miescher. However, it took well over one hundred years before the industry began to develop and grow at a consistent rate. Government programs and a relaxation of the laws on genetic engineering in the 1990s led to a growth phase that was further bolstered by a rush of venture capital firms anxious to fund start-up biotechnology businesses. The result has been a steady stream of headlines, not the least of which was the cloning of a sheep named Dolly in 1997. The future looks even better, with analysts predicting that biotechnology will represent the next revolution.

Spurred by this strong growth, particularly in the United States and the United Kingdom, the biotechnology industry is nearing the end of the Opening Stage and moving rapidly into the Scale Stage. Smaller start-up biotech companies continue to compete for venture capital money and move toward initial public offerings (IPOs) but, as the Endgames curve predicts, their numbers are dwindling as the industry matures. Meanwhile the larger players are wasting no time in moving up the Endgames curve by consolidating: MedImmune bought Aviron for about US$1.5 billion and Millennium Pharmaceuticals purchased COR Therapeutics for US$1.75 billion. Apart from leaders such as Amgen and Genentech, most lack profitability despite their rapid growth.

At this stage of industry consolidation, companies make acquisitions primarily for two reasons: to expand globally and to achieve critical mass, both technologically and financially. And the deals grow in both size and scope. In the United States, for example, the number of biotech mergers increased from 46 in 1999 to 77 in 2000. Although the number of deals declined to 52 in 2001, the total value of acquisitions rose from a mere US$6.3 billion in 2000 to US$23.2 billion in 2001. It's likely that 2001 could mark the beginning of a long trend of fewer but richer deals as the industry continues its ride up the Endgames curve.

Merger activity has not been limited to the United States: Rhein Biotech's acquisition of Korean Green Cross Vaccine in February 2000 ignited a series of merger activities in Europe. Soon after, German-based GPC AG acquired U.S.-based Mitotix, creating the world's first transatlantic genomic company, GPC Biotech AG. Other consolidation activity includes British Celltech Group's acquisition of Chiroscience Group in 1999 and Medeva in 2000, making the combined entity a fully integrated pharmaceutical company.

In terms of size, however, the majority of these acquisitions are small when compared with the US\$16 billion merger between market leader Amgen and Immunex in 2001—the biggest ever in biotech. The reason for the deal, of course, is synergy: Amgen hopes to combine the strong products of both companies while leveraging the capabilities of its high-powered sales force.

Analysts have begun referring to the emerging group of larger companies as "biopharmaceutical" companies, differentiating them from the research-driven, loss-making groups of smaller businesses that still make up the largest portion of the biotech industry. There are relatively few industry-founding companies, but they hold significant market share. In the United States, Amgen, Genentech, and Immunex have a combined market capitalization of more than US\$100 billion. MedImmune, the fourth largest company, has a market capitalization of less than US\$10 billion. From there, the roster gets smaller very quickly. Still, with breakaway companies speeding toward consolidation, the industry's climb into Stage 2 is well under way.

Online retailers. Few industries have sped from 0 to 60 faster than online retailing. Attracted by compelling value propositions and robust-sounding business models, venture capitalists in the 1990s lined up to invest large sums of money in Internet-based businesses. The horsepower behind most of these outfits was the blood and passion of young, wide-eyed enthusiasts with visions of mind-boggling wealth—all working long hours for low wages while waiting for their stock options to mature.

Of the thousands of these new companies, online book retailer Amazon.com led the pack from the beginning. For the first few years of its life, in fact, Amazon went unchallenged by its offline counterparts, giving it time to capture hefty market share. Soaring stock prices and strong funding also gave Amazon the freedom to set its prices low— some below cost, even—and provide such depth of service that it easily outpaced its rivals and cemented its first-mover advantage.

First-mover advantage can be fleeting, however. Today, Amazon faces many competitors, from the bricks-and-mortar rivals that have set up their own e-business operations to a host of rival online-only interlopers. The news has not been all bad. Amazon has garnered some strategic victories, including taking over the Borders.com Web site—simultaneously eliminating a brick-and-mortar rival from the online space while gaining its online customer base—although other competitors, such as Barnes & Noble, are closing the gap.

In response to its competitors, Amazon has leveraged its speed and value pricing to move beyond books to create a virtual online department store, selling everything from CDs and DVDs to toys and household electronics. In addition, it continues to extend its business-to-consumer commerce capabilities to other manufacturers in a variety of industries. The result has been that many of its competitors have been driven out of business.

Of course, Amazon's long-term survivability as a dot-com model remains in question because even today the company generates little profit. eBay, on the other hand, is one of the few Internet-based companies that can boast solid—and rising—profits, even in light of the dot-com implosion. By charging a small listing fee for each item sold through its buy-and-sell matching service, eBay turned the promise of the Internet into reality. Phenomenal growth has been at the core of eBay's success, but is its Endgame strategy strong enough to propel it into the Scale Stage? Its first steps look promising.

Nearing critical mass in the U.S. market, eBay began establishing a stronger presence beyond American borders. In 2001, international operations took in US$114 million (15% of the total), but eBay's Chief Financial Officer, Rajiv Dutta, predicts this number will top US$800 million in 2005. In addition to launching new country-specific sites on its own, the online auction house began acquiring leading auction providers in target markets, including Ibazar, S.A in Europe, Internet Auction Co. Ltd. in Korea, and NeoCom Technology in Taiwan. In addition to global expansion, however, eBay has also focused on line extensions, trying to gain a foothold in everything from selling cars to providing a marketplace for professional services. Of course, the key to eBay's long-term success will be not just to grow market share, but to protect it.

Nanotechnology. Newer still are industries that build practical applications from emerging technologies. Nanotechnology, for example, is based on the relatively new science of building infinitesimal devices that can manipulate single atoms or molecules. Proponents claim that practical applications will include everything from building better computers to fighting cancer. The U.S. National Science Foundation echoes this optimism with predictions that the market for nanotechnology products and services will reach US$1 trillion by 2015. Although it is still in the early stages, governments, venture capitalists, established companies, and entrepreneurs alike are funneling money into creating marketable products. Last year alone, world governments invested more than US$2 billion in nanotech research. Similarly, tech leaders such as IBM, Intel, and Hewlett-Packard have all embarked on nanotechnology projects. In fact, IBM plans to introduce commercial products in the next two or three years. Although North America has about half of the world's nearly 500 nanotechnology companies, no single region dominates the industry.

Clearly, this industry remains early in Stage 1. As technology advances and companies begin to reap the benefits of their current R&D, look for tremendous growth, quickly followed by consolidation, as it moves through this stage. However, developing nanotechnology products is time-intensive, with many estimated to take as long as 10 years. As a result, this time lag will greatly affect how long it will take the industry to climb into the Scale Stage.

Spin-Off Subindustries

Other industries in the Opening Stage are those that emerge from the fallout from one of the later stages of industry consolidation. These industries form when subindustries reach a critical size and create a dynamic of their own. They may also emerge due to a new industry-forming technology, or as a result of a restructuring due to a market or economic event.

PepsiCo, for example, firmly in the Stage 4 soft-drink industry, fueled the development of the bottled water, sports drink, and flavored sparkling water subindustries. Each of these subindustries was in an

earlier Endgames stage: they were fragmented and growing strongly—
characteristics of Stages 1 and 2—and thus presented opportunities for
PepsiCo to get onto a new growth track. (*For more on Pepsi's strategies,
see Chapter 6.*)

Similarly, the global high-technology industry has created dozens
of spin-off industries as technology advances and the core technology
industries mature. Consider the following examples:

- In the early 1960s, economies of scale opportunities in servic-
  ing IBM mainframe computers led to the creation of the IT outsourcing industry.
- New communications technologies led to the creation of satel-
  lite, cable television, broadband, and cellular telephone communication networks, each competing with traditional telephone
  service providers.
- Advances in communication and software technology led to the
  formation of thousands of dot-com companies, creating dozens of
  new Stage 1 subindustries in a matter of a few years.

Deregulating Industries

Another major segment of industries in Stage 1 is that of deregulating
industries. This group emerges from previously state-owned or state-
regulated monopolies and includes such companies as energy, water,
gas, postal services, and, to some extent, banks and insurance. When
state monopolies of telecommunications were broken up, dozens of
specialized providers, such as the cellular phone companies, entered
the market.

Over the years, many industries have been liberalized or, in effect,
made more competitive via legislation or alternative steps that man-
dated opening up their markets to more players (see sidebar:
"Development Bank of Singapore"). When this happens, industries
that were dominated by single players suddenly explode and produce
two, three, or perhaps as many as 10 players.

Generally, this is good news for consumers, because when monopolistic pricing mechanisms are at work, companies can charge much
more than they would in a competitive market environment. In a pure

DEVELOPMENT BANK OF SINGAPORE

Government action can often spark an inflection point in a local industry, as it did in the late 1990s when the Singapore government decided to open the banking sector to outside players. The Development Bank of Singapore (DBS) is a classic example of a Stage 1 company that changed its strategy due to a shift in the environment.

In the wake of the Asian crisis in 1997, DBS brought in a new CEO, John Olds, to pursue an Endgames strategy across Southeast Asia. Olds, an American banker from J.P. Morgan, surveyed the Southeast Asian banking landscape and saw an interesting competitive picture: several mammoth global competitors in Citibank, HSBC, and Standard Chartered; a host of fragmented, country-specific banks in each of the neighboring Southeast Asian countries, including Malaysia, Thailand, and Indonesia; and some aspiring start-up regional competitors, such as the Commonwealth Bank of Australia.

Olds believed that the only strategy available to ensure DBS's success in the future was to embark on a rapid regional consolidation strategy. His first major deal was the acquisition of the POS Bank in Singapore in 1998—the old Post Office Savings Bank, with thousands of depositors from the heartland of Singapore's economy. Next he branched out and acquired the Thai Danu Bank in 1999, one of the largest purchases by a Singapore company outside of Singapore ever. The Thai Danu deal provided DBS with a wealth of post-merger integration experience and capabilities, which it would later use to its advantage in the 2001 acquisitions of Dao Heng Bank in Hong Kong and Vickers Ballas, a Hong Kong-based brokerage business.

Building on this success, DBS is now recognized as a regional banking powerhouse and is well positioned to complete several more deals in the future. A good thing, too, as DBS has raised its profile enough in this hot sector of the Singaporean and Asian economy to attract increasing attention from foreign banking giants such as Citibank, which has a license to offer full-service banking in DBS's local markets.

monopoly situation, for example, there is no competitive pressure to optimize business processes or make services cost-efficient. Staffing often becomes padded with extra layers and redundancies creep into

business processes. Without pressures being applied by the marketplace, such as corporate governance or competition, there are often
more employees than needed to deliver services and little investment
in implementing new market efficiencies.

Consider the following experiences of companies in deregulating
industries:

Telecommunications. In Germany, Deutsche Telekom was a state-
owned monopoly until it went public via a stock offering in 1996. As
the markets opened up elsewhere in Europe, Deutsche Telekom struck
a major joint venture deal with France Telecom. The two organizations
had other cross holdings in such telecommunications companies as
Switzerland's Multilink and the United Kingdom's MetroHoldings. But
after Deutsche Telekom announced a merger with Italy Telecom, which
subsequently failed, the joint ventures between the two rivals collapsed. They unwound their mutual investments, which left Deutsche
Telekom with 100% of Multilink and France Telecom with a 50% stake
in MetroHoldings. Deutsche Telekom has since acquired stakes in
additional telecom companies: a 51% stake in Slovakia Telecom when
it was transformed from a state-owned enterprise to a joint-stock company by the Slovakian government in 1999 and a majority stake in
Pragonet when the ministry opened the Czech Republic market in
2000. It also formed a strategic partnership with Hrvatski Telekom of
Croatia following its separation from HPT—Croatian Post and
Telecommunications. These are just a few of its dealings in opening up
emerging markets in Europe.

Deutsche Telekom also launched other star-crossed deals that
never succeeded: Qwest and Freeserve. When it finally purchased its
first U.S. company, VoiceStream, consensus was that Deutsche
Telekom vastly overpaid for those assets when compared with other
values in the industry. However, according to its critics, the "root cause
for these blunders appears to be an inability by Deutsche Telekom's top
management to bridge cultural divides and different corporate cultures, skills essential to making cross-border mergers work."[1] In
Chapter 9, we discuss the challenges of creating a global culture and
offer some key lessons on how to foster it.

Financial services. Deregulation of the global financial services industry has led to a large increase in merger activity and consolidation, both within individual countries and across borders. Once restrictions governing interstate banking were removed in the United States, the commercial banking industry went on a consolidation rampage, with thousands of mergers taking place in the 1990s. By the same token, once long-standing laws forbidding commercial banks from owning investment banks were overturned, commercial banks aggressively expanded the scope of their businesses, moving into investment banking, brokerage, insurance, and financial planning services.

In Europe, the introduction of the Euro paved the way for a frenzy of cross-border mergers, with the largest banks in each major European country trying to stake out a leading competitive position across the continent.

> *Deregulation of the global financial services industry has led to a huge amount of merger activity and consolidation, both within individual countries and across borders.*

In Asia, following the Asian economic crisis and the continuing deterioration of the Japanese financial services industry, leading global financial services competitors have gone on a buying spree to position themselves favorably to serve some of the largest and fastest-growing markets in the world.

MOVE TO SCALE

Industries with low entry barriers stay in the Opening Stage until a large industry consolidator changes the rules of the game by using its scale to dominate the others. In the beginning there is excitement, plenty of venture capital, and a buzz about "opportunities." Eventually, however, imitators and improved versions of the original business model begin to horn in on the venture capital action. Before long there are so many companies serving the same market that all the ideas are out on the table—and the venture capital spigot suddenly turns off.

When the consolidation wave begins, competition can become particularly fierce. TMP Worldwide (owner of Monster.com, the largest Internet employment recruiting firm in the world) offers a unique example of an Internet company that moved quickly to become a first consolidator (see sidebar: "TMP Worldwide"). In just two years, the online employment recruiting industry consolidated from 10 major players to

<blockquote>
Industries with low entry barriers stay in the Opening Stage until a large industry consolidator changes the rules of the game by using its scale to dominate the others.
</blockquote>

just three top-tier players—TMP, CareerBuilder, and Yahoo!. These three companies now control 66% of online recruitment Web site revenues. Yahoo! beat out TMP in the race to acquire a leading player named HotJobs.com last year, and CareerBuilder acquired HeadHunter.net.

Of course, not all consolidation occurs at this speed, but all industries consolidate nevertheless. For example, with the invention of steel melting, there were immediately hundreds, if not thousands, of steel mills around the world trying to capture a part of the market. The same held true for the automobile industry and the hotel industry. The hotel chains—which classically originated in North America—are now dominating the world hotel market, where establishments were traditionally family-owned businesses and therefore highly fragmented.

With too many companies chasing a finite share of market, the stronger companies in the space begin looking around for candidates they might buy to achieve synergies. At the most deconsolidated level, too many companies are doing the same thing.

At this point, competition can continue only in two ways. The first is for the more efficient operator—the one that has the best product or service, the best organization, and the most efficient means of serving the customer—to drive the less efficient rival out of the market through aggressive competition. The other option, of course, is to buy the competitors out. Automatic Data Processing (ADP) used these methods when it started consolidating the payroll processing business.

The incentives for mergers are clear: aside from achieving a synergy in which the whole is greater than the sum of the parts, the combined revenues of the two entities could result in higher overall profits as well as an increase in market share, while the combined cost of doing business goes down. Consider the following two industry examples.

U.S. car dealerships. The single biggest business expense in any auto dealership is the cost of carrying inventory. Dealers have an enormous amount of capital and real estate tied up in vehicles. On a local level, two neighboring car dealerships—each with 500 cars in inven-

TMP WORLDWIDE

TMP Worldwide is a fascinating example of a company moving through Stage 1 of the Endgames consolidation curve. Founded in 1967, TMP was originally a Yellow Pages advertising agency. As part of an acquisition it made in the early 1990s, TMP stumbled upon an Internet-based résumé posting board that it built up and relaunched as Monster.com.

Soon, Monster.com emerged as an integral part of TMP's famous "Intern-to-CEO" strategy to dominate the global recruitment solutions industry. Right in the middle of the Internet boom, TMP managers realized that to dominate this space they would have to enter a rapid acquisition and consolidation stage. In just four years, TMP acquired and integrated more than 70 companies globally. These included many of the start-up and established Internet career portals such as FlipDog.com (United States) and Jobline (Sweden), employment agencies and recruitment firms such as QD Legal (United Kingdom and Asia), TASA (Hong Kong), Morgan & Banks (Australia), and Melville Craig (Scotland), and online advertising services companies, including IN2 (United States).

In typical Internet time, TMP swiftly executed its Endgames rapid consolidation phase. Without its foresight, which made the Internet the rallying cry for its future business model, it would have become an "also-ran," almost certainly bought out by a faster, stronger company. Instead, TMP moved quickly and decisively, building the company's success on three critical pillars:

1. Deep knowledge of potential acquisition candidates and the ability to screen, weed out, and close deals with the highest-potential players. TMP developed a powerful capability to identify the best players on a country-by-country basis among thousands in a highly fragmented industry.
2. Global vision and foresight to execute Endgames consolidation worldwide from the outset.
3. Merger-integration know-how that was embedded into all facets of the business. Because most of TMP's acquisitions were small (well under US$100 million) and it completed so many deals, the company often had several merger integration efforts going on simultaneously around the world.

tory—could combine. But when joined to form a super dealership, they might need only 750 cars. That's a much larger selection than the customer originally had access to at each car lot, so it's better for the customer. And the synergies gained in terms of cost savings to the combined dealership are obvious. In addition, larger dealerships can more easily afford to invest in technology such as computer systems that can lower costs and make the operation run more efficiently. Add such cost-saving benefits such as pooled purchasing of direct and indirect goods and cash flow improves dramatically. So do profits.

Looking back, the 1950s were the heyday for U.S. auto dealers. More than 50,000 dealers sold about 6.5 million cars, surpassing the previous peak set in 1929. By 1996, however, the number of dealers had declined by 50%. The group that suffered the greatest drop was the smaller firms that sold fewer than 150 new cars per year: nearly 65% of these dealerships disappeared between 1976 and 1989.[2] Meanwhile, larger dealers are on the rise.

Another tectonic shift in the industry lies in the dramatic increase of used (or pre-owned) car dealerships, which has been largely fueled by the rise in the number of late-model used cars coming out of leasing programs. This launched a new type of auto superstore in the early 1990s that typically holds an inventory of well over 1,000 cars, employs sales consultants rather than high-pressure salespeople—often on salary, not commission—and offers no-haggle pricing. Some auto superstores are public companies whose access to capital markets gives them a low-cost way to finance their inventories. Some also sell new cars. Car manufacturers, in turn, are buying up some of these auto superstores and consolidating them.

The first "pure" industry consolidators began appearing in the late 1990s. These consolidators combine a large number of formerly independent dealerships from many states into a "megastore" for new and used cars as well as auto repairs. They are branded as one-stop shops designed to simplify the car buying process for consumers. Consolidators continue to grow as many dealerships—especially marginal ones—prefer to join with them rather than continue struggling as independent dealers. According to Forrester Research, another 7,000 independent dealers will vanish by 2022.

While industry costs are being squeezed, some companies continue to thrive. United Auto Group—a public company and the third-largest player in the United States with 127 franchises—has seen earnings grow by an average annual rate of 31% since 1999. Now United Auto Group has cast its eyes across the seas, announcing expansion plans to sell Mercedes-Benz passenger cars in the United Kingdom. The strong consolidation activity that is well under way among U.S. auto dealers remains at a much earlier stage of the cycle in Europe—but this is about to change.

In fact, deregulation in the European Union is spurring consolidation in the car dealership industry. Before February 2002, the law allowed European car dealers to enter into exclusive contracts with a single manufacturer. In return, the manufacturer could not supply the same models to another dealer in the same region. This law also restricted dealers to go cross-border.

With the abrogation of this law, car dealers will now be able to sell multiple brands without regional restrictions. Car dealers from other countries are free to open stores in any area. This puts pressure on the dealerships to lower their prices to compete with foreign dealers and on car manufacturers to increase their market share.

The demise of the law, combined with a less regulated market, marks the Opening Stage in the European car dealer industry. Industry analysts are already predicting a consolidation wave, with smaller family-owned businesses being gobbled up by larger dealers. Eventually, analysts expect the shakeout to result in a small network of strategic core dealerships—comparing it to the shakeout that is occurring in the U.S. automotive supplier industry. And the dealers expect competition to grow increasingly fierce in tandem with consumers' demands that companies sell and provide services via the Internet.

Railroads. Because many railroads fell into the state-owned or state-regulated category, many are consolidating—or even deconsolidating—depending on their nationality. One of the biggest consolidation moves in European history took place between the German state-owned freight rail company, DB Cargo (Mainz), and its Dutch counterpart, NS

Cargo (Utrecht). The combined company was named Rail Cargo Europe. At the time of the announced merger, its projected revenue was US$3.5 billion based on the transport of more than 310 million metric tons of freight annually. One of the greatest benefits of combining the two entities involved the elimination of stops at the Dutch/German border, which required changes for both locomotives and drivers because of differences in power, signaling and safety systems. The two companies pledged to convert their locomotives to make them compatible and announced further plans for a nonstop freight rail service between Rotterdam and Germany. A year and a half prior to the effective date of the merger, the two firms placed joint orders for new locomotives that would operate between both countries. They also began cross-training engineers so they could operate in both countries.[3]

In the United States, railroads have been consolidating and pursuing market solutions since the passage of the Staggers Act in 1980. Since then, productivity has increased, more than US$200 billion has been invested in equipment and infrastructure improvements, the accident rate has fallen by 70%, and shipping rates have been sliced in half. In addition, the U.S. Surface Transportation Board also approved several cross-border acquisitions of U.S. regional freight lines by the Canadian National Railway (CNR) in an effort to further improve end-to-end service for customers in key areas. CNR serves all of Canada, parts of the U.S. Midwest, and Buffalo, New York.

Finally, in the United Kingdom, the state-owned rail system is being replaced by new companies that carve up territory on the state-owned rails, but will provide their own service. Of course, there must be some coordination among the service providers, but these should be easily solved by private industry.

STAYING AHEAD OF THE CURVE: STRATEGIC LESSONS FOR THE OPENING STAGE

Build up entry barriers to prevent deconsolidation. Defend territory at all costs. Once all available market space is staked out, it becomes too expensive or time-consuming for a new company to enter the field. This is a time for industry pioneers to protect their first-mover advantage. The key is to prevent competitors from proliferating, but how? If you work in the nanotechnology business, you would want patents approved for as many products as possible. In e-business, Priceline.com was able to patent its business model. The same logic holds true for almost every other business as well, high-tech or otherwise. What does your company have that's worth defending, patenting, copyrighting, or service marking?

> Defend territory at all costs. Once all available market space is staked out, it becomes too expensive or time-consuming for a new company to enter the field.

Capture market share by focusing more on revenue than profit. To the swift go the spoils, at least in the market share wars. True, many dot-com companies went too far with this lesson and ignored profits altogether—and have since disappeared. Still, the emphasis for Stage 1 companies should rest more with amassing market share than hitting profitability targets. In a sluggish economy, investors may not be as patient as they were with Amazon, for example, but with a solid Endgames strategy profits will follow.

Closely monitor the external political environment to profit fastest from any legal changes. The first companies to act in a changing environment will capture mind share, thereby extending market advantage, just as the Development Bank of Singapore did. Lobbying can be a great tool for staying in the loop: By knowing what's happening in legislative circles, you may be able to influence outcomes. In the same vein, tracking major legislation efforts and employing lobbyists or funding political action committees that mirror your business interests will also be useful. For retailers and manufacturers, this may entail monitoring trade agreements such as the North American Free Trade Agreement (NAFTA) for new developments on the horizon.

If you foresee that an outcome will not be desirable, be prepared to act accordingly. When deregulation of the power industry was approved in the United States, there was advance notice for those who sought to react with a new strategy or make aggressive moves to strengthen their market position.

If you cannot dominate the whole industry, focus on the most attractive industry segments where your company can win. Winners in the Opening Stage learn to dominate an area where opportunity is substantial, rather than trying to spread their expertise across the entire industry. A pharmaceutical company, for example, is best served by focusing on a single condition. AstraZeneca has mastered this by holding patents on Prilosec and Nexium, the number-one and -two drugs for treatment of acid reflux, a chronic condition affecting as much as 10% of the middle-aged population. Similarly, TMP was successful because it carved out the online recruiting space rather than the entire (online *and* offline) recruiting space.

> *Winners in the Opening Stage learn to dominate an area where opportunity is substantial, rather than trying to spread their expertise across the entire industry.*

Master—then accelerate—the acquisition process to capture volume. Perfecting acquisition skills takes time and experience. The sooner these are developed, the better the chances for market leadership later on. Integration skills are key to making the majority of consolidations work. In *After the Merger*, Max Habeck, Fritz Kroeger, and Michael Traem discuss the seven rules for merger success, namely: vision; leadership; going for the growth; looking for early wins—in assets, with customers and knowledge; cultural integration; communication, communication and communication; and prudent risk management. (*For a detailed explanation of these rules, see Chapter 7.*)[4]

Form an open, integrated culture that will become the backbone for future growth. As a first mover, part of the advantage in preempting competitors lies in preserving and nurturing key employees. Building an environment that encourages people to stay is just as important as erecting entry barriers to keep competitors out—and both help sustain a first-mover position. Luring top employees away from other organizations, in fact, is a key strategy for fast movers and other companies looking to establish market share in a start-up industry. After all, they know the core processes—such as sourcing, logistics, and fulfillment—of the lead players.

And once they are aboard, the company must foster their development and ensure that the key employees stay a long time—not just for the two- to five-year strategic planning horizon. The corporate culture must therefore be both satisfying and challenging. It is only through a competitive and strong workforce that companies can offer the best products and services.

For merging companies, ensuring stability and openness within employee ranks—from both organizations—is particularly critical. Companies with a closed and uniform culture often experience difficulties in taking over other companies or even employees who have worked outside their own company for some time. Although a strict culture can be a strength in its own right, it also has severe limitations when the company experiences a growth spurt.

The only sure way to get new employees who will stay is to imbue them with the specific company culture. Companies that excel in this area include Wal-Mart and the German discounter Aldi. On the other hand, such a strong and specific culture makes it difficult to acquire companies as a whole, and sometimes requires specialists from outside to refresh the company's ranks.

Be prepared for anything in a deregulating industry. Once privatization or new competitors arrive—and can't be stopped—look outside your borders for best practices and clues to prepare for the new environment in which you will be competing. See what's happening and what has occurred in other states or countries where markets have opened up.

The global utilities industry is an excellent example. As Figure 3-2 illustrates, the growth performance of most of the global utility companies is concentrated in a narrow band because of their regulated legacies. But we are beginning to see stratification of performance among the U.S. utilities that have been deregulated for several years. Many have used mergers aggressively to gain economies of scale and to expand internationally as part of their Endgames strategy. As the global level of regulation in the utilities industry falls, there will be a massive shakeout as the effects of Endgames transform the industry. By benchmarking what's happened in other places, executives will have a better sense of how to react to certain market changes and anticipate common problems.

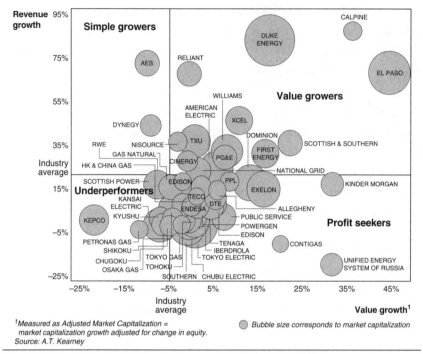

Figure 3-2. Global utilities industry (CAGR 1996–2001)

Also, when a monopoly situation ends, it's critical for companies to examine both their pricing structure and customer relationships. When no choices exist—as was the case with railroads, airlines, and telecommunications companies—it's easy to overlook customer loyalty and customer satisfaction, as well as price point issues. In a deregulated environment, pricing becomes paramount. With little loyalty, customer attrition can be high and defection to lower-price competitors swift. To realign prices, companies must look at costs and, if adjusting or lowering prices means that costs get squeezed, then it's a sign that processes must be reexamined or even reengineered entirely to eliminate fat and waste.

READY FOR SCALE?

As companies reach the end of the Opening Stage, the landscape takes on a much different look and feel. The open space is gone and groups of lead players are beginning to emerge. At this point, the strategy shifts from claiming ground to building a corporate powerhouse.

This is just what Stage 2 is about. As the name implies, the Scale Stage is when growth becomes paramount—and the stakes are raised accordingly. Just as in the Opening Stage, only a handful of players that begin will live to tell the tale by the end. For the best chance of survival, players need a solid Stage 2 strategy from the beginning ... so read on.

Notes

1. Stephan Richter, "Quo Vadis, Deutsche Telekom?" *Chief Executive*, December 2000.
2. 1950 dealership data is from the National Automobile Dealers Association, Industry Analysis division. Later data is from the Bureau of Labor Statistics. In 1976 there were 13,200 dealerships selling fewer than 150 units per year and by 1998 that number had dropped to 4664.
3. Ian Young, "Rail Merger Raises Industry Hopes," *Chemical Week*, September 22, 1999.
4. Max M. Habeck, Fritz Kroeger, and Michael R. Traem, *After the Merger: Seven Rules for Successful Post-Merger Integration* (London: Financial Times Prentice Hall, 2000).

Chapter Four | The Scale Stage

If it's not growing, it's going to die.
—Michael Eisner
Chairman and CEO, Walt Disney Company

Having risen through Stage 1, companies have laid claim to all of the available territory. Now it's time for them to build scale. Leaders must devise new strategies to expand, grow, capture market share and protect their turf—all to continue their climb up the Endgames curve. Stage 2 is when industry leaders stand tall. Whether or not they are conscious of their Endgames strategy, as they look across the landscape they must constantly analyze their next acquisition target or assess a new growth plan. Typical Stage 2 industries include hotel chains, breweries, banks, homebuilders, automotive suppliers, restaurants and fast-food chains (see Figure 4-1). The race for position and market share capture comes into full swing and, as it progresses, positioning of the leaders frequently changes (see sidebar: "Changing Positions"). Even the partners that the leaders choose for customers, suppliers, and allies may change.

> The race for position and market share capture comes into full swing and as it progresses, positioning of the leaders frequently changes.

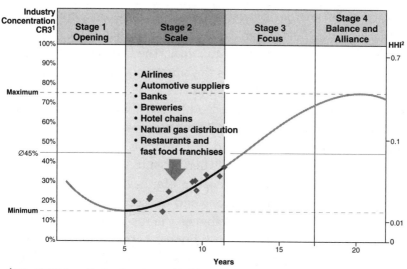

Figure 4-1. Industry concentration rate in the Scale Stage

CHANGING POSITIONS

A scorecard can often come in handy in Stage 2. A merger may be announced one day and the number-three player quickly takes the number-two spot. The following week, another merger between the third- and fifth-ranked companies propels the combined entity into second place. The old number two reacts by going after additional companies to regain its position. The game quickens and the stakes are raised. A war of attrition is often not enjoyable, even for the victor.

In some cases, strategy has been more reactive than proactive. In discussing the paper industry's US$18 billion M&A binge, Kari Toikka, senior vice president of Finland's UPM-Kymenne, said: "We simply followed what was happening in our customers' industries. Global publishers of magazines like *Elle* want a consistent look and quality around the world. Their approach is to reduce their number of suppliers, because they can get better products and better terms."

In situations when only a few players remain, another phenomenon occurs. A merger between the number-one and -three players actually creates a more stable market and provides a safe—and profitable—harbor for the number-two rival. The lawn and garden long-handled tools market illustrates this situation. The number-one company, Ames (a Division of U.S. Industries until recently) acquired Tru-Temper from Huffy Corporation. Although the combination of the number-one and number-three companies created a business three times the size of number two, Union Tools (a division of Acorn Products), the move was actually beneficial to both companies.

The reasons are simple: retailers prefer having alternative suppliers, both for competitive reasons and for security of supply. When numbers one and three are combined, the top three become the top two—and the player in second suddenly becomes more important strategically to their mutual customers. The market leader could try to overwhelm the second-position competitor with a massive lower-price, cost-cutting attack, but that's a dangerous move. The result of such a step often is lower profits for the leade—and a new (perhaps more troublesome) replacement in the number two slot. So the number-two supplier's position is stable and safe in this scenario. This small industry represents a microcosm of what happens in many larger industries as companies move through the Scale Stage to fortify their market share and position.

In Stage 2, the increase in scale improves production, spreads fixed costs and earns profits. However, profits are still slim because pricing becomes extremely competitive. And, as always, strategy is key to gaining or maintaining a winning position. Companies must determine which market segments to stake out, and not all of them are equally rewarding. Some segments may be unattractive because they require disproportionate investments; others may be desirable because they offer a foothold into a new or newly accessible market. As a result, companies must determine how much investment is required or, more specifically, estimate the return on capital that will be provided in their desired segments.

Similarly, while companies must be quick to consolidate and grow, they must be careful to avoid taking on more than they can handle financially. During a consolidation wave, the intense desire to grow and acquire sometimes overcomes this financial reality. When this happens, companies find themselves strained for working capital. As a result, they incur excessive borrowing costs, and ultimately struggle under the burden of what looked like valuable acquisitions. The problem may be exacerbated if the new acquisitions are not well integrated. Sheer size is no guarantee of genuine long-term market leadership, unless that size is properly leveraged for financial advantage or market positioning—and ideally both.

> *Sheer size is no guarantee of genuine long-term market leadership, unless that size is properly leveraged for financial advantage or market position—and ideally both.*

In fact, this point—size and scale do not automatically confer industry-leading market capitalization—is the most important lesson companies in Stage 2 must master. Consider the global automotive industry. Over the past decade, most of the largest competitors in this space have used mergers as a tool to add to, or maintain, their market share. General Motors, the world's largest automotive company, took significant equity positions in a number of automotive companies including Saab, Isuzu, Subaru, Suzuki and now Daewoo. Similarly, Ford acquired Volvo and Jaguar; Daimler-Benz snapped up Mitsubishi and Chrysler to form DaimlerChrysler; and Renault bought Nissan. Toyota, on the other hand, has rarely used mergers as a strategic tool. It is the third largest automaker and holds about 10 percent of the global automotive market, well behind GM and Ford. Nonetheless, Toyota has had the biggest market capitalization of any auto company at several points in the past decade. Why is this so?

A key reason is one that we just mentioned: size, especially in the automotive industry, does not always equate to superior business performance. Japanese carmakers, for example, do not have the additional cost burdens of unionized labor contracts and hourly paid employee pension funds that their U.S. and European competitors do. Also, technology and production strategies vary widely among automotive competitors, producing significant cost differences.

With regard to the Endgames strategy, merely announcing—or even completing—a merger does not guarantee a boost in market capitaliza-

tion. Only by successfully integrating the two companies will beneficial long-term results emerge. Once again, the automotive industry's
track record has not been good. Other, more pressing internal business
problems have hampered Ford's merger integration timetables, and
DaimlerChrysler experienced numerous challenges in integrating the
different cultures, management styles and business models of Daimler-
Benz and Chrysler. Toyota, though, stuck to its business model and has
been successful as a result. The Scale Stage of the Endgames curve is
one of brutal competition. The players that grow strategically, and successfully use mergers as a competitive weapon, emerge victorious.

The Stage 2 landscape is also different than Stage 1 in that there is
much more stratification of the growth performance of the global players. For example, in the global banking industry, as shown in Figure 4-
2 (next page), a few competitors are beginning to emerge as the global
leaders, but there is a huge middle pack that could overtake them. And
for the leaders, there are still hundreds of acquisition opportunities for
them to expand their business footprint and continue their journey up
the Endgames curve.

STAGE 2 SNAPSHOTS: WHO'S WHO

By the end of the Scale Stage, freedom of choice is widely limited
because the major players have formed their empires, and few valuable
picks remain. In other words, much of the blueprint for the final
Endgame has been drafted. Those companies
that have fallen behind or have not been
acquired during this stage may be forced to
choose niches as temporary hiding places until
they can become attractive to consolidators.
Even storied companies such as BMW must
consider this as a future challenge. Time, as

> *Those companies that have fallen behind or have not been acquired during this stage may be forced to choose niches as temporary hiding places until they can become attractive to consolidators.*

we've established, is critical, and companies that are in Stage 2 must
move quickly yet carefully. For snapshots of industries—and individual companies—traversing the Scale Stage, take a look at the following examples.

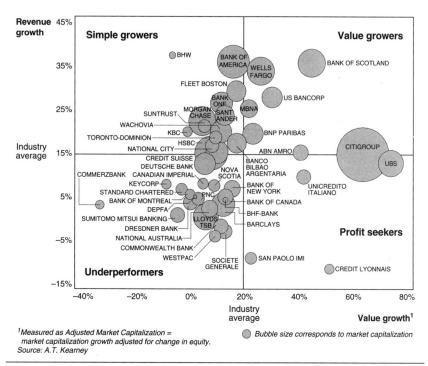

Revenue growth 45%

Simple growers
Value growers

35% — BHW, BANK OF AMERICA, WELLS FARGO, BANK OF SCOTLAND

FLEET BOSTON

25% — SUNTRUST, MORGAN CHASE, BANK ONE, SANTANDER, MBNA, US BANCORP

WACHOVIA
TORONTO-DOMINION — KBC, HSBC, BNP PARIBAS

Industry average 15% — NATIONAL CITY, ABN AMRO, CITIGROUP

CREDIT SUISSE
DEUTSCHE BANK
COMMERZBANK   CANADIAN IMPERIAL — NOVA SCOTIA, BANCO BILBAO ARGENTARIA, UBS

KEYCORP
STANDARD CHARTERED — PNC, BANK OF NEW YORK, UNICREDITO ITALIANO
5% — BANK OF MONTREAL, BANK OF CANADA
DEPFA — BHF-BANK
SUMITOMO MITSUI BANKING — LLOYDS TSB, BARCLAYS
DRESDNER BANK
NATIONAL AUSTRALIA — **Profit seekers**
-5% — COMMONWEALTH BANK
WESTPAC — SOCIETE GENERALE, SAN PAOLO IMI

Underperformers   CREDIT LYONNAIS

-15%

-40%   -20%   0%   20%   40%   60%   80%

Industry average

Value growth[1]

[1]*Measured as Adjusted Market Capitalization = market capitalization growth adjusted for change in equity.*
Source: A.T. Kearney

Bubble size corresponds to market capitalization

Figure 4-2. Global banking industry (CAGR 1996–2001)

Software industry. Customer relationship management (CRM) software, like other e-business related areas, has moved from the Opening Stage into the Scale Stage and is right at the inflection point of consolidation. New industries begin with a single successful company that achieves a generous market capitalization. That company, in turn, begins to attract competitors. These hopeful competitors proliferate; however, many don't get enough traction in the market to achieve critical mass and remain unprofitable until the consolidation begins.

The most successful companies consolidate their early gains by acquiring market share—they gobble up the fingerlings. In CRM, a specialty software area, this plot is unfolding pretty quickly. CRM software sales stood at US$11.8 billion in 2001 and were expected to reach US$14.2 billion in 2002. Siebel holds a 28 percent market share, Peregrine has 9 percent and Oracle follows with 7 percent. PeopleSoft, SAP, Trilogy and Epiphany hold a combined total of 12 percent, and the remaining market share is divided among smaller players. In sum, seven players have 56 percent concentration, with the rest sharing 44 percent. Also, the fact that the top three players—although Siebel is far and away the leader—hold a combined market share of 44 percent means that the industry is moving up the Endgames curve rather quickly.

The smaller players, including Kana Software, Onyx Software and Primus Knowledge Solutions Inc., are struggling, making the market ripe for takeovers. Clearly, battles will erupt over market share in such a fast-growing area. Of course, Oracle and Peregrine also have products that serve other markets, as does SAP. It's also possible that a new competitor could enter the marketplace in a diversification move (IBM, perhaps?) and scoop up several small players to take a major position if it sees CRM as a high-growth market.

Automotive parts industry. The global automotive business is characterized by a never-ending battle for margins between automotive parts suppliers and automotive original equipment manufacturers, or OEMs. In recent years, this turf war has been a fascinating example of merger Endgames in action.

In the mid- to late-1990s, larger first-tier automotive parts suppliers pursued a systems integrator strategy by consolidating their individual sub-industries. They believed they could reap higher margins from OEMs by offering "plug-in" modules such as integrated door assemblies or entire car interiors, as opposed to simply offering the individual parts. Some examples of this Endgames strategy include:

- TRW purchased LucasVarity in 1999 to become the leading braking systems supplier in the world.
- Lear Corporation bought United Technologies' automotive division in 1999 with the goal of supplying OEMs with "full-service modules" that integrate interior systems with electrical systems. In the same year, Lear purchased Ovatex and Polovat, two smaller automotive interior suppliers, in addition to Donnelly Corporation's 50 percent interest in Lear-Donnelly Overhead Systems, an overhead interior systems business.
- Johnson Controls bought Ikeda Bussan, a Japanese automotive

seating company and the main supplier of seating systems to Nissan. This purchase served as a starting point for selling Johnson's entire range of seating systems to the Japanese OEMs in 2000.

More recently, private equity firms such as Ripplewood Holdings have led the consolidation of second-tier automotive parts suppliers, largely with the same objectives as the first-tier consolidation wave.

The emergence of these systems integrators raises an interesting question: Just how much manufacturing does an OEM need to do in-house? Volkswagen has a well-known assembly plant in Brazil that is a great example of this emerging large-scale outsourcing trend. Third-party suppliers deliver all the major parts of the vehicle—including rolling chassis, interiors, engine drive trains—to the plant, where it is merely assembled into its final form. The erstwhile manufacturer, in the Scale Stage, has now become a designer, marketer, brand name, and systems integrator. The capital, asset and labor-intensive parts and systems manufacturing and assembly has been pushed back down the integrated supply chain to large suppliers.

> *The erstwhile manufacturer, in the Scale Stage, has now become a designer, marketer, brand name and systems integrator.*

Does a potential new business model emerge during the Scale Stage? Perhaps along with the Scale Stage a new platform or basis for competition emerges—as a designer, marketer and branded systems integrator—and not as a basic producer. Such diverse companies as the Sara Lee Corporation, Puma, Sony and Nokia (among others) have chosen this model. Is the Scale Stage also leading to new business models and new definitions of scope?

Health care products industry. Johnson & Johnson, one of the world's leading health care products companies, has taken an innovative approach to its Endgames strategy. Clearly in a Stage 2 industry, it has not followed the path of its main competitors such as Pfizer, Bristol-Myers Squibb, and Eli Lilly, which have divested all of their non-pharmaceutical businesses. Instead, it has segmented the pharmaceutical industry more finely and built an Endgames strategy around creating scale in each of its three core businesses: consumer products, medical devices and diagnostics, and pharmaceuticals. The resulting strategy has been executed through three guiding principles:

1. Acquire to build or reinforce Johnson & Johnson's competitive position in each of its core businesses. Examples include its acquisitions of Centocor and Inverness Medical Technology (biotechnology and diabetes care businesses, respectively) to help build competitiveness in pharmaceuticals; DePuy, an ortho-pedics device company, for its medical devices business; and Neutrogena for its consumer business.

2. Acquire to create or enhance synergies among its core business-es. An example of this was Johnson & Johnson's 2001 acquisi-tion of Alza, which designs controlled-dosage drug systems such as skin patches. Alza's prescription pharmaceutical business will increase the scale of Johnson & Johnson's pharmaceutical busi-ness, while its drug delivery capabilities allows Johnson & Johnson to improve the effectiveness of many of its products in both its pharmaceutical and consumer businesses.

3. Actively review the portfolio of businesses and divest or spin off businesses that become commodities, or suffer from reduced margins. While Johnson & Johnson has made more than 45 acquisitions over the past dozen years, what is less widely recog-nized is that it has divested more than 20 businesses, typically lower-margin commodity businesses, such as surgical gowns, latex gloves and other units that no longer fit the company's long-term growth strategies.

Johnson & Johnson has lowered its Endgames risk profile by pur-suing an Endgames consolidation strategy across many sub-industry segments at the same time. It is also successful at extracting value from acquired companies because it empowers business unit leaders to implement the merger integration themselves. As a result, Johnson & Johnson's core businesses—not the acquired companies—are always the driving force and focal point of the business. In addition, merger integration know-how has become widely dispersed throughout the company—a powerful embedded capability.

Brewing industry. One of the world's oldest and perhaps favorite industries is the brewing business. With nearly 500 years of history behind it, the industry has clearly been slow to move up the Endgames curve. In large part, this was due simply to logistics: Like dairies, which produce perishable milk products, breweries struggle to find the right geographic locations to assure economical distribution and product freshness. Smaller countries can accommodate a proliferation of local breweries, whose higher production scale costs are offset by lower, local delivery costs. In larger countries such as the United States, it's not unusual to find placement of Anheuser-Busch breweries in strategically efficient distribution locations. Coors beer, for example, was brewed in a manner that required refrigeration during transit, so its distribution area—and thus potential market—was limited primarily to the Western United States through the 1970s.

Most of the world's beer markets are mature and offer only limited potential for further volume development: aside from Germany, where the industry is still quite fragmented among small companies, only a few players dominate in each market (see sidebar: "Is Bigger Better for German Brewers?"). For example, only two breweries, Brasseries Kronenbourg and Brasseries Heineken, lead the French market. In Spain, Grupo Cruzcampo, San Miguel, Mahou, El Aguila, and Damm were the five remaining players left in the market before Heineken formed a Spanish conglomerate integrating Grupo Cruzcampo and El Aguila. In the United States, market leaders Anheuser-Busch, Miller, and Adolph Coors hold 80% of market share.

Is Bigger Better for German Brewers?

Few industries can boast such a long, rich heritage and storied traditions. By 1516, beer had become such a popular beverage that Wilhelm IV of Bavaria created a special law, the "Reinheitsgebot," which dictated the exact ingredients allowed in beer. Even today, German breweries follow the quality standards set by this law, and international breweries that want a share of the German market abide by it as well.

As a result, Germans tend to think of themselves as the founding fathers of beer and continue to value their breweries and beer quality. When compared with the international competitors, however, German breweries are only minor players: Anheuser-Busch (United States) has annual sales of about 130 million hectoliters (hl), Heineken (Netherlands) about 100 million hl, and Interbrew (Belgium) about 90 million hl. By contrast, the largest German brewery, Warsteiner, has sales of about 5 million hl per year.

Similar discrepancies in production volume are found in the markets for malt beverages across the world. The German market remains extremely fragmented, with more than 1,200 breweries active today. Thanks to strong consumer loyalty, many small family-owned breweries still exist in Germany and have avoided being swallowed up by the consolidation waves affecting the rest of the world.

Still, many of the country's small companies are under pressure to consolidate. Nonalcoholic beverage companies are gaining market share, consumers are becoming more health conscious, and general consumption is on a downward trend. 30 years ago, the annual per capita consumption in Germany was at roughly 140 liters; in 2000 it was down to 120 liters. Today, as nonalcoholic beverages make inroads in the market, companies have raised their marketing spending and sponsorships, shrinking profit margins in the process. Only the well-known brands with strong marketing enjoy healthy profits.

The current condition in the German brewery industry is already evidence of a maturing market and the beginning of consolidation: Interbrew first bought Diebels and spent DM3.5 billion for Beck & Co.; Heineken formed a joint venture with Paulaner. The German market will eventually become oligopolistic, as is the case in all other countries around the globe. Smaller family-owned businesses ultimately must join the larger conglomerates that offer needed economies of scale.

Such regional maturity sets the stage for increased cross-border mergers and globalization. Scottish and Newcastle, the biggest brewer in Britain, has been a steady growth company in its home market, while its larger competitors—Carlsberg, Heineken, and Interbrew—looked to Eastern Europe for emerging growth opportunities. However, Scottish and Newcastle's takeover in early 2002 of Finland's largest brewer, Hartwall, for US$1.7 billion clearly changes the picture. The hidden gem in the Hartwall deal is its stake in Baltic Beverage

Holdings, which gives Scottish and Newcastle an instant market presence in Russia, Latvia, Estonia, and Lithuania, where growth has been steadily upward. The deal also puts the company on a probable collision course with Carlsberg, which also has a stake in Baltic Beverages.

Just a few months after Scottish and Newcastle acquired Hartwall, another major industry shift was announced: Following months of speculation, London-based South African Breweries, PLC (SAB) purchased Miller Brewing from Philip Morris for US$5.6 billion. The merged company—SABMiller—will be the world's second-largest brewing company and a leading player in the United States, the industry's most profitable market.

Eventually, as the industry continues its climb up the Endgames curve, smaller companies will fall victim to the emerging global powerhouses that benefit from economies of scale.

SCALING THE SCALE STAGE

Clearly, Stage 2 is about growth—healthy growth, that is—and about gaining scale as quickly as possible. What do we recommend for companies struggling to scale Stage 2? Of course, there is no one-size-fits-all diet that will transform a relative lightweight into a heavyweight overnight: Different companies and industries require different approaches. Still, the basics for growth are immutable: mergers, globalization, brand consolidation, and market extension. Mastering all of these may not be necessary, but if you don't excel in most of them, your competitor (the one that's growing over in the corner) will.

> Stage 2 is about growth—healthy growth, that is—and about gaining scale as quickly as possible.

Making mergers work. Historically, mergers have not added value in proportion to expectations. This fact reveals a fundamental flaw in the strategy behind most mergers. There are two kinds of benefits that must be reaped. The first is the rationalization and consolidation of economies, which may be substantial. The second, and perhaps more important, is the ability to capitalize on the scale, size, and scope of the new, larger company. Unless this latter strategy is well conceived and executed, the result is a short-term surge in profits followed by a long-term sag, often sinking below pre-merger levels.

The more carefully the acquirer considers the potential synergies and leverage of the acquisitions, the more likely a successful financial outcome. Obviously, markets—by which we mean both customers and financial investors—respond to well thought-out acquisitions and reject ill-advised ones. Without a favorable reaction from these constituencies, the acquirer may struggle to generate the positive returns to match the "buzz" around the acquisition.

In Stage 2, executives must ask themselves what, specifically, is the unique competitive advantage on which the consolidated company will build future growth and long-term profitability. Simply buying competitors is not enough. Remember: in mathematics, the sum of two negative numbers is an even larger negative number. The same holds true for combining companies. Alternatively, choosing companies with unique, proprietary, and complementary value propositions can create genuine synergies that result in dominant market positions earned, not bought.

Industry titans such as GE, Cisco Systems, Newell Rubbermaid, and Medtronic, to name a few, lead in the game of strategic acquisitions. These companies have set the bar not only in terms of number of acquisitions, but more important, in terms of successfully integrating them (see sidebar: "Integration Checklist"). In other words, companies must be able to not only integrate an acquisition target, but effectively run it as well. Integrating IT systems, for example, is a critical—and complicated—step (see sidebar: "The IT Platform Is a Consolidation Linchpin"). The Newellization approach, in which the acquired company achieves the same level of efficiency as its parent in approximately two years, has been the most successful, despite some high-profile stumbles.

Mapping out globalization. In the Opening Stage, industries may be concentrated on a local, regional, or maybe even national scale. But once the Endgames move to Scale Stage, the geography changes. Going global is a critical means of increasing mass. To be a true world leader, a company must participate in a meaningful way within the global triad—the Americas, Europe, and Asia Pacific. International expansion presents significant market opportunities to gain the resources

INTEGRATION CHECKLIST

Thinking of acquiring a new company? Choosing the right target is only half of the battle: some of the best "fits" fail to live up to their potential due to missteps after the ink dries. The necessary due diligence is intense and for long-term success companies must master it—there is no getting around it. Although each acquisition is unique, having a set strategic framework that addresses the following integration categories is key:

- **Price.** Pay the right price and take write-offs up front.
- **Processes.** Learn the processes and eliminate misfits.
- **Integration.** Seamless integration of key functions, particularly IT systems, is critical and must occur as soon as possible. Additionally, companies in each industry must identify their own unique systems—procurement and logistics for the retail industry, for example—and ensure that they are a top priority.
- **Culture.** Create an open culture and communicate aggressively.
- **People.** Retain key people and know-how, eliminating those who must go, fast and cleanly.

Of these lessons, the single most important one is fostering an open culture that readily embraces the employees of the acquired company. If the employees don't feel comfortable with the new owners, they will leave, thus destroying a substantial part of the acquisition's value. Of course, grants, patents, processes, and goodwill all fall into the value equation as well, but in most cases, the people matter most.

If there are key contributors who came with the acquisition (and if there aren't, why was it acquired?), create positions that will motivate them and keep them from jumping ship. Key actions for this include:

Decide on the right structure. A decentralized organizational structure—with key people in the right position—that pushes decisions downward to lower levels often helps new organizations adapt.

Understand and simplify the processes. Putting two companies together is difficult enough when they do things in similar, flexible ways—but nearly impossible if they cling to old, provincial processes.

Choose the culture to build around. Look at the culture of the target company. Is it uniform? Is it open or is it insular? In other words, is it one where very few outsiders come in at a higher level, such as Wal-Mart and Procter & Gamble, or does top management welcome executives from a variety of backgrounds? Understanding the organizational culture of the target company helps executives take the necessary steps to reshape their own organization accordingly.

In Chapter 7, we offer some more merger integration lessons in the sidebar, "Seven Steps to Merger Success."

THE IT PLATFORM IS A CONSOLIDATION LINCHPIN

One of the most critical—in fact, indispensable—elements of the Scale Stage is that the acquiring company must have an IT platform/system capable of serving the combined companies. Islands of separate, incompatible systems cannot be sustained. Depending on the nature of the business, the IT platform must at least include an enterprisewide (enterprise resource planning or ERP) base system upon which all core transactions can be handled. Companies such as SAP, Oracle, Computer Associates, and J.D. Edwards are among many that provide such systems.

Converting the acquired company immediately to ERP is an important step in successful integrations and achieves three goals:

- It puts core transactions into a system that permits accounting to be done and financial controls to be put in place.
- It reveals process incompatibilities that must be fixed.
- It defines who is in control and what mode of operation the combined company will follow.

Next, depending on the nature of the business, the IT systems must be combined into the best-of-breed operations within the company—either in the acquirer or, less often, in the acquired. In product companies, supply chain software is important. In almost all kinds of businesses, data warehouse and knowledge management systems are valuable. In service businesses, communications, transaction tracking, and customer interaction systems are important. IT is critical because it is the key enabler for decision-making—arguably the most vital management task.

Underestimating the importance of physical integration (people, processes, places) with the parallel integration of information and

> systems can be a fatal mistake. Putting together two large companies is challenging enough. Trying to do it in the dark or speaking different systems languages is a formula for failure.

that become necessary in the Scale Stage. Many of these opportunities will require finding new and different partners—businesses that are cognizant of what is needed to win in unfamiliar global markets (see sidebar: "Avis Drives a Global Strategy").

AVIS DRIVES A GLOBAL STRATEGY

Cendant is a globally diversified hotel and real estate franchisor, with US$9 billion in annual revenue and operations in more than 50 countries. For years it has supplemented its organic growth with strategic acquisitions around its core competencies.

In 2001, for example, Cendant purchased Avis, the second-largest car-rental company in the industry. Avis has demonstrated exceptional skill in building scale with a strong—and consistent—global presence. Once a customer registers for its Wizard program, the process for picking up, paying for, and dropping off rental vehicles at airports, hotels, and Avis centers becomes quick, easy, and familiar. The company has locations at roughly 1,700 centers across North and South America and Asia Pacific. It also has marketing agreements with Avis Europe, PLC, a separately owned U.K.-based company that owns or franchises an additional 3,050 Avis locations throughout Europe, the Middle East, and Africa. For frequent travelers, the ability to deal with a familiar and ubiquitous service provider becomes a high-value benefit.

Avis faces a continuing challenge in its competitive environment. Ranked number two, it operates as a first-choice alternative to market leader Hertz. If Avis does its job well, its convenience and global scale can help it overcome lesser competitors with different value positions (Budget, National: low price; Enterprise: door-to-door pickup and delivery; Alamo: very low price, but less convenient non-airport locations).

The challenge Avis faces is one that all large competitors must deal with in the Scale Stage. To grow, Avis must clearly identify its target customers and deliver the service and value those customers find

> most desirable at competitive prices—better than the few remaining competitors—while maintaining acceptable profitability.

Although globalization can open doors to new markets, it can just as quickly turn into a trap. The complexity of conducting business in other countries can be overwhelming. Most business metrics for national markets ignore or underplay the intricacies of crossing borders, such as product or customer proliferation, language and currency differences, different cultural norms, market restrictions, government intervention, and the distances (and time zones) across which information and people must move.

Acquiring foreign companies with resident knowledge provides a solid foothold in the new market. Then, the acquirer must subdue its tendency to ignore the local cultures and knowledge. International business, like all businesses, follows the old 80-20 rule: 80% of all business activity is the same or very similar regardless of where it is done; the remaining 20% of what must be done in foreign markets is very different.

The company that recognizes the 80-20 rule, that understands and properly deals with the 20% difference while building scale economies and reducing complexity in the areas of 80% similarity, will be the winner. Study any successful global company and these points are evident, even if only in hindsight (see sidebar: "Wal-Mart Finds a World of Difference").

WAL-MART FINDS A WORLD OF DIFFERENCE

From the day Wal-Mart opened its doors in 1962, it has followed a tremendous growth path. In 1990 it became the largest retailer in the United States and began to work on its global expansion plans. Since then, Wal-Mart has emerged as the number-one retailer in the world, with superior market share in the United States, Canada, and Mexico, and smaller operations in South America, Asia, and Europe.

But not all of Wal-Mart's expansion plans have been a success. In 1998, the retail giant targeted the German market and began a series of acquisitions, including 21 Wertkauf stores in 1998 and 74 Interspar stores in 1999. But it quickly became evident that Wal-Mart's culture conflicted with that of its newly acquired stores. Take the issue of cost control. For Wal-Mart executives, keeping costs low is an ingrained fact of life. Managers on business journeys traditionally share a hotel room to keep expenses low. For the German managers, however, such arrangements were unacceptable. Additionally, the Germans perceived Wal-Mart's motivation exercises at the beginning of a normal working day as silly. Bringing an abrupt end to the honeymoon, most members of the German management team quit their jobs shortly after the acquisition, leaving Wal-Mart with insufficient knowledge about the German way of doing business.

The lack of local expertise quickly caused problems. Wal-Mart was unaware of administrative regulations that can defer its launch by up to five years. Furthermore, the retailer realized too late that its strategy of undercutting its competitors' prices would be scrutinized by the German Cartel Office (Bundeskartellamt), hindering its ability to follow its traditional business plan. Combined, these obstacles kept Wal-Mart's German market share at just 2%, providing it with too little scale to operate profitably. In 2000 it suffered a loss of US$200 million on roughly US$3 billion in sales.

Building better brands. Brand management becomes an increasingly complex issue as consolidation speeds up in the Scale Stage. Frequently companies in the Opening Stage become "roll-ups"—companies created as the result of a series of acquisitions in a fragmented industry. These roll-up companies typically have good business fundamentals, but it is important for their leaders to present a unifying strategy that articulates how the new company will be worth more than the sum of its parts. Branding can be an important strategic tool to bind the various groups together and position them for growth in the Scale Stage.

Magnetek is an excellent example. Formed in the mid-1980s through a series of more than 10 acquisitions in the electric motor, electrical equipment, and lighting industries, Magnetek was a roll-up of related and adjacent businesses, put together through private equity money and the acquisition of such companies as Plessey SpA and Century Electric. Management renamed the company as Magnetek and built the Magnetek brand as the unifying theme for the businesses. The Magnetek brand became a lightning rod in defining the company's acquisition strategy and face to the market, allowing the company to successfully progress through the 1990s in the Scale Stage.

Banks, in particular, have experienced the challenges of maintaining brand awareness as they have gone through a wave of industry consolidation. Many have chosen to use hyphenated hybrid names during a transition period until the brand equity has been reasonably transferred to the new parent company. Space prohibits making a list of the progression of bank consolidations and brands here, but several name changes over the past five years no doubt spring to mind. Two industries obviously benefit from this stage: printers and signage makers. Some banks have gone through three sets of signs on the front of their buildings and offices in the past five years!

Expanding through extension. Companies with strategic vision anticipate when their industry will reach the saturation point and begin branching out or developing a new business model in preparation. Consider the evolution of Yum! brands, formerly known as Tricon Global Restaurants. Yum! was originally formed by PepsiCo when it acquired the restaurant chains of KFC, Taco Bell, and Pizza Hut. Unable to attain the same levels of profitability in the restaurant business as in its core businesses, PepsiCo spun the three restaurant chains off to form Yum! Once independent, Yum! management aggressively drove synergies across the restaurant brands to squeeze out costs and grow.

> Companies with strategic vision anticipate when their industry will reach the saturation point and begin branching out, or developing a new business model.

Yum!'s first step was to reengineer its business model to form the foundation for acquisition-based growth. The company consolidated human resources and recruiting programs across the three restaurant chains, consolidated procurement to reduce costs, created an integrated global restaurant development plan, and pursued common product development programs. These actions led to a competitive cost structure, a harmonized global growth strategy, and a template for folding prospective acquisitions into Yum!'s business model.

Most important, Yum! began to cross-market the three restaurant brands, which led to a critical innovation—restaurant multibranding. In 2000, Yum! tested the restaurant multibranding concept in an alliance with Yorkshire Global Restaurants, the owners of Long John Silver's and A&W All-American Food Restaurants. Over the next several months, Yum! and Yorkshire opened 83 KFC/A&Ws, six KFC/Long John Silver's, and three Taco Bell/Long John Silver's. Consumer acceptance was so great that Yum! ended up acquiring Yorkshire in early 2002. As David C. Novak, Yum! Chairman and CEO, said in the press release announcing the merger, "One of our major strategies is to drive global growth by leading the way in multi-branding innovation—offering the consumer two brands and more choice in one restaurant.... We are confident multibranding is a key enabler for accelerating the renewal of our existing asset base and adding new units with excellent returns for our shareholders."

McDonald's also is branching out. It has acquired Donato's Pizza, Chipotle Mexican Grill, Aroma Café, and Boston Market (formerly Boston Chicken) restaurant properties. McDonald's has failed with most of these menu items as dinner offerings on its regular restaurant menus. Why? Because, as Al Reis and Jack Trout constantly remind us in their books on positioning, "Once you have a position in the mind of the consumer, it is terribly hard to change it." And you shouldn't try anyway. McDonald's is hamburgers and fries. Why fight it? Simply make the best-tasting, fastest, most consistent and inexpensive hamburgers and fries.

What is the marketing value of Donato's Pizza, Chipotle Mexican Grill, Aroma Café, and Boston Market to McDonald's? As brands, their value is just so-so. As line extensions, these are competing restaurants. Nevertheless, these acquisitions may be strategically brilliant. They can leverage McDonald's immense buying power, its management base, and its financial resources. In other words, McDonald's has the potential to keep non-hamburger and fries customers in its fold.

Staying Ahead of the Curve: Strategic Lessons for the Scale Stage

Reinforce core strengths. In the Scale Stage, companies run the risk of losing a hold on their core culture as new acquisitions are brought into the fold. Consequently, they must pay close attention to fostering a strong culture that can absorb acquired companies, yet still maintain their original strengths and characteristics. Also, because key employees are often the most valuable assets of a newly acquired company, retaining them is critical. At the heart of a successful cultural integration is a strong management team that can build on the unifying features of the two companies and remove the differences. Building an information technology platform that is scalable, can rapidly integrate acquired companies, and causes minimal disruption to operations and customer service will also go far in paving the path up the curve.

With internal strength and stability under control, a company is in a stronger position to craft its Focus Stage Endgames strategy. Attention must turn to building superior insight based upon other industry players—monitoring what their competitive strategies are and finding ways to beat them up the curve. Much of this insight depends on gathering the right information. Today, approximately 10% to 20% of information is gathered externally; this proportion should be doubled.

Build momentum. The imperative is simple: consolidate the industry by growing with maximum speed. Inherently, this must involve a high rate of acquisitions because organic growth alone won't get you there. A company jockeying to reach Stage 3 must be among the first players in the industry to capture the major competitors in the most important markets. The deals toward the end of the Scale Phase move beyond small acquisitions and should instead lead to quantum-leap jumps in scale.

Become a consolidation leader. Companies must build up the deepest integration know-how in the industry, using internal as well as external sources. The idea here is to build a merger integration model that clearly documents a proven methodology. There should also be a critical mass of experienced employees who can perform the necessary tasks, in addition to a regular influx of new employees. Soon, the company will master the skills to take over operational control of the main functions of an acquired company in less than three months. Additionally, choosing the right targets should also become routine: Warren Buffett is famous for saying yes or no to deals within five minutes. Assessing acquisition targets may never meet Buffett's strict time-line, but with the right knowledge base and methodologies in place, losing critical time up front will no longer be an issue.

Other factors in becoming a top consolidator are cultivating investor relations to get optimal funding and expanding global reach to gain strategic geographical coverage.

AN EYE ON FOCUS

As companies move from Stage 2 to Stage 3, the strategic emphasis shifts from speed to finesse. The deals become fewer and farther between, but each one carries significantly more weight. The room to misstep, while never great, continues to shrink. In fact, the space to maneuver in general is decidedly tighter.

As a result, players entering the Focus Stage must develop new strategies: gobbling up competitors to gain scale no longer works, simply because there are fewer and fewer competitors to gobble. Thus, while mastering merger integration gets companies through Stage 3, it won't get them to Stage 4. To find out what does, let's move on.

Chapter Five | The Focus Stage

What we need to do better is be predictive. We have to be proactive. We have to develop the capability to anticipate attacks. We have to develop the capability of looking around corners.

—Robert S. Mueller III, F.B.I. Director,
New York Times, 30 May 2002

The third Endgames Stage, the Focus Stage, is characterized not so much by a blizzard of merger activity, as we saw in Stages 1 and 2, but by mega-deals and large-scale consolidation plays. The goal in this stage is to emerge as one of the small number of global industry powerhouses.

In this stage the number of merger deals begins to subside, but the size of mergers continues to rise as competitors battle to be among the last ones standing. The race is far from over, but the strategy changes as future Endgames winners begin acquiring their competitors with an economic return in mind, rather than with an eye primarily toward gaining market share. Companies that have made a lot of acquisitions in the past will begin fine-tuning their business portfolios to peel off units that are outside their core competencies. Some of these spin-offs will generate new businesses—and even new industries—as the number of industry players dwindles to those that are the most efficient operators.

Internally, companies typically focus on integrating mega-mergers made in late Stage 2 or early Stage 3. Once the merger process is wrapped up, they turn their attention to maximizing shareholder value and satisfying the demands of equity markets. Externally, the near oligopolistic structure of many Focus Stage industries results in the commoditization of products and services. Unfortunately, companies in the Focus Stage often pay more attention to operational efficiencies and survival, and less attention to satisfying their customers. The balance beam that bridges the gap to the final stage of consolidation is progressively more challenging.

> *The strategy changes as future Endgames winners begin acquiring their competitors with an economic return in mind, rather than with an eye primarily toward gaining market share.*

Typical industries in the Focus Stage include electric power and gas companies, steel producers, glass manufacturers, coal producers, magazine publishers, ship builders, and distillers (see Figure 5-1). A number of subindustries also fall in the Focus Stage; the pharmaceutical subindustry, for example, falls under the larger umbrella of the healthcare products industry. The rules of the game have been well established at this point, and only an outside event or an industry incumbent will have enough power to effect significant change.

Often, the most important competitive levers that come into play in the Focus Stage come down to economies of scale, size and global reach, and cost position. An interesting example of this in action is the dynamic around cost position versus capacity versus demand. When new low-cost competitors rapidly infuse large amounts of capacity into an industry (think of Wal-Mart in the large-scale retail industry and Nucor in the steel industry), they often end up eventually squeezing out higher-cost competitors with large amounts of pre-existing capacity (think of Kmart and Bethlehem Steel). This dynamic is exacerbated and accelerated in an economic downturn when demand shrinks.

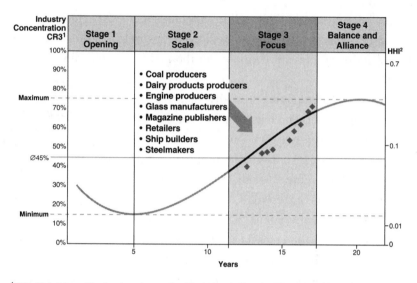

[1]CR3 = Market share of the three largest companies of the total market based on Value-Building Growth database (25,000 companies).
[2]HHI = Hirschman-Herfindahl Index corresponds to the sum of the squared market shares of all companies and is greater than 90%; the axis logarithmically plotted.
Sources: Value-Building Growth database; A.T. Kearney analysis

Figure 5-1. Industry concentration rate in the Focus Stage

STAGE 3 SNAPSHOTS: WHO'S WHO

To illustrate the forces at work in the Focus Stage, we present a number of case studies from the retailing sector. As opposed to the steel or shipbuilding industries, where the dynamics of Stage 3 consolidation are fairly well established and widely known, the retailing industry highlights several fascinating variations on Endgames dynamics in action.

First, the retailing industry appears to be bimodal in its Endgames positioning. In other words, the industry has some parts (specialty retailing, for example) that demonstrate characteristics of the Opening and Scale Stages (Stages 1 and 2) and other parts (large-scale retailing—Wal-Mart—and discount retailing) that are clearly in the Focus or even the Balance and Alliance Stage (Stages 3 and 4).

Second, the typical, overt Endgames "M&A driven" consolidation we have come to expect in other industries is less prevalent in the retailing industry. Instead, retailers often use the tactic of "implicit consolidation" to achieve their strategic goals, including:

- Focusing on market share and cost position, and implicitly consolidating their industry by forcing competitors to go bankrupt (rather than acquiring them).
- Forming cooperatives (rather than acquiring competitors) to gain scale, reach, and purchasing power.
- Buying out minority equity partners that initially helped a retailer to grow and expand, particularly into international markets.

All told, the richness of its examples prompted us to derive all of the snapshots for this section from this single, albeit massive industry. Combined, these case studies create a microcosm of Stage 3 activity. The lessons U.S.-based retailers have learned—and have yet to learn—will undoubtedly resonate with companies and industries around the globe.

> *The lessons U.S.-based retailers have learned will undoubtedly resonate with companies and industries around the globe.*

Mega-retailers. First, consider the retailing giants. We assign the venerable Big Three retailers from decades past—Sears, Montgomery Ward, and J.C. Penney—to this category. Two of these companies, Sears (1886) and Ward (1873), predate the 20th century, with J.C. Penney (1913) closing in on 90 years of retailing.

In 2001, however, Ward filed Chapter 11 after a five-year struggle to survive in a market being squeezed from all sides. And although Sears is on its second "turnaround CEO," several strategic moves have put it in a stronger position. Sears' US$1.9 billion acquisition of the mail-order retailer Lands' End in 2002 was widely applauded for its potential synergies. As the *New York Times* headline succinctly declared, "Sears to Buy Lands' End in a Deal That Unites Pants and Power Drills." Lands' End's vast Web-based distribution channels, in addition to its quality brand name, will go far in helping Sears improve its clothing product portfolio.

J.C. Penney took steps to alter its merchandise position and presentation in the late 1980s and early 1990s. In effect, this turned its clock back a bit, and bought the company some time. But Penney now faces a full frontal attack from a new nemesis, Kohl's, which is outdoing Penney at what it once did best—and with better, low-cost locations outside of expensive malls.

And J.C. Penney is not alone. Retailers everywhere are vulnerable to new and formidable competitors that are closing in on all sides. In 2001, Marks & Spencer, a venerable English retailer, became locked in a battle for survival. Faced with plummeting market share, it embarked on a massive reorganization plan that included closing 38 stores throughout Europe, shuttering its catalog operation in the United Kingdom, and divesting its Brooks Brothers clothing stores and Kings Super Markets chains in the United States—all in an effort to refocus on its traditional core strengths of food and clothing. One year later, Marks & Spencer seemed to be on the road to recovery: profits were up and it had regained some of its lost market share. But the cost for losing its way was high, and the lessons of its U.S. counterpart, Montgomery Ward, serve as a reminder how fragile this comeback may be.

Beyond the retailing industry, such harsh competition and dramatic defensive maneuvers characterize the Focus Stage. It's a mistake to believe size and scale can insulate a company from the pressures of the Endgames curve. Remember: the bigger they are, the harder they fall.

Discount retailers. Sam Walton may be forever known as the CEO who built an empire on discount retailing, but without the pioneering—and somewhat duplicitous—efforts of Eugene Ferkauf, Walton might not have enjoyed the same success. In 1948, Ferkauf opened one of the first discount stores in the United States, E.J. Korvette. But there was a problem: the Robinson-Patman Act of 1937 dictated that retailers must charge the manufacturers' suggested retail price. To circumvent this law, Ferkauf claimed his store was a "membership store" that was not open to the general public, which effectively exempted him from the Act; Ferkauf then simply passed out membership cards at the door. Eventually Ferkauf was challenged in court, but support for the Act had waned and Ferkauf and his successors were free to stay in business. The E.J. Korvette chain peaked at 58 stores; it performed well in the Opening Stage, but never mastered the Scale Stage and went bankrupt in 1980. It did, however, set the stage for subsequent discount retailers as well as for the current spate of membership retailers such as Sam's Club and Costco.

By the 1960s, with changing demographics and the rise of the suburbs, the freestanding general merchandise discount store came into its own. Kmart evolved from the five- and 10-cent chain S.S. Kresge. Target Stores were spawned by department store chain Dayton's as an off-price entry into what appeared to be a logically emerging market segment. And last but not least, in 1962, former J.C. Penney employee Sam Walton opened, in a small town in Arkansas, the first store of what has become the largest and most successful retailer in the world, Wal-Mart.

Soon, discount stores swept the retail landscape, not just in America, but also in some European countries, and then globally as well (Carrefour and Hypermarché in France, Tesco in the United Kingdom, and Wing On in Hong Kong, to name a few). These stores—led first by Kmart and now by Wal-Mart—are fully into the Focus Stage. Of the many regional chains that were spawned by the discount stores during Scale Stage, most of the regional ones have failed, including Lucky Stores, Treasury (Penney's attempt), Fedmart, Gibson, Howard, Venture, Gold Circle, and Caldor.

These chains all followed essentially the same model through the Opening Stage and rapidly grew to what they thought was Scale Stage. They soon fell to the behemoths as they discovered that their understanding of Scale Stage was flawed. This lesson is useful as it is repeated often in other industries (including automotive and heavy industry).

Conversely, aggressive discount retailers such as Wal-Mart recognized the risk of a one-size-fits-all approach and experimented. These chains found which merchandise categories would fit, compete well, and survive in their store assortments and which didn't. Freestanding drugstore chains such as Walgreen's and its next competitor, CVS, are establishing beachheads against large general merchandise leaders such as Wal-Mart and Target. By setting up shop at busy intersections—and making the old "drugstore" a combination drug, convenience, food services, and mini-discount store—they are attracting shoppers who do not want to traverse huge parking lots and 100,000+ square foot discount stores to find a few items.

This is classic Focus Stage behavior of the "trading players" mode—but in this place it is "trading customers."

Kmart has already fallen into Chapter 11. The company is exhibiting the classic Focus Stage illness of being caught between two huge, tough competitors and *not* being able to achieve parity of cost/delivery necessary to compete. Only Kmart's size and locations give it a small chance to emerge from bankruptcy and move past the Focus Stage, but it faces many of the same issues as Holzmann.

As the industry gears up for the final stage of the Endgame, Wal-Mart and Target are choosing sides, garnering the best suppliers, the best deals, the best merchandisers, and the best talent. "Trading players" is going on and Kmart risks not being attractive enough to play the game. Few regional, niche competitors remain: ShopKo Stores, Fred Meyer, and Meijer are among the survivors. These retailing giants are moving to compete in the same retailing format that Fred Meyer (in turn owned by Kroger) and Meijer had competed in for a decade or more—"superstores" that incorporate grocery stores into discount stores.

> *As the industry gears up for the final stages of the Endgame, Wal-Mart and Target are choosing sides, garnering the best suppliers, the best deals, the best merchandisers, and the best talent.*

Wholesalers. Sol Price, an innovative retailer, founded the early department store chain FedMart in southern California and rapidly built it into a success before selling it. As he departed that venue, he realized that all retailing efforts were ignoring one large and newly growing market segment—small business owners.

As more and more small businesses sprung up in the 1980s, they were forced to either pay premium retail prices for routine supplies (office and maintenance supplies, small equipment, coffee and cups, for example) or spend precious time buying from a multiplicity of local distributors, one for each need. An opportunity was emerging.

Price considered the economics. Small businesses could shop weekly if they could come to one place and get everything at great prices. Location meant little. In fact, industrial locales were where the customers were clustered and real estate was much cheaper. Ambience also meant little. These business people would gladly prowl a warehouse-like setting with industrial carts, collecting the supplies they needed. No merchandising was necessary because no reason existed to offer more than a single brand or type of each item.

These decisions cut the costs of overhead dramatically and

reduced the assortment of items required from the 50,000 and up available in discount stores to less than 10,000. Bulk packages were acceptable and non-perishable food items could also be good sellers.

By paying a membership fee (US$25), the people who shopped at the first Price Club somehow felt special, like "insiders." Price realized that he could achieve unprecedented inventory turn way over the norms experienced in this business, usually selling goods before he had to pay for them under standard 30- to 60-day terms. The low-overhead locations, low-overhead presentation, and negative working capital model allowed Price Clubs to earn a profit on a 10% gross margin—fully 15 points below what traditional discounters charged.

People flocked to the first Southern California Price Clubs, leading to volume of more than US$2 million per week per location. This model spread like wildfire, moving rapidly to metro markets across the United States, and led to a raft of competitors including Pace, Costco Wholesale, BJ's, and Wal-Mart's Sam's Clubs. In fact, more than a dozen smaller chains began operations and then quickly merged into the larger companies during a rapid consolidation in the mid to late 1980s. By the mid-1990s, only three clubs still existed: Costco acquired Price Club, Sam's bought Pace, and BJ's staked out a regional presence.

As the clubs moved into the Focus Stage, they found that the Scale Stage had dragged them off course. Their profit model was no longer as sound as the original. Opening membership early to consumers and establishing a 5% higher price tier than for business members stimulated growth tremendously, but it also created proliferation of items and resulted in some loss of focus on core customers. After a period in the Focus Stage, both Sam's and Costco have restructured their locations and assortments to meet the new mix of consumers and small businesses. During the Focus Stage, it is easy to get off track by trying to artificially stimulate growth at the cost of lower profit and, often unrecognized, potential financial failure.

Office products retail and wholesale industry. For decades, the industry had been a sleepy distributor-based business-to-business segment. Large companies evolved to serve other large companies, thus the "contract stationers" became discrete intermediaries, doing more than distributors to serve large corporate clients. Mail order emerged to serve small businesses and individuals, and a few retail stores existed here and there.

This was the scenario circa the mid-1980s, when former grocery merchant Tom Stemberg conceived Staples, the office products superstore. Within five years after Stemberg opened a handful of Staples stores, several dozen emulators had appeared—typical of the Opening Stage of a new segment shift.

Within five more years, there were once again only three superstore chains: Staples, Office Depot, and Office Max. And, like their discount store counterparts (Office Max was once a division of Kmart), two of the three are dominant and the third, Office Max, hangs on but remains at risk. This new form of distribution—think of it as a retail store to serve small business office products needs—totally disintermediated the comfortable industry structure. It drove the entire industry through the Scale Stage and into the Focus Stage in less than a decade. As the superstores grew, they negotiated better deals from suppliers and competed with contract stationers at the lower size range of their markets.

Clearly, large companies were not going to give an administrator US$5,000 cash and a small truck to go shop for supplies and equipment—but they would provide a company credit card and ask the administrators to go pick up a few hundred dollars' worth of supplies on their lunch break. As the superstores grew, they became wealthy enough to acquire a few of the better contract stationers and two or three leading mail-order companies, thus broadening their reach and extending their scale for purchasing leverage. In defense, specialty distributors and smaller contract stationers banded together to form buying groups or simply merged outright. This is reminiscent of what the hardware trade did a decade earlier (see sidebar: "Hardware Retailers Build New Strategies").

Finally, the industry now finds itself moving into the Focus Stage. A few large distributors remain, as do a handful of large "consortia" and three superstores. The segment patterns revealed in other retailing/products repeat. If this case covered the "category killers" industries like toys (Toys 'R' Us), sporting goods (The Sports Authority, Gart

---

HARDWARE RETAILERS BUILD NEW STRATEGIES

No mom-and-pop store or other niche player is immune from the forces of the merger Endgame. However, in the hardware retail industry, smaller competitors have developed an interesting survival strategy.

Sears' much-vaunted Craftsman brand and its lifetime products guarantee combined with ubiquitous stores and its mail-order catalog forever changed the hardware retailing landscape. Those competitors that survived managed to do so by banding together into cooperatives such as Coast to Coast, Servistar, Sentry Hardware, Hardware Wholesalers Inc., Liberty Group, Cotter & Co. (True-Value/ V&S), and Ace Hardware, along with a host of other less notable groups that pulled together purchasing and distribution services.

In an attempt to emulate Scale Stage economies for non-Scale Stage competitors, these groups were formed to provide administrative and financial help, volume discounts, program merchandising, centralized distribution, and coordinated advertising on a scale otherwise economically impossible. These were just the five largest benefits. Members paid fees to use them and any profits gained at the end of the year were distributed among group's members.

Such groupings took place in other industries as well, essentially moving an entire group of small Opening Stage competitors into the Scale Stage, at least temporarily.

Sports Company), and electronics (Best Buy, Circuit City), the same patterns of consolidation would be evident. As the Endgame plays out, the strong either crush or acquire the weak.

The participants move segment by segment through the Opening Stage to the Scale Stage to the Focus Stage, where they may reinvent themselves to initiate a new start. Or they move to the Balance and Alliance Stage where they "choose sides" and "trade players" in a fight for survival until reinvention can occur. Such is the progression of the Endgame in industry after industry.

MOVING THROUGH THE FOCUS STAGE

The path through the Focus Stage is as treacherous and difficult to manage as all of the other Endgames stages. But there are some specific make-or-break strategic challenges and enablers to keep in mind. Harnessing the power and innovation of all of the employees in your company and focusing exclusively on the strategic imperatives of your core business are the "must-dos" for the Focus Stage. At the same time, sidestepping the effects of disruptive technologies and refocusing on the basics of competitive strategy can make the journey through the Focus Stage relatively smooth.

Harness People Power

The strain on senior management teams, as well as rank-and-file employees, in getting to and competing in the Focus Stage is enormous. Companies in the Focus Stage often have hundreds of thousands of employees. They have often been through mergers and mega-mergers, restructurings, change management initiatives, and competitive onslaughts. As a result, harnessing and focusing the power of all employees becomes particularly important (see sidebar: "GE Raised the Bar").

GE RAISED THE BAR

From aircraft engines to turbines to locomotives to plastics and chemicals, General Electric competes in several prototypical Focus Stage businesses. One of the most important things that GE senior management realized was the need to build advanced people management processes to focus the entire organization on the critical success factors for competing in a Focus Stage business.

What Jack Welch, the retired CEO of GE, accomplished was to build a superior organizational advantage using people development techniques that have been widely publicized. The purpose of this explanation is not to cover this ground again, but merely to put it into context. In the Focus Stage, many competitors have relatively comparable size, scale, scope, resources, and market technology. Thus a critical source of competitive advantage and profitable growth in the Focus Stage often comes from people—how they work together and what they work on.

Welch pioneered several innovative people management principles and borrowed others and tailored them to fit GE's requirements. Several were particularly useful in the Focus Stage:

- **"Boundarylessness":** The open sharing of (often confidential) market, competitor, and customer service information across all levels of management. The boundarylessness concept led GE to extend its value chain to create profitable new service businesses and implement innovative financing vehicles to grow its core Focus Stage businesses.
- **Workouts:** A team-based, non-confrontational approach to resolving cross-functional or cross-business issues and problems. Therefore, employees with different backgrounds and from different levels in the organization (excluding top management) meet for one or several days to find ways to make the organization more efficient and effective. Workouts led, for example, to GE consolidating much of its purchasing power and reducing its procured costs across its many business units.
- **Peer Review of Strategic Plans and Budgets:** A transparent process of having leaders of unrelated business units review and challenge the strategic plans and budgets of each other's businesses. This process, while somewhat confrontational, led to the best minds and creativity of GE focusing on raising the bar of GE's financial and business performance.
- **Six Sigma Focus on Quality and Excellence:** Borrowing this concept from a number of successful Japanese companies (and Motorola in the United States), Welch championed a call to excellence that spanned the globe. By spreading a Six Sigma culture and expectation, Welch focused GE on exceeding customer expectations and outperforming weaker competitors.
- **Digital Transformation:** Although GE was somewhat late to embrace the Internet, when Welch realized its potential, he moved aggressively. He coined the phrase "destroyyourbusiness.com" to emphasize the importance of the Internet to all GE employees. Welch believed that people's efforts are only as good as what they know is happening in their company and within their competitive arena—especially vis-à-vis their immediate partners: suppliers and customers. Building on this principle, Welch implemented a number of strategic Internet initiatives to transform GE's interactions with its customers, suppliers, and internal stakeholders.

> Finally, Welch put an enormous amount of time and effort into selecting the right people for leadership roles. He championed a massive effort in training and leadership development, showcased in GE's management training center in Crotonville, and during quarterly business reviews, he devoted significant amounts of time to career progression and succession planning of his senior managers.

CEOs must conceive and launch companywide initiatives that capture the spirit and commitment of all employees—and focus them on achieving important strategic, customer, supplier, and internal goals.

Maintain Unwavering Focus

The best Focus Stage companies do just what the name implies: focus. They focus on creating and building the advantages of size, scale, scope, brands, organization, and information. They focus on sticking to their knitting and emphasizing what they are best at across their industry's value chain.

For all industries in the Focus Stage, the leaders strive for world-class status and undisputed market leadership. Consider Diageo. Based in London, Diageo has a portfolio of businesses in the beverage and food areas. It owns United Distillers and Vintners, a liquor and wine purveyor, in addition to the Guinness label (beer) and Burger King (fast food). But in 2000, it began to restructure itself to focus solely on the beer, liquor, and spirits businesses. In October 2001, Diageo sold its Pillsbury food business to General Mills; in December 2001, Diageo jointly acquired the Seagram spirits and wine business from Vivendi Universal with Pernod Ricard. Diageo also launched a significant marketing program to leverage its spirits businesses and sold off its Burger King chain to an investor consortium led by Texas Pacific Group.

Focusing a superior amount of resources against selected competitors permits a Stage 3 company to win the competition without the pain of a full frontal assault.

Focusing a superior amount of resources against selected competitors permits a Stage 3 company to win the competition without the pain of a full frontal assault. Recognizing start-up competitors early on allows the Focus Stage competitor to decide whether to crush them, acquire them, or simply emulate them. When used properly, this can become a tremendous advantage and, as each win is racked up, the advantage grows.

Beware Disruptive Technologies

One of the greatest threats to Focus Stage companies lies in "disruptive technologies," as described by Clayton Christensen in his book, *The Innovator's Dilemma* and a series of *Harvard Business Review* articles. Disruptive technologies can change the dynamics and economics of a Focus Stage industry quickly—often resulting in an overhaul of the competitive landscape.

Nucor Steel and its mini-mill emulators revolutionized the U.S. steel industry, essentially redefining what cost-competitiveness means, and plunged several older-technology steel mills into bankruptcy or closure in the process. The publishing industry faces similar disruptions by Web publishing and (self-published) print-on-demand books.

Some companies, however, use emerging technologies to their advantage. Old-line glass companies such as Corning have moved from their Focus Stage core business into the world of fiber optics—with a host of new market and competitive dynamics.

Consequently, Stage 3 companies must keep a close eye on their competitors—especially those hiding in the shadows. It is easy, but dangerous, to overlook or discount non-traditional competitors. New competition often comes from some of the least likely places: Digital Equipment's failure to recognize the threat of personal computers to its minicomputer business until it was too late underscores the potential danger. To avoid repeating Digital Equipment's blunder, companies must keep a close watch on both primary competitors and troublesome start-ups with disruptive technologies.

Develop—and Redevelop—Competitive Strategy

Competitive strategy takes on a new dimension in the Focus Stage. Companies are so big that mergers and acquisitions are no longer the most viable strategic option, and they must look to "blocking and tackling" as a primary growth strategy. Focus Stage companies have often exhausted backward integration as a source of competitive advantage; and vertical integration can be a double-edged sword:

> Companies are so big that mergers and acquisitions are no longer the most viable strategic option, and they must look to "blocking and tackling" as a primary growth strategy.

powerful if industry technology changes little or not at all—and deadly if there is a major shift in technology.

To advance to the Balance and Alliance Stage, companies can no longer depend on taking share by directly encroaching on competitors' markets. There is more parity of market power, resources, and financial clout. As a result, companies must develop a combination of business excellence and strategic initiatives that maximize the effectiveness of both people and capital investments.

STAYING AHEAD OF THE CURVE: STRATEGIC LESSONS FOR THE FOCUS STAGE

The top of the curve is well within sight at this point—but reaching it is far from a given. Companies preparing for the final push into the Balance and Alliance Stage can strengthen their positions by taking a fresh look at their efforts in three areas:

Retool your competitive strategy. Every company approaching the final stage must find its strike zone. In other words, it needs to clearly define its true strengths and make them the focal point of the Endgames strategy. Now is the time to either shore up or part with weak businesses; the competition is just too well entrenched at this phase to resist attacking underperformers.

Companies should also identify the major players that will survive the Endgames—and either agree to a tacit ceasefire or avoid full-frontal assaults. Competitors may reach an implicit understanding at this point, essentially "swapping" lines of business or other opportunities. When they do so under the right conditions, no market share is lost and the competitive landscape becomes cleaner.

Focus on financial affairs. Getting the company's financial house in order takes on a new level of importance at this point. Companies should increase their focus on profitability and rid their portfolio of low-growth or marginally profitable segments, while exploiting higher-growth or more profitable segments.

As we mentioned earlier, Diageo is doing just this by focusing on its core capabilities—alcoholic beverages—and divesting noncore businesses (such as Burger King). Companies in asset-intensive industries often rationalize their global manufacturing footprint during Stage 3 as well. Achieving "fighting" weight for the final stage also means keeping resources lean and fit—in part by employing fewer, better people. An efficient organizational structure that leverages key talent is essential.

Sharpen your marketing message. Companies that move through Stages 2 and 3 rapidly through mergers and acquisitions often need to consolidate and unify their branding and marketing focus during Stage 3 as well. Especially following a mega-merger, a company's marketing message and brand identity may be diffused in the eyes of customers. Stage 3 is the perfect time to sharpen your marketing message, consolidate your sales force, and successfully implement cross-selling and cross-branding strategies.

PREPARING FOR THE FINAL PUSH

These steps are prerequisites to the final, and most challenging, phase of the Endgames. It is during the Balance and Alliance Stage that some businesses reach a natural maturity and decline—while others find renewed life. Which group will your company or industry fall into?

Chapter Six | The Balance and Alliance Stage

Unless you try to do something beyond what you have already mastered, you will never grow.
—Ralph Waldo Emerson

The top of the Endgames curve, the Balance and Alliance Stage, is the final step in the Endgames journey. The industry landscape in Stage 4 includes such heavy hitters as tobacco, aerospace and defense, shoe manufacturing, and soft drinks (see Figure 6-1). These industries are populated by a very few, very large companies that are the winners in their industry consolidation race. They are the unquestioned leaders in their field and can be successful in this space for a long time depending on how they handle and protect their prime position.

But the room to maneuver is considerably smaller and strategic opportunities are increasingly hard to come by. In this stage, big mergers are no longer a significant option simply because the industry has already been consolidated. Instead, Stage 4 companies harvest their competitive position by maximizing their cash flow, protecting their market position, and reacting and adapting to changes in industry

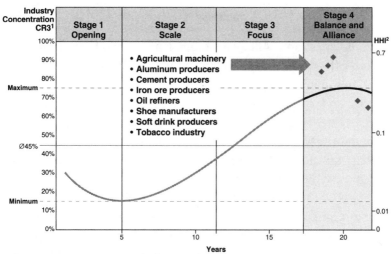

[1] CR3 = Market share of the three largest companies of the total market based on Value-Building Growth database (25,000 companies).
[2] HHI = Hirschman-Herfindahl Index corresponds to the sum of the squared market shares of all companies and is greater than 90%; the axis logarithmically plotted.
Sources: Value-Building Growth database; A.T. Kearney analysis

Figure 6-1. Industry consolidation in the Balance and Alliance Stage

structure and new technological advances (see sidebar: "Trading Places"). Stage 4 companies often experience difficulty in growing market share because they have maximized their market penetration. But they are often subject to government regulation or scrutiny because of their perceived oligopoly or monopoly market position.

> In Stage 4, the room to maneuver is considerably smaller, and strategic opportunities are increasingly hard to come by.

Typically, one of the most significant challenges Stage 4 companies face is knowing what to do with the significant amounts of cash they generate. Some opt to return their profits to their shareholders by increasing dividends or buying back their stock. Some choose to break into pieces by redefining their market scope, to enable their businesses to pursue new growth (and Endgames) strategies. Still others decide to diversify into new or unrelated industries, leading to a new Endgames path. Finally, some try to maintain a "business-as-usual" mindset, but get blown away by breakthrough technologies and simply disappear. The ice distribution businesses in the early 1900s, for example, were crushed by the new

TRADING PLACES

In the Balance and Alliance Stage, leaders climb onto—and are knocked off—their pedestals constantly. This phenomenon is particularly common in the high-tech field, where the velocity at which technologies and companies can move between stages is difficult to match.

In about two decades, IBM's large mainframe systems were undercut by Digital Equipment Corporation's (DEC) powerful minicomputers, which were in turn rendered unimportant by Compaq's low-cost, PC-based servers (as Compaq acquired DEC).

Now Compaq has been acquired by Hewlett-Packard (HP)—and the combined entity is being defeated by Dell's superior production model, which features a close-knit supply chain. Who will beat Dell? And when? Will it be a personal digital assistant (PDA) company such as Palm or Handspring? Doubtful. Or a cell phone company such as Nokia? Not likely, but possible. Or will the Balance and Alliance Stage produce some strange new combination of bedfellows that drives this industry back to the Opening Stage?

The Balance and Alliance Stage drives massive acquisitions and divestitures in technology companies. IBM, Intel, Microsoft, and Cisco bought literally hundreds of small companies to gain technology, talent, and market entry. But the tech giants have been busy shedding large viable companies, too. For instance, HP has been doing more than buying: it spun off Agilent Technologies in 1999.

Another industry ripe for partnerships and alliances, as well as fast consolidation, is the telecom equipment business. It's populated with major players—Cisco, Nortel, Motorola, Qualcomm, Alcatel, and others—surrounded by numerous smaller companies—Powerwave, CommScope, Corvis, Marconi plc, ONI Systems, and Sycamore Networks, to name just a few. When Lucent spun off cellular telephone equipment supplier Celiant, the company was independent for less than a year before another public telecommunications equipment company with about US$1 billion in sales—Andrew Corp.—snapped it up and increased annual revenue by 70%.

CIENA recently purchased ONI Systems for nearly US$400 million to acquire a position in the metropolitan area optical networking

> market to balance out its position in long-distance optical networking. Others, no doubt, are also seeking to use the current market climate to balance out their markets.

refrigeration technology. Or, more recently, look to Polaroid's photography technology, which was supplanted by digital technology. In other words, stability at the top of the curve is no more guaranteed than at any other point along the way.

Let's examine some case studies to bring some of the issues and challenges of Stage 4 companies to life.

STAGE 4 SNAPSHOTS: WHO'S WHO

In reading through the following examples, remember what we noted in the beginning: *all* industries are global and *all* industries will consolidate. Which retailer that is currently stuck in Stage 3 will be its industry's next Nike? Which Stage 2 brewery will rise to become the next Coca-Cola?

The lessons such industry titans offer to those who follow in their footsteps are invaluable. They are, after all, the best of the best. But their position is not—and never will be—secure. These leaders have shattered corporate boundaries, set new records, and created global empires, but the challenge to stay on top of the Endgames curve proves just as rigorous as the climb to the peak. Which ones have the strongest foothold? And which are resting precariously at the top? Read on.

> These leaders have shattered corporate boundaries, set new records and created global empires, but the challenge to stay on top of the Endgames curve proves just as rigorous as the climb to the peak.

Tobacco industry. With roughly 400 years of history behind it, the tobacco industry has emerged as a triumphant contender in the final stage—and offers valuable lessons for those in its shadow (see Figure 6-2). About 15 years ago, the buzzword was diversification. Rising health concerns and increasing legal restrictions prompted analysts to believe that the U.S. tobacco segment had reached its peak of profitability. As a result, traditional tobacco companies invested in snack

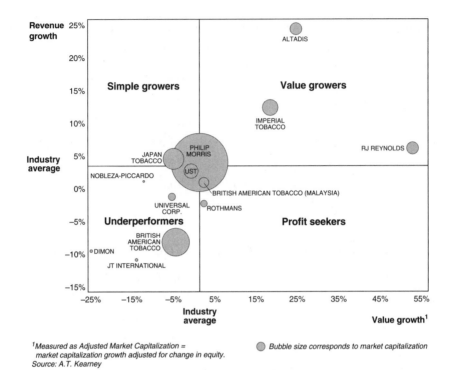

Figure 6-2. Global tobacco industry (CAGR 1996–2001)

foods, retail stores, and financial services to take part in future growth markets. However, despite the predictions, the tobacco industry continued to thrive, becoming the cash cow for many diversified companies. Soon, companies began to divest their portfolios to focus on their tobacco business.

Although much of the industry was still fragmented in smaller, national companies—including several that are state-owned—a few had mastered the global stage. Philip Morris and British American Tobacco (BAT) embraced two distinct strategies that led them to become global leaders in the tobacco industry. Philip Morris followed the strategy to grow organically. It emphasized its main brand, Marlboro, around the world, particularly in countries where health concerns and legal restrictions do not prevail. Only occasional acquisitions, such as Cigatam in Mexico and Tabaqueria in Portugal, punctuated its strategy. Conversely, BAT adopted an acquisitions-based strategy.

In 1999, a dramatic consolidation wave swept over the global tobacco market. The mega-deals that year included BAT's merger with Rothmans and its purchase of Imasco; the merger between the Japanese tobacco giant JTI and R.J. Reynolds International (RJRI); the merger between the Spanish Tabacalera and the French Seita, which created the new company Altadis; and, most recently, the acquisition of Austria Tabak AG by the British Gallaher Group PLC. The mergers moved JTI to the number-two slot with annual sales of about US$40 billion, after Philip Morris with annual sales of about US$80 billion. BAT fell to third place with annual sales of about US$35 billion. The deals clearly demonstrate how national companies must join the consolidation trend in order to grow or risk becoming the next target for a takeover by the large conglomerates.

While economies of scale and privatizations of state-owned tobacco monopolies are still the main catalysts that will continue to drive consolidations on a global scale, the trend has slowed down considerably over the past two years. There's still room for the smaller players to consolidate, as the industry remains fragmented. However, the main wave of consolidations has passed.

Modern tobacco companies have been money machines through the Scale and Focus Stages. However, tobacco use is lower in the United States (and Canada) than in the past because of intensive, health-related anti-smoking campaigns. In less developed countries, and in many European countries, smoking remains a common, widespread practice.

Although the United States was once tobacco's most lucrative market, a series of never-ending obstacles—including advertising bans, label warnings, liability lawsuits, activist complaints, and public education programs—continues to plague the industry. Despite these challenges, this mature industry controlled by a few behemoths has battled through the regulatory thicket of the Focus Stage and is entrenched in the Balance and Alliance Stage.

The tobacco industry has learned how to manage its way through its implicit re-regulation. Tobacco companies have restructured to contain and absorb the effects of government claims and restrictions, as well as consumer product liability lawsuits. From an Endgames stand-point, though, the effect has been to eliminate many of the industry's strategic options. In an effort to isolate the potential impact of lawsuits, tobacco companies have spun off or sold their non-tobacco businesses. Unrelated diversification is no longer an option. And, as mentioned earlier, all of the major M&A deals within the industry have already been done. The relatively simple business model of the industry does not lend itself to creating spin-off industries. Thus, as one senior tobac-co industry executive says, "the only remaining strategic option for our industry is to make as much cash as possible and pay it out to the gov-ernment and to our shareholders."

Shoe industry. Shoe manufacturing, especially for sports or athletics, has traversed a slippery slope over the past several decades. As the production of nearly all such shoes moved to low-wage labor markets in Asia, winning market share became a marketing, styling, endorse-ment, and brand management contest. Sales of fad brands such as LA Gear soared seemingly overnight—and collapsed just as quickly. Global sportswear maker Fila spent fortunes on shoe endorsements with minor success—although sales by counterfeiters in Asian coun-tries were brisk. Reebok rode up the soft leather, cross training, fitness craze—and back down the other side.

Financial success has been fleeting for many in the sports shoe business, but Nike continues to stay ahead of the pack. Without a sig-nificant change in its strategic game plan, however, long-term success is uncertain. Nike's marketing windfall with superstars Michael Jordan and Tiger Woods has effectively counterbalanced a weak acquisitions record, and pegging corporate growth on sports stars can be just as short-lived as their careers.

As a company at the top of the curve, Nike's best bet is to move into new categories by acquiring companies in the Opening Stage that are poised for superior growth. And it did, in fact, make some moves in this direction that met with moderate success. In 1988 Nike acquired Cole-Haan to tap into the business-casual shoe and accessories market and in 1994 it purchased Canstar to establish a foothold in the ice and inline skate market. But that was the extent of Nike's external growth activities. With regard to its Endgames strategy, the list of missed opportunities is a red flag. In 2001, Nike's then-president of outdoor products, Gordon McFadden, lobbied for the company to purchase outdoor-gear and clothing maker North Face, Inc. McFadden claimed, "It would have doubled the business overnight and made Nike the dominant player." CEO Phil Knight, however, rejected the acquisition, just as he turned down a similar opportunity to purchase mid-priced shoemaker Converse.

> *As a company at the top of the curve, Nike's best bet is to move into new categories by acquiring companies in the Opening Stage that are poised for superior growth.*

With sales and market share declining, strategic acquisitions could rebalance the scale in Nike's favor. Remember: leaders in this stage must not only be strategic experts in the final stage, but also be skilled in managing their individual companies across the curve.

Software industry. Of all the Balance and Alliance Stage industries, software is the one most vulnerable to start-ups in the Opening Stage. Unlike many Focus Stage industries, barriers to entry are low—as are required capital assets—and switching costs are easily overpowered by superior innovation. The only requirement: intellectual capital. And for the right reward, as we have seen over and over, such valuable knowledge will allow a company to leapfrog from a Focus Stage or Balance and Alliance Stage company to a start-up in the blink of an eye.

Some software companies, especially those rich with cash (think Microsoft), can buttress their dominance by acquiring promising competitors before they can become a threat. Indeed, Microsoft's legendary acquisitions strategy has been a key element of its storied rise to the top: from 1994 to 2002, the firm purchased more than 50 companies. As it gained market share and moved up the Endgames curve, it began aggressively acquiring Stage 1 companies to protect its position. Microsoft's ongoing growth strategy also includes targeting new lines of business, such as video games, through its Xbox console, and media, through its joint venture with NBC to create MSNBC.

Microsoft's acquisition spree slowed considerably, however, in the early 2000s when Microsoft faced antitrust charges brought by the U.S. government. Having emerged from its legal battles in 2002 relatively unscathed, it's almost certain that the software giant will quickly revitalize its acquisitions strategy. And, by making more than US$38 billion available in cash reserves in early 2002, Microsoft is clearly repositioning to start shopping again to stay on top of the curve.

Aerospace and defense industry. The aerospace and defense industries wage war through the Balance and Alliance Stage, with "countries" vying against "companies." When Europe blocked the GE-Honeywell merger, it sent a clear message that the industry's consolidation had gone far enough, at least in the minds of European regulators. What was once a raft of companies in Europe and the United States has diminished to a handful of large contractors. Will large defense contractors continue to "choose sides" and partner against comparable combinations? A logical evolution of the Balance and Alliance Stage is just that—surviving participants in a market will "choose partners," just like teams pick players in a sandlot ball game. Will the odd player out be out of the business? Will regulators allow via alliance what they frowned upon with GE-Honeywell? Only time will tell. As aircraft and weapons systems grow in terms of complexity, cost, and development time, such alliances are inevitable. Start-ups or small players have little or no chance in this industry.

But this doesn't mean the outcome is predictable. Sometimes a wild card—new, agile entrants or an external event—can precipitate consolidation. With the sudden turn of events post-September 11, 2001, for example, weapons procurement spending in the United States will vault from US$60 billion to US$90 billion annually for the next five years, precipitating a rush to further consolidate an industry already in the Focus Stage.

Northrop Grumman's acquisitions of Litton Industries and Newport News Shipbuilding pushed it to the top of the shipbuilding industry and made it the world's third-largest defense contractor. With sales approaching US$14 billion, Northrop is targeting engineering company TRW to pick up another US$7 billion in defense spending after selling off the target company's auto unit, which has larger sales and lower profits. If the Northrop takeover is successful, it would be a match for Lockheed Martin, with US$24 billion in revenue.

Even if TRW succeeds in defeating the Northrop move, it will have to divest itself of the auto unit anyway to please shareholders, since the aerospace and defense business has higher margins and will benefit greatly from the current spending boom. In the process, this sale would push the auto parts business along its industry consolidation curve.

Soft drink industry. Global markets for carbonated soft drinks are growing slowly—if not stagnating—as befitting a Balance and Alliance Stage business. But non-carbonated drinks are growing handsomely, and offer Scale Stage opportunities—which Pepsi is seizing. Even carbonated, low-alcohol drinks are cutting into carbonated soft-drink sales by eliminating the need for "mixers" in many drinks sold in bars.

While Coca-Cola stuck with its soft-drink competency, PepsiCo began diversifying into snack foods and juices. Pepsi also embarked on several other solid Endgames strategies: it acquired other soft-drink brands; it formed alliances and partnerships with food chains, such as Burger King; and it created marketing partnerships with, for example, Universal Studios.

Coke realized it made an error after it decided to focus solely on being the leader in carbonated drinks; it was effectively shutting out the non-carbonated market—and missing a significant opportunity. To rectify the situation, Coke attempted a deal with consumer goods giant Procter & Gamble. The proposal called for Procter & Gamble to bundle its Pringles (potato chips) and Sunny Delight (juice-based drink) with Coke's Minute Maid juice business. However, before a final agreement was reached, both parties opted to back out, leaving Coke back where it started—right behind Pepsi (Tropicana dominates Minute Maid, Aquafina leads Dasani in the water business, and Pepsi may gain an edge by its acquisition of the sports drink Gatorade). Although Coke retains its lead in carbonated beverage sales, it has already begun to find new ways to combat Pepsi's impressive expansion into the non-carbonated drink market. In April 2002, Coke entered into an agreement with Group Danone to distribute Evian bottled water in North America. One month later, Coke announced that it was acquiring the Seagram's line of mixers, tonic, ginger ale, and seltzer from Diageo and Pernod Ricard.

However, in evaluating future growth plans, both Pepsi and Coca-Cola must run a gauntlet of legal tests set by the Federal Trade Commission in the United States and other government regulatory agencies throughout the world. Acquisitions and alliances are the fastest mode of further growth, but legal restrictions limit expansion opportunities for many Stage 4 companies.

STAYING AT THE TOP: PROSPERING IN THE BALANCE AND ALLIANCE STAGE

This chapter is different from the three previous chapters in the sense that companies don't move *through* Stage 4—they remain *in* it. Whereas in Chapters 3, 4, and 5 we presented a roadmap of how to move through each stage successfully, in this chapter we discuss how to remain in this stage and flourish.

> All companies in Stage 4 industries "hit the wall" in one way or another.

All companies in Stage 4 industries "hit the wall" in one way or another. What separates successful Stage 4 companies from less successful ones is the way that they tackle five critical challenges:

1. *Manage the growth challenge.* Companies must find new ways to grow the core business in a mature industry.
2. *Address the potential for industry regulation.* Stage 4 companies must be alert to the constant threat of governments, consumers, or competitors perceiving oligopolistic or monopolistic behavior by the leading industry participants.
3. *Create spin-off businesses.* Even the most entrenched Stage 4 companies can create a new wave of growth by spinning off new businesses into earlier Endgames stages.
4. *Fight complacency.* Stagnation is perhaps the biggest threat to Stage 4 companies if they become too comfortable with their industry position and either get blindsided by competition or wither away.
5. *Set a good example.* Stage 4 companies are always in the spotlight and thus must hold themselves to even higher standards than companies in other stages to avoid media, consumer, or government backlash.

Let's dive into the details of these challenges and see how leading Balance and Alliance Stage companies address them.

Manage the Growth Challenge

As companies move into the final stage, they must confront the challenge of how to grow their core business. Typically, Stage 4 companies are in extremely mature industries and their growth options are limited. But growth continues to be a critical success factor, and companies with strong internal growth will be rewarded in the stock market.

> Growth continues to be a critical success factor, and companies with strong internal growth will be rewarded in the stock market.

Consider the tobacco industry. Faced with huge legal battles and regulatory constraints in the United States and Europe, they turned to less-developed countries in Asia and Eastern Europe to make acquisitions, form alliances, and grow their business. Now, tobacco companies have some of the most sophisticated supply chains and organization infrastructures of any industry serving these markets.

Consider also the growth path of Japanese-based Canon. Its cameras and optical products spawned photocopiers ... which led to printers ... that now are used with digital cameras ... which brought Canon right back to photography. If it had rigidly defined its total market as any one of these segments, the company might have limited or constrained its growth. Canon's competitors, Kodak and Xerox, made this mistake and ran into significant problems as a result. Canon, however, remained flexible and innovative. And it prospered.

To find growth, companies must adopt a growth mindset and redefine the market(s) in which they compete. Look at "next door" markets: expand the definition of market scope by zooming out until your market share is under 25% and preferably closer to 10%. Suddenly, plenty of growth opportunities will materialize.

Address the Potential for Industry Regulation

Because Balance and Alliance Stage industries are so concentrated, the most successful companies are often lightning rods for government scrutiny and regulation, as well as public backlash. Second-tier competitors often cite unfair advantages given to the leaders; consumers become concerned about the power the industry wields in terms of pricing or service; and suppliers get squeezed so much that they can't make decent profits. Individually or combined, these dynamics—whether perceived or real—can cause problems for Stage 4 companies.

The threat of government regulation is prevalent in all Endgames stages, but is most prevalent in the Focus and Balance and Alliance Stages (Stages 3 and 4). Consider the following examples:

- The heavy regulation and massive payouts from the tobacco industry to the U.S. government.
- The European Union's Competition Directorate General rejection of the proposed GE-Honeywell merger (mostly comprising businesses in Stage 3 and Stage 4 industries).
- The intense scrutiny, or rejection, of mega-mergers that may be indicative of an industry transition from Stage 1 or 2 to Stage 3 or 4 (for example, the proposed WorldCom merger with Sprint in 1999).
- The intense scrutiny of pricing practices, and the length and complexity of the FDA approval process, for new products in the pharmaceutical industry.

The key for management of Stage 4 companies is to realistically recognize the position of their industry vis-à-vis the government and to identify and address potential areas of government concern or action.

Create Spin-Off Businesses in Subindustries

At this final stage of consolidation, market potential lies in identifying pockets of opportunity or niches where the company can add value to the business. From an Endgames perspective, Stage 4 companies can achieve new waves of growth by identifying and building businesses that are launched from their core business, but create new industries or compete against new players in earlier stages of the Endgames curve. This dynamic enables the Stage 4 company to achieve future growth in a newly created Stage 1 or Stage 2 industry. Think back to the Pepsi case study: as a Stage 4 company, its acquisitions are geared toward emerging, high-potential markets, including the sports drink (Stage 2) and bottled water (Stage 2) industries.

For another example, look to IBM and Oracle. In the late 1990s, both companies spun off units in the sizeable, Stage 1 corporate training industry. Annual spending on corporate training exceeds US$8 billion in the United States, and of that about US$5 billion is spent on IT training. According to Lifelong Learning's Market Report, the number-two training company in 1998 was Oracle Education, a division of

> At this final stage of consolidation, market potential lies in identifying pockets of opportunity or niches where the company can add value to the business.

the software giant, with a 5.4% share worth US$443 million. The number-one trainer was IBM Learning Services, with an 8.5% share worth nearly US$700 million. The training market, while sensitive to economic trends, has been growing at a steady rate. And these two Stage 4 innovators did not miss the opportunity of an attractive spin-off business opportunity with lots of growth potential.

Fight Complacency

Stage 4 companies must engage in a never-ending battle with complacency, and those that succumb to contentment with their position risk imminent competitive onslaught.

Once again, consider the ongoing battle between Stage 4 giants Coca-Cola and PepsiCo. It has been a battle of give-and-take for decades. In the early 1990s, Coke became complacent in its marketing and product strategy. Then, intimidated by Pepsi's rapid gain in market share, Coke changed the taste of its flagship product, causing it to go into a tailspin. In the mid-1990s, however, the tables turned as Coke beat Pepsi in the race for international expansion and became the dominant brand in several strategic countries in Asia and Eastern Europe. More recently, Pepsi has been on a faster growth track than Coke, thanks to gains in its new non-cola beverage businesses. This epic battle highlights the consequences of taking your eye off the ball in the Balance and Alliance Stage.

As a result, Stage 4 companies must avoid complacency at all costs. Effective human resources management can often take on a strategic dimension in Stage 4 and help mitigate this risk. Reward and compensation systems, promotion and succession planning processes, and recruiting and people development are all critical processes that can encourage innovation and risk-taking and reduce susceptibility to competitor advances.

Set a Good Example

Companies in the Balance and Alliance Stage are so big, so global, and so prominent that they attract undue media, consumer, and government attention. When they make a mistake, the consequences can be disastrous. As a result, they must develop and maintain a sense of overriding responsibility for the global marketplace, offer superior customer service, establish strict environmental protection policies, promote economic development, and foster strong, cooperative relationships with governments.

Stage 4 companies must realize they can do well by doing good. Shell learned this lesson the hard way when it tried to sink the Brent Spar drilling platform in the North Sea. The cost savings wasn't worth the loss of revenues through a consumer boycott, the bad press and damaged reputation it gained with consumers and environmentalists. Now it's working its way back into favor with a greener policy.

Nike has had its issues in the past, with accusations of using child labor in foreign factories and closing U.S. manufacturing plants to move production offshore. But it is moving to the vanguard of corporate responsibility with recent initiatives such as recycling programs, voluntary removal of PVC from its shoe materials, and introducing organic cotton into its T-shirts, which reduces environmental pollution caused by agricultural chemicals.

Nike has also turned to corporate reporting to raise awareness of its efforts to address the labor abuse practices it was charged with. Its Web site contains open self-criticism about findings in some of its factories. However, the site also reports that Nike gave a grant of nearly US$8 million to the International Youth Foundation—an organization dedicated to improving the lives of young people.

Other examples of Stage 4 companies seeking to improve their corporate image abound. Philip Morris, for example, has spent tens of millions of dollars on cultural sponsorships and smoker education programs, and Microsoft has emerged as a prominent charitable donor.

Unfortunately, trust in Stage 4 companies is long and slow to build and easy to lose. It takes a concerted long-term effort to achieve lasting results. Stage 4 companies need to develop and implement public relations, consumer awareness, and charitable donation programs. They need to build the high skill levels required to both lobby governments and involve nongovernmental organizations. Finally, companies must use sponsorships and corporate contributions to mitigate mistrust and fear.

BEYOND THE CURVE

This chapter concludes the long journey through each of the four Endgames stages. By now, you should have a sense of the power and inevitability of the Endgames curve and you should accept that Endgames dynamics *will* affect your business and that of your competitors, suppliers, and customers.

Understanding the Endgames progression, though, is only half the battle. Some of the most interesting facets of the Endgames concept lie in its implications for business managers and investors. How should a CEO manage each Endgames stage? How should the Board of Directors carry out its duties across the Endgames spectrum? What are the implications of Endgames for investors? How will Endgames transform the business landscape between now and 2010? These questions will be the focal point of the third and final section of the book, "New Imperatives and Future Outcomes."

Chapter Seven | CEO Strategies for Endgames

There is no point at which you can say, "Well, I'm successful now. I might as well take a nap."
—Carrie Fisher, actress and author

Want to generate some excitement and emotion? Try announcing a big merger. Nothing makes a CEO as famous. Nothing gets Wall Street buzzing like the prospects of a mega-merger. And rarely is anything quite as exciting for a CEO professionally as carrying out a merger.

CEOs such as Jack Welch (GE) and Carleton (Carly) Fiorina (HP) became household names primarily because of their involvement in Endgames (see sidebar: "The Jack Welch Phenomenon"). They each presided over hundreds of mergers and led consolidation in their respective industries. In addition, mergers can make CEOs wealthy. For example, Carly Fiorina, the CEO of Hewlett-Packard, reportedly received a merger success fee of tens of millions of dollars for the merger between HP and Compaq. But both the glory and financial windfall dissolve in an instant if that one big deal turns sour.

> The skills required from a CEO vary according to a company's position on the Endgames curve.

THE JACK WELCH PHENOMENON

Jack Welch demonstrated many unique talents while he was CEO of General Electric, but his implicit understanding of Endgames dynamics was perhaps his greatest strength. He epitomized the Endgames strategy through four GE strengths:

- Predicting industry consolidation and deconsolidation
- Building a strong post-merger integration competency
- Maintaining primary focus on GE's core business despite a high volume of M&A activity
- Structuring and using the Board of Directors as an effective Endgames sounding board

Welch anticipated the consolidation of the medical systems, plastics, and aircraft engine industries (to name a few) well ahead of his competitors and forced GE to become the consolidation leader in each. He also recognized that the mining industry had reached the Balance and Alliance Stage and divested it before its financial performance and market valuation dropped off—again well ahead of any competitor. Finally, Welch reinforced the Endgames strategy across GE by insisting that any GE business unit be the number-one or -two competitor in its industry or be sold off. Most of the time, this strategy led to anticipating Stage 4.

Welch also empowered his senior line managers to fully integrate newly acquired businesses into the GE business model. The acquired companies were fully assimilated into GE; from day one, their primary focus became the business success of GE's core business. The only time Welch negotiated special concessions in an acquisition, he regretted it. Following the acquisition of the investment bank Kidder Peabody, the investment bankers were reluctant to be fully integrated into the GE Capital business model. What especially irritated Welch was that the bankers felt they were entitled to hefty bonuses even when their financial performance came in below their commitments. Welch tolerated the Kidder differences until a 1994 insider-trading scandal involving the head of its government trading desk, Joseph Jett. At this point, Welch put in GE executives to manage Kidder and fully integrate it into GE Capital.

Finally, Welch relied heavily on his Board of Directors for advice and insight on potential acquisitions. In a number of deals, Welch counted on his Board to establish contacts with acquisition candidates, as well as act as a sounding board for the strategic rationale for buying them. He also chose or recommended potential new Board members in part based on their ability to introduce GE to acquisition candidates or ideas in new industries.

In this chapter, we examine what CEOs must do to successfully carry out an Endgames strategy and the new onus placed upon the Board of Directors to manage the Endgames execution.

The most important issue for a CEO and a Board of Directors to realize is the inevitability of Endgames consolidation. The reality is that *every* company in *every* industry will go through the four Endgames stages—or disappear. Some industries may consolidate faster or slower than others, and one Endgames stage may last longer than another, but Endgames consolidation *will* happen. Period.

Although the beauty of the Endgames model is its promise as a predictive tool, this potential will be realized only through strong execution by the CEO and the Board of Directors. Senior leaders must always be aware of where their industry and company lie on the Endgames curve and plan their strategies accordingly. The key question, then, becomes how the CEO and the Board should react to and lead through Endgames consolidation dynamics.

Our research reveals that the skills required from a CEO vary according to a company's position on the Endgames curve. From Stage 1 through Stage 2, CEOs must drive aggressive growth and lead their industry in consolidation: brute force, bold leadership, and vision are key success factors. In Stage 3 through Stage 4, however, CEOs become more like master chess players: careful planning, anticipating competitors' strategies, identifying and implementing a mega-merger, and mastering portfolio management become paramount.

CEO IMPERATIVES: STAGE 1 THROUGH STAGE 2

Positioning the CEO as the primary architect of an Endgames strategy has the potential for great success, if properly managed. To illustrate this point, we looked at the evolution of two companies, WorldCom and Bank of America, when they were successfully executing a consolidation strategy, moving their companies through the first stages of the Endgames curve (Opening and Scale).

Obviously everyone would have wanted to be shareholders in these companies during this stage! What did these chief executives do to successfully implement their Endgames vision?

The path to success in the early Endgames stages is relatively straightforward and comprises three distinct phases:

- Develop an Endgames vision.
- Create a merger integration engine.
- Prepare for Endgames Stages 3 and 4.

Develop an Endgames Vision

First, the company must develop an Endgames vision. In many industries, the necessity of consolidation is apparent. In steel, paper, and chemicals, the economics of scale argue compellingly in favor of consolidation as one of the few strategic levers to achieve superior profits.

However, in other industries, CEOs must have a rare talent to gain first-mover advantage by spotting an Endgames play before any other competitor. In these situations, the Endgames vision is not so obvious. At this point, it is imperative for CEOs to develop a success model for acquisitions. As Figure 7-1 illustrates, the first step is to identify the most promising acquisition candidates.

> In many industries, the necessity of consolidation is apparent... In others, CEOs must have a rare talent to gain first-mover advantage by spotting an Endgames play before any other competitor.

Take the case of NCNB under CEO Hugh McColl. In the early 1980s when McColl became CEO of NCNB, a small bank based in North Carolina, interstate banking was not permitted under U.S. law. This clearly positioned the U.S. banking industry in the Opening Stage of the Endgames curve.

McColl believed that the only way for NCNB to control its destiny and achieve superior returns was to create a regional, multi-state bank. In 1982, NCNB began its interstate banking M&A activities by exploiting a regulatory loophole and acquired a bank in Florida. He

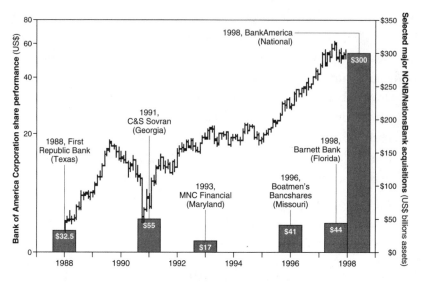

Sources: www.finance.yahoo.com; Thomson Financial Mergers & Acquisitions database; Mergerstat

Figure 7-1. NCNB/NationsBank share performance through the Scale Stage

successfully lobbied regulators in the southern United States and eventually, in 1985, the law changed to permit regional bank holding companies. By this time, McColl had acquired banks in Florida, South Carolina, and Georgia and achieved a big lead over his competition.

In 1992, NCNB merged with C&S/Sovran to become NationsBank, the fourth-largest bank in the United States. McColl completed more than 40 acquisitions and grew the banks' assets twentyfold to US$120 billion. With a new federal interstate banking law in place, McColl's strategy kicked into a new gear and, in 1998, McColl completed his biggest deal ever: the US$60 billion merger with BankAmerica to create Bank of America. At this point, the original NCNB had gone from a single state bank with less than US$20 billion in assets to the largest depository bank in the United States, with US$570 billion in assets, US$10 billion in earnings, and operations in 22 states—clearly McColl had a well-developed vision for Endgames consolidation. (See Figure 7-1.)

Although WorldCom is better known for its recent accounting scandals, management turmoil and subsequent fall from grace rather than for its rise to power, it still serves as an example of a breakthrough Endgames vision in Stage 2. In fact, WorldCom's troubles also illustrate—in dramatic fashion—how many companies fail to make the transition from the rapid growth of Stage 2 to the slower growth of Stage 3. It also shows the risks that CEOs face when taking the lead in consolidating an industry—and the consequences of consolidating too early, ahead of the Endgames curve.

The WorldCom Endgames vision began in 1983 with Long Distance Discount Calling (LDDC), a small long distance reseller. When Bernie Ebbers became CEO of the company in 1985, he recognized several important trends in the U.S. telecommunications industry: deregulation, rapidly increasing growth in data communications among large U.S. corporations, and a fast-changing technological environment.

Ebbers' Endgames vision was to create a coast-to-coast competitor of AT&T, focusing on the corporate data communications market. From 1985 to 1989, he restructured LDDC to position it for rapid consolidation. From 1989 to 1997, he carried out more than 70 mergers, primarily buying long distance resellers and companies that could bolster his corporate data capabilities.

Also, the new technological advances created by the Internet heavily favored WorldCom in a big way. WorldCom's corporate data strategy seemed to be the right strategy at the right time and Ebbers had visions of carrying huge amounts of Internet traffic across WorldCom's global network. Soon, M&A fever hit the telecommunications industry like a pandemic, with global telecommunications giants snapping up wireless, broadband, and cable companies at an astonishing rate.

WorldCom merged with MCI in 1998, which at the time was the largest merger in history (US$40 billion). MCI solidified WorldCom's U.S. and European corporate data network and positioned WorldCom as the second-largest long distance provider in the United States. WorldCom's acquisitiveness reached its nadir in late 1999 with its proposed purchase of Sprint for US$129 billion. The rationale for the Sprint deal was to put WorldCom within striking distance of AT&T's U.S. long distance market share (34% versus 45% for AT&T), to consolidate its position as the leading Internet traffic carrier, and perhaps

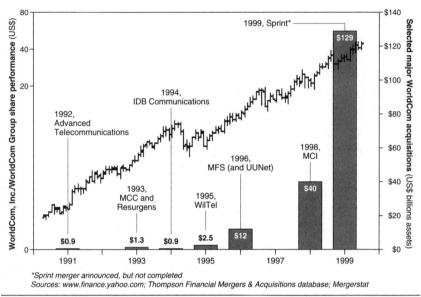

*Sprint merger announced, but not completed
Sources: www.finance.yahoo.com; Thompson Financial Mergers & Acquisitions database; Mergerstat

Figure 7-2. WorldCom's share performance through the Scale Stage

most important, to acquire a nationwide wireless network.

Unfortunately for Ebbers and WorldCom, however, they were forced to abandon the Sprint acquisition due to regulatory concerns. This effectively ended the company's Endgames rapid consolidation phase. WorldCom's business then deteriorated with accounting scandals, management changes, and Chapter 11 bankruptcy. (See Figure 7-2.)

Create a Merger Integration Engine

Once a company's Board of Directors embraces an acquisition strategy and the first wave of deals is completed, the vision is usually confirmed and validated. This marks the beginning of the Scale Stage. At this point, a company in Stage 1 or Stage 2 will often carry out dozens of deals a year. The key differentiating success factor, however, becomes a company's ability to successfully integrate the high volume of acquisitions into its core business (see Figure 7-3).

Most successful companies build what is often referred to as an "integration engine." Hugh McColl and NCNB, for example, aggressively integrated acquisitions to fit NCNB's core business model. They developed an integration template for each core function and process

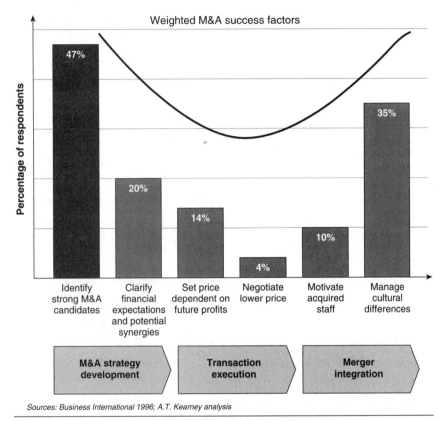

Figure 7-3. Critical capabilities for M&A success

of the business and deluged a newly acquired company on day one with integration specialists. These specialists completely integrated the new company in all areas, from IT to lending systems and processes to credit scoring systems. As one senior NCNB executive said after NCNB acquired First Republic Bank Corp. in 1988, "[McColl] gave us two things: an airline ticket and a red book with the battle plan."

In some of its acquisitions, NCNB was prepared to lose up to 20% to 30% of the acquired company's customer base as well as a certain portion of the management team. Senior management accepted this as a necessary part of achieving the company's objectives—and believed that a 70% retention rate added to its core business was good progress.

This brings up an important point: a critical success factor for executing an Endgames strategy is ensuring that Wall Street understands and supports the Endgames rationale. Not every merger will be a complete success, but investors will be somewhat more patient if management takes the time to get buy-in for an Endgames strategy (see sidebar at end of chapter: "Seven Steps to Merger Success").

Like NCNB, WorldCom also created a straightforward merger inte-

Not every merger will be a complete success, but investors will be somewhat more patient if management takes the time to get buy-in for an Endgames strategy.

gration strategy and capability. Because margins were so thin in the long distance market, Ebbers focused on rapidly assimilating an acquired company's customer base and revenues into WorldCom's network and cutting costs to the bone. This strategy worked to perfection through the early 1990s as WorldCom completed a series of small- to medium-sized acquisitions.

Finally, it is important to note that conglomerates and companies executing roll-up strategies sometimes take a different approach and delegate merger integration issues down the chain of command. When Berkshire Hathaway makes acquisitions, for example, the incumbent management team is generally left in place. Even if acquired companies compete in the same industry, they are rarely integrated. On the other hand, Cisco Systems is an integration powerhouse. As an industry leader, Cisco focused on smaller acquisitions during its consolidation phase. The company's guiding belief is that acquisitions should be friendly, not hostile, and that acquired companies should be fully integrated into the Cisco business model immediately. Senior Vice President Peter Solvik explains, "We've learned, sometimes the hard way, that the only way to make an acquisition is to fully and seamlessly integrate all aspects of the new company into Cisco. There are no exceptions." One of the most striking examples of this, Solvik relates, is that one acquired company had just upgraded all of its employees' computers—more than 1,000 of them. Nevertheless, Cisco replaced them all after the acquisition to ensure compatibility within the Cisco business model.

Prepare for Endgames Stages 3 and 4

Sometime during Stage 2 or the early part of Stage 3, competitors begin to think about a defining, industry standard-setting mega-merger.

Companies in these stages typically face several new competitive realities. Their market share has grown substantially and their largest industry competitors are taking notice. There aren't as many deals available because targets are too big and competitors also become "deal hungry." Companies experience a "stick to their knitting" renaissance and the core business performance becomes the key driver of a company's stock price. As a result, the CEO faces a whole new set of business dynamics.

Once companies arrive at Stage 3, they reach a crossroads: either they continue along the path to glory or they die by the sword. Both NCNB/NationsBank and WorldCom chose to continue along the acquisition path, each capping off their Stage 2 journey with massive acquisitions. Same strategy, perhaps, but the results couldn't be more different.

Although both WorldCom and NCNB enjoyed great runs during their consolidation heydays, they ultimately suffered setbacks on the stock market when their companies reached the end of the rapid consolidation Endgames phase. As Figure 7-4 illustrates, Bank of America's stock price has stalled since NationsBank acquired it in 1998 and WorldCom's stock price has plummeted since it made the Sprint announcement in 1999.

At NCNB, McColl's deal-making prowess ultimately became the driver of NationsBank's stock price—NationsBank had to sign bigger deals, faster, to keep increasing its share price. As the size and pace of deals increased, management's ability to integrate the acquired companies became compromised. At the same time, the acquisition price per dollar of assets acquired increased substantially, almost quintupling between the C&S/Sovran deal in 1991 and the acquisition of Barnett Banks in 1998. These issues came to a head with the BankAmerica deal (which created what is now Bank of America) and the stock price has been flat, never regaining its US$70 per share peak since the announcement of the transaction.

In retrospect, the BankAmerica deal signified the bank's arrival into Stage 3. However, the size and scope of the post-merger integration overwhelmed McColl and his senior management team, forcing the company into a protracted transition period. Since the merger, Bank of

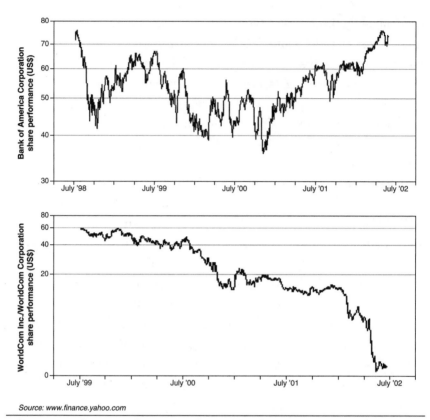

Source: www.finance.yahoo.com

Figure 7-4. Share performance for Bank of America and WorldCom since their largest acquisitions

America has reorganized and gone through a major senior management and CEO change. It has had to realign its strategy and objectives to adjust to its new position in Stage 3. In addition, the economic slow-down of 2001 and 2002 has delayed the realization of the merger benefits, and it is not yet clear whether the merger will create significant incremental shareholder value.

By the same token, at WorldCom, Ebbers also stepped up the size and pace of acquisitions in 1996. The US$14 billion acquisition of MFS Communications in Omaha, NE, that year was almost five times larger than his previous biggest deal, the WilTel acquisition in 1995. WorldCom's winning formula of integrating customers and cutting costs took longer to fully implement and realize than with previous acquisitions. Then came the MCI deal, which at US$40 billion was almost off the scales. At the same time, telecommunications companies' share prices boomed during the Internet bubble, which meant that when the bubble burst (just after the time of the Sprint announcement), WorldCom's share price plummeted, both due to the erosion of the Internet premium built into the stock and because of underlying core business profitability (due in part to the slower pace of integration of MCI).

Similar to the NationsBank example, the telecommunications industry moved rapidly from Stage 2 to Stage 3 on the Endgames curve. The size, scope, and pace of mega-mergers carried out by WorldCom eventually overwhelmed the company's management team. It became difficult to realize the synergies from all of the acquisitions in a timely manner and post-merger integration timetables lagged. From its peak of over US$60 per share at the time of the Sprint announcement, WorldCom's share price plummeted more than 90% to less than US$3 in April 2002. Bernie Ebbers resigned as CEO, leaving the company to put together a new senior management team. The company is in turmoil and its future in its current form is in question.

> Companies must undergo a major strategic transition when their industries move from Endgames Stage 2 to Stage 3. This transition can wreak havoc with a company's business strategy and management processes.

While each company has its own unique circumstances and the force of the business cycle always is a shaping factor, A.T. Kearney's Endgames research shows that companies must undergo a major strategic transition when their industries move from Endgames Stage 2 to Stage 3. This transition can wreak havoc with a company's business strategy and management processes. It may forewarn of the need for a company's senior management team to seriously rethink its medium- to long-term strategic plan to ensure its strategies will lead to success in the Stage 3 environment.

Let's look at some of the warning signals and red flags that management and their Boards should watch for:

- Mergers and consolidation become the focal point of corporate strategy (the means instead of the end) and of share price performance.
- Operating managers are so overly burdened by integration issues that they neglect core business performance.

- The company can become "too big to manage" as a result of the cumulative effect of so many mergers.
- The CEO achieves a certain degree of fame or notoriety in the business community, usually accompanied by a significant bonus or stock award (hundreds of millions of dollars).
- The CEO evolves into a "one-trick wonder" rather than an industry visionary.
- The CEO makes one deal too many... or too big... or both.

Any of these trends can signal the end of Stage 2 and indicate the need for a new strategy. But the complication is that they are often realized simultaneously—sometimes with disastrous effects. CEOs must read the Endgames tea leaves, heed the Endgames warning signals, and adjust their companies' strategy for the realities of Stages 3 and 4—or risk disastrous consequences for their shareholders and their tenure as the organizations' leaders.

CEO Imperatives: Stage 3 Through Stage 4

Why did Pepsi offer such a significant acquisition premium for Quaker Oats' Gatorade business? What was the underlying strategic rationale for Philip Morris to undertake an initial public offering (IPO) of its Kraft Foods business unit and contemplate selling its Miller Beer business? The answer is the Endgames curve.

> *Unlike the dealmaker skills and bold leadership traits required in Stages 1 and 2, the prototypical Stages 3 and 4 CEO is a shrewd chess player and portfolio manager.*

Managing Stage 3 and Stage 4 of the Endgames curve requires a particular set of CEO attributes. Unlike the dealmaker skills and bold leadership traits required in Stages 1 and 2, the prototypical Stages 3 and 4 CEO is a shrewd chess player and portfolio manager.

Consider Johnson & Johnson, a leader in the pharmaceutical and health care industry, which is transitioning into Stage 3. Johnson & Johnson has carried out more than 30 acquisitions over the past 10 years, but has always stuck to its core businesses: prescription and over-the-counter pharmaceutical products, medical devices and diagnostics, and consumer and baby products. Well-known for being a decentralized company, J&J empowers each business head to identify and execute acquisitions.

As a result, J&J has acquired companies across its entire portfolio of businesses; examples include Neutrogena (consumer products), ALZA (pharmaceutical), Centocor (biotechnology), and DePuy (medical devices). While J&J has carried out some big deals over the years (ALZA was the biggest, at almost US$12 billion), the company has stayed away from deals big enough to risk changing its culture or business model.

In addition, J&J has pursued its acquisition strategy over the tenure of several CEOs, not just one, which has meant that M&A and consolidation have become embedded as an integral part of the company strategy. Finally, the Board of Directors reviews J&J's portfolio of businesses on a regular basis to assess whether J&J should shed underperforming businesses and whether J&J as an overall entity is more valuable to shareholders as is or as separate companies. In other words, through regular meetings, the Board validates J&J's Endgames strategy.

Many companies in Endgames Stage 4 industries adopt a strategy of creating spin-off growth businesses from their core business. Typically, these spin-off businesses launch new industries or subindustries that are in an earlier Endgames stage and lead to new opportunities for these companies to fuel their future growth. PepsiCo is a good example of a Stage 4 company that took advantage of this strategy. Faced with the prospects of low growth in its core (Stage 4) soft-drink business, PepsiCo identified two new spin-off industries: the sports drink subindustry and the bottled water subindustry.

These subindustries were both much less concentrated than the soft drink industry, showing characteristics of Endgames Stage 1 or 2. PepsiCo managers believed that both of these subindustries could provide growth to boost the top line of the overall company. They acquired the Gatorade sports drink business from Quaker Oats, paying a significant premium over a competing offer from Coca-Cola, and have since used Gatorade as a focal point for developing their sports drink business.

Another Stage 4 management strategy is to "isolate" a Stage 4 business in a portfolio company and use the cash thrown off from it to either fuel other businesses in the portfolio or return it to investors. In this light, Philip Morris has set the standard for excellent management of a particularly tough Stage 4 business—the tobacco industry. In the late 1980s and early 1990s, when it became clear that the tobacco industry was advancing toward Stage 4, Philip Morris diversified into the Stage 2 food industry. With the acquisition of Kraft, General Foods, Jacob Suchard, and others, Philip Morris diversified into a food industry powerhouse.

In the late 1990s, though, the impact of government regulation of the tobacco industry for health-related claims led Philip Morris to change its Stage 4 strategy. It is now in the process of isolating its tobacco business, with a strategy of containing it with respect to litigation claims and maximizing its cash dividend payments to shareholders. In the process, it sold 16% of its Kraft shares in an IPO, is spinning off other businesses, and has sold its Miller Beer business. This type of bold, shareholder-focused leadership in Stage 4 led shareholders to give retiring CEO Geoffrey Bible a 10-minute standing ovation at Philip Morris' 2002 annual shareholder meeting.

Nestlé has been successful in supplementing its core Stage 3 food business with acquisitions of businesses in earlier stages. This strategy enables Nestlé to continually realize new growth opportunities and grow the company aggressively. Nestlé consolidated the Stage 2 bottled water industry with the acquisitions of Perrier and San Pellegrino, among others, and appears to be in the process of consolidating the Stage 2 pet food industry as well. Like Johnson & Johnson, which executes a similar strategy, Nestlé has built strong capabilities in merging large acquisitions quickly and effectively on a global basis.

The bottom line on managing through Stages 3 and 4 is that there are few winners and many losers. CEOs must accept the position of their industry on the Endgames curve and plan their strategy accordingly. A few brilliant strategic insights can make a CEO famous in these stages.

IMPLICATIONS FOR ENDGAMES SURVIVAL AND SUCCESS

In this chapter we have discussed some of the challenges CEOs face at each Endgames stage. In the coming years, the scale, pace, and complexity of business will surely increase as more and more industries consolidate and move along the Endgames curve.

What can CEOs do to lead a successful Endgames strategy? Let's summarize this chapter by looking at three key implications of our research and the tools and strategies available to CEOs to manage in the Endgames environment.

1. **Take a global view and adjust your strategy to reflect your position on the Endgames curve.** Endgames consolidation is a global phenomenon. It may be a cliché, but it's no longer enough for CEOs to think local, regional, or even national in strategic planning. Scope must be global and corporate strategy has to be significantly adjusted several times over the course of the Endgames journey. Ignoring this concept leaves you vulnerable to being surpassed, or acquired, by your most feared competitors.

2. **Capitalize on cross-industry opportunities.** Because consolidation is universal and all industries consolidate, look beyond your own industry to see what can be learned from others. If necessary, bring in fresh thinking from the outside to incorporate cross-industry thinking. At the same time, the strategy of creating new products that lead to subindustries in earlier Endgames stages can be a growth accelerator for any company, and CEOs need to be creative and innovative in identifying these new potential growth engines.

3. **Leverage the Board of Directors.** Although the CEO has been the focal point of this chapter, the Board of Directors must also take on new roles in the successful execution of Endgames strategy. This represents a renewed vision for how a Board carries out its duties and reinforces the need for CEOs and shareholders alike to ensure that Boards are structured for success. Some imperatives include:

   ■ *Contributing deep expertise and relationships in customer and supplier industries, as well as adjacent industries.* The Board must be able to assist the CEO in determining when one Endgames stage is over and when another is beginning. In addition, Board members should become a source of acquisition ideas and contacts and be able to assist in closing deals.

■ *Assessing the strengths and weaknesses of a CEO in managing in a particular Endgames stage.* The Board must ensure that the CEO has the appropriate skill set to lead the transition from one Endgames stage to another and, if necessary, determine if the CEO should be replaced.

■ *Thinking carefully about how to appropriately reward a CEO in each Endgames stage.* Best practice suggests that big payouts or tying compensation to the number or size of deals completed should be avoided at all costs. Rather, focusing on the health and success of a company's core business should continue to be the focal point.

Some of these imperatives may require many Boards to significantly restructure their current objectives and membership. Ultimately, however, the Board and the CEO must take ownership for the successful execution of an Endgames strategy through detailed, hands-on deliberation and decision-making.

> The Board and the CEO must take ownership for the successful execution of an Endgames strategy through detailed, hands-on deliberation and decision-making.

FROM CEOS TO STOCKS

As strategists, orchestrators, and leaders, CEOs play a pivotal role in driving their companies up the Endgames curve. But other constituencies wield considerable influence as well, including Wall Street and the investor community. In discussing Endgames strategies with our clients, those in the private equity community have been our most interested listeners. The implications of Endgames on investment timing and choice of target industry are enormous for private equity investors.

What are the implications of Endgames on the stock market? What strategies should investors adopt along the Endgames curve? Let's turn to the next chapter to see.

SEVEN STEPS TO MERGER SUCCESS

The numbers are startling: more than half of mergers ultimately fail to create the value top management had envisioned. But heeding the pitfalls of the past is a big step toward a successful future. Analysis based on an A.T. Kearney survey completed in 1999 reveals that seven steps are key to making mergers work. Highlights of the research first appeared in the book, *After the Merger: Seven Rules for Successful Post-Merger Integration*, by Max M. Habeck, Fritz Kroeger, and Michael R. Traem.

Create a clear vision and strategy. While companies devote a great deal of thought to strategy and vision when embarking on a merger, nearly 80% of companies place corporate "fit" ahead of corporate vision. Learning about a potential partner may win the battle; still, the companies that learn to live with each other are the ones that ultimately win the war.

Vision is the only acid test as to whether companies are on the right track as they prioritize, execute, and interpret post-merger integration tasks. Many merging companies learn the hard way that fit flows from vision—and not vice versa.

Establish leadership quickly. It is impossible to overestimate the importance of immediately establishing strong leadership when a merger deal is completed. The faster the merged company solidifies management—by working out compromises, minimizing or preventing defections, and making the most of available talent and knowledge—the faster it can exploit the growth opportunities inherent in its "one business" vision. Yet, nearly 40% of all companies in the A.T. Kearney study faced a leadership vacuum because they failed to put the establishment of leadership at the top of the priority list. With no one to secure buy-in or provide a clear direction, conflicts simmer, decisions go unmade, and constituencies—from employees to customers to market analysts—lose patience.

Merge to grow. As important as cost-cutting and similar synergies are in mergers and acquisitions, they should be a secondary issue in the post-merger integration. It is clear that almost all mergers offer opportunities to save money. But the primary reason for the merger decision—and the obvious focal point during post-merger integration—should be growth. Merging companies must unlock the "merger added value" by taking advantage of the positive combinations offered by their combined resources. One example: the "growth" synergies identified during due diligence cannot be trumped by "cost" or "efficiency" synergies. Companies run the risk of cutting too much and for too long.

In short, there are two kinds of synergies: "efficiency" and "growth." Our survey clearly shows where the emphasis currently—and unfortunately—lies. Some 76% of companies surveyed focused too heavily on the "efficiency" synergies. Some 30% of the companies surveyed virtually ignored attractive growth opportunities such as cross-selling possibilities or knowledge sharing in research and development.

Focus on results and communicate them. Merger announcements consistently spread uncertainty, not only among employees, but among suppliers, customers, and shareholders as well. It is critical to inform stakeholders of plans and goals, but addressing these longer-term issues is not enough. Companies need to also communicate "early wins"—successful and sustainable moves made quickly after the merger. This offers the audience the first glimmers of the potential of the deal. The result is solidified support and increased buy-in, both inside and outside of the new company.

Where do early wins come from? Areas to consider inside the company include asset sales, knowledge sharing, and improvements to the work environment. And there is a rich source of early wins in a place few companies look: outside of the company. Relationships with suppliers or customers may improve after a merger—offering additional potential for positive communication.

Companies that look internally often fall into the trap of citing job cuts as early wins. Some 61% of merged companies search for early wins, but frequently tread on dangerous territory by turning to job shedding, factory closings, or inward-looking cost moves. The negative emotions these moves produce can quickly turn them into "early losses."

Fortunately, when business due diligence has been conducted properly, several sources of early wins should be readily apparent.

Be sensitive to culture clashes. Cultural differences represent one of the most intractable problem areas in mergers and acquisitions, both before and after the deal is done. The term culture, of course, refers to a collection of elements, including behaviors, objectives, self-interest, and ego, that people are reluctant to discuss openly.

Successfully integrating cultures is key to making any merger work. When this challenge is approached in a structured way, it becomes more manageable.

When we looked at 115 transactions around the globe, we discovered one reason why many mergers are unsuccessful and why cultural differences are blamed. Cultural imposition is standard practice—whether or not it is the most appropriate strategy. While this tactic is valid in some cases, in others it destroys the value the merger was supposed to create.

Problems frequently arise when the organizations that are coming together serve very different markets; in such cases, it is often best to leave the two cultures intact. If full integration of the two organizations is critical to release value, a "compound" culture should be created, one that takes the best elements from each of the parent organizations.

Communicate throughout the process. Managers who can persuade constituencies to believe in a vision and to act on it fare much better at achieving their merger integration goals. In other words, the most compelling communicators come out ahead. This may appear to be the easiest aspect of merger integration. It's not. Communication doesn't just happen; managers must take responsibility, plan it carefully, and then control it over time.

Behind every effective communications program is a combination of communications goals, flexibility, and feedback. The effort is part art, part science—and often inadequate, as most companies acknowledge. Some 86% of respondents said that they failed to communicate their new alliance sufficiently in their merger integration phase.

For most companies, the biggest barrier to merger integration is failure to achieve employee commitment. Some 37% of respondents listed this as their primary challenge, well ahead of obstructive behavior and cultural barriers.

Successful companies emphasize their ultimate communications goal—a company that works seamlessly to realize the value of the merger. Taking this perspective encourages the deep-seated commitment required to achieve buy-in, provide proper direction and orientation, and properly manage expectations.

Manage risks aggressively. The most common reaction to risk is to avoid it. That's understandable: risk carries a negative connotation in many people's minds. Unfortunately, any endeavor involving high returns and strong growth—including a merger—comes with comparably strong risks as well. Companies need to recognize and confront these risks instead of ducking them; when they do, they ultimately maximize the returns on the merger. Fortunately, the corporate world is acknowledging this need. Our global survey of 115 transactions showed encouraging signs that companies are making efforts to proactively face their risks. Some 32% of companies that are merging actively pursue formal risk management.

Effective risk management can lead to early wins. Some of these companies have developed enough expertise in risk management that it has become a source for both early wins and long-term growth.

Yet on the other side of the coin are the two-thirds of all companies that integrate after a merger without the benefit of the risk management process. This statistic is alarming today—and will be more so tomorrow. In the future, the complexity of risk will grow in proportion with the opportunities large deals offer.

Chapter Eight | The Stock Market Connection

The history of the market is clear: in the short term, stocks have extreme ups and downs ..., but in the long term, stocks go in only one direction. Up.

—James K. Glassman and Kevin A. Hassett
Dow 36,000, 1999

From the beginning, we've noted that there is a connection between the Endgames curve and the performance of equities markets worldwide. Now it's time to take a closer look. The basis of this discussion stems from several conclusions that we've drawn from the Endgames analysis so far.

First, the competitive and economic dynamics in each of the four Endgames stages present crisper acquisition and consolidation strategies to companies than ever before. Companies that lead their industries will have unprecedented opportunities to outgrow their rivals, make superior profits, and lead the pack in stock prices.

Second, the Endgames model is a predictive tool that looks as far as 20 years into the future. One major implication from the model is that the pace and size of mergers across most industries will accelerate.

Today, with merger activity generally idle while the economy recovers from the recession, the stock market has been moving sideways for some time. However, as the economy recovers and consolidation resumes, there is significant potential for stock prices to be boosted by merger premiums and the superior economic returns offered by the successful implementation of Endgames strategies. On this basis, the stock market has the potential to increase several times over.

Third, the Endgames analysis implicitly predicts and forecasts industrial deregulation in Stage 1 industries, trade liberalization as a means to achieve growth and transition from Stage 1 to Stage 2 or Stage 3, and increased corporate governance. As this happens, several outcomes are clear: companies will have new opportunities to increase profits and lead their industries; the size and number of mergers will increase; and macroeconomic and regulatory factors will be more conducive to growth and expansion—all of which, in turn, point to rising stock markets.

GLOBAL CONNECTIONS

Looking back on history, a rising stock market and increased merger activity usually go hand in hand. A detailed analysis of the number of M&A deals and the market indices shows a strong correlation between the Dow Jones index and acquisition activity in North America. As Figure 8-1 illustrates, from 1989 to 2001, there is a correlation of 93% between the number of U.S. mergers and the Dow Jones Industrial Average (R^2 of 93%). This implies that, at least to a certain degree, rising stock prices form a currency for making M&A transactions possible and are therefore a key driver of acquisition and consolidation booms.

How many of the mergers of the 1990s would have taken place without the high stock valuations of the equities used by acquirers to pay for the transactions? And don't forget the favorable accounting treatment of mergers completed via share swaps. Still, timing plays a key role in the success of acquisition strategies; a high stock market alone means little. For example, in what was considered a bold move at the time, Tyco International purchased CIT Financial in a highly

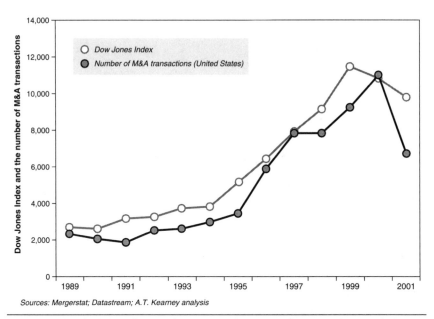

Sources: Mergerstat; Datastream; A.T. Kearney analysis

Figure 8-1. The correlation between the Dow Jones Index and the number of M&A transactions in the United States (1989–2001)

leveraged move to diversify into the financial services field. One year later, however, Tyco began looking to unload CIT Financial—for a loss—when the balance sheets of highly debt-leveraged companies (like Tyco) came under scrutiny for possible financial irregularities in the backwash following the failure of Enron. Rising stock markets and lots of merger activity don't always guarantee a *successful* acquisition strategy.

> Rising stock markets and lots of merger activity don't always guarantee a successful acquisition strategy.

Expanding our field of vision a little further, the same holds true for the European markets, where Figure 8-2 shows that the Euro Stoxx and merger activity are 80% correlated.

In Japan, however, a different picture emerges (see Figure 8-3). Merger activity was relatively flat while the Nikkei Index plummeted in the early- and mid-1990s. However, in the midst of the Asian economic crisis in 1998, merger activity rocketed upward. This discrepancy can be traced to a number of Endgames-related factors:

■ In Japan, financial services companies, automotive companies,

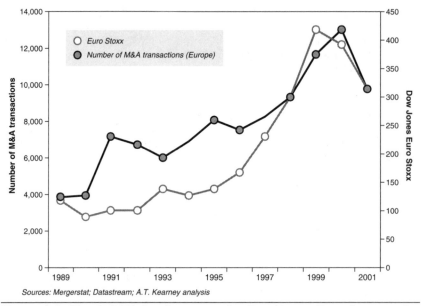

Figure 8-2. The correlation between the Dow Jones Euro Stoxx and the number of M&A transactions in Europe (1989–2001)

and real estate assets industries had fallen so much in value that investors believed they could be acquired for a reasonable price. These companies were all in Stage 2 industries, prompting foreign banks to jump in and make a number of acquisitions as part of their global Endgames consolidation strategy.

- The Japanese government "encouraged" the merger of several troubled financial services institutions as it began to deregulate and reform this huge industry.

- Although acquisitions of Japanese companies by foreign companies were rare, after the Asian crisis the Japanese government could no longer insulate national companies from foreign acquirers. The market began to open up and globalize, primarily in Japan's Stage 2 and 3 industries.

Although merger activity in Japan is not as closely correlated with markets as it is in Europe and North America, it is still driven by Endgames phenomena. And when we combine the data for North America, Europe, and Japan, we see that the strong correlation

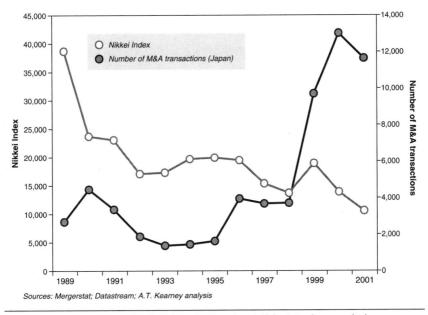

Sources: Mergerstat; Datastream; A.T. Kearney analysis

Figure 8-3. The correlation between the Nikkei Index and the number of M&A transactions in Japan (1989–2001)

between share prices and M&A activity also holds true globally. If this long-term trend stays intact, the entire global market capitalization for the year 2010 could amount to between US$60 and $80 trillion (see Figure 8-4). The size of this number suggests that there is more than enough room for mega-mergers—and the acceleration of merger activity in general—that the Endgames model predicts.

THERE ARE WINNERS IN EVERY ENDGAMES STAGE

Investors can profit at every stage along the Endgames curve. In this section, we look at some of the best practices of companies across the entire Endgames spectrum and explain how identifying those practices can lead to superior investments.

We began by creating Endgames stage-specific indexes based on industry indexes from Dow Jones and plotting their development from the beginning of 1992 until the first quarter of 2002. The Stage 1 index is the combination of the utilities, financial services, and railroads indexes; Stage 2 is chemicals and retailers; Stage 3 is aerospace, auto-

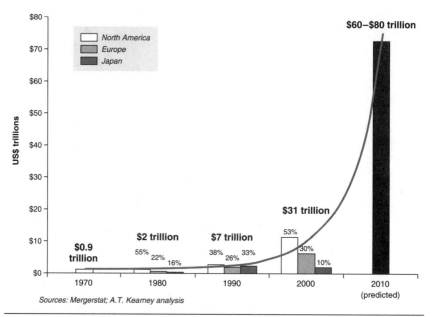

Figure 8-4. The value of the world capital markets

motive manufacturers, distillers and brewers, and food services; and
the Stage 4 index is made up of soft drinks and tobacco. As Figure 8-
5 illustrates, our analysis revealed that there is no significant variation
in the stock market returns between stages (and industries within those
stages) along the Endgames curve.

The key to using the Endgames analysis as an investment tool,
then, is the ability to choose companies that

> The key to using the
> Endgames analysis as an
> investment tool is the abil-
> ity to identify companies
> that apply Endgames prin-
> ciples particularly well.

apply Endgames principles particularly well. In
turn, this means being able to identify companies that have the highest probability of becoming the ultimate winners in the Endgames consolidation battle.

In each industry, regardless of where it is along the Endgames
curve, there are leaders and laggards. The value building growth
matrix, described in earlier chapters, should serve as the starting point
for identifying top-performing companies in any industry on the basis
of revenue growth and growth in value creation. How concentrated is
the industry? What core competencies separate leaders and laggards?

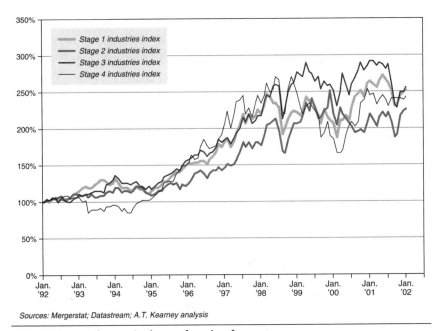

Sources: Mergerstat; Datastream; A.T. Kearney analysis

Figure 8-5. Industry indexes for the four stages

Regardless of what Endgames Stage their industries are in, companies that exhibit revenue growth and value growth above their industry averages are the starting point for good Endgames-based investments.

With this industry growth framework in mind, the second step is to look at the specific dynamics in each Endgames Stage for clues as to which companies may perform best.

In the Opening Stage, it is important to choose companies that have financial backing and a sound business model. This may sound obvious, but because industries are often fragmented in Stage 1, there is plenty of room for big winners … and big losers.

A company called Northpoint illustrates this example well. Verizon, a telecommunications leader in the United States, offered to acquire Northpoint, a pioneering "last-mile" DSL communications provider that sold discounted DSL service to its local phone customers. But when it appeared that the economy was headed into a recession, Verizon walked away from the deal. Despite Northpoint's fundamental attractiveness to Verizon, like so many other DSL providers that were undercapitalized and suffered from slower adoption rates than predicted, it soon went bankrupt. Verizon ultimately purchased Northpoint's assets for pennies on the dollar, triggering rapid consolidation of Northpoint's entire industry. Phoenix, for example, a rival to Northpoint, ended up being acquired for a bargain-basement price as well.

In the Scale and Focus Stages (Stages 2 and 3), look for potential mergers of near equals as the pace of consolidation increases rapidly. Recent examples include:

- Exxon and Mobil, Chevron and Texaco, Conoco (a spinoff from DuPont) and Phillips, BP and Amoco, and Arco and Castrol from the Focus Stage (Stage 3) oil industry.
- Pfizer and Warner Lambert, Pfizer and Pharmacia, Glaxo Wellcome and SmithKline Beecham, Bristol-Myers Squibb and DuPont's pharmaceutical subsidiary, and Sandoz and Ciba-Geigy to form Novartis from the Scale Stage (Stage 2) pharmaceutical industry.
- Citigroup and Associates First Capital, and Morgan Stanley and Dean Witter from the Scale Stage (Stage 2) financial services industry.

Also, look for Scale and Focus Stage companies that stick to their knitting. Ventures too far afield from a company's core competencies usually yield poor returns. Consider Starbucks, which turned designer coffee into an industry among a galaxy of little players. It is dominant in its field, but when it decided to embrace the Internet, it made a number of investments in dot.coms—Living.com, Cooking.com, Kozmo.com, and TalkCity.com—that left a bitter taste in the mouths of shareholders. Starbucks has written off the majority of its dot-com investment and no longer considers the Internet as part of its core business strategy.

Another example is Tyco International, a conglomerate of companies in Stage 2 and 3 industries. After an aggressive series of mergers in unrelated industries, Tyco has fallen on hard times because it became so big and diversified it was unable to extract synergies from its far-flung portfolio of acquisitions.

In Stage 4, look for companies that reinvent themselves and spin off new businesses into earlier Endgames stages. These spin-off companies can create the next wave of growth and shareholder value. A good example is the defense electronics industry. Following the September 11, 2001 terrorist attacks in the United States, the U.S. Congress approved the largest increase in U.S. defense spending in a decade. This augurs well for the core business of defense electronics companies, but also opens them up to develop whole new spin-off subindustries such as aircraft security, airport security, and passenger screening technologies, effectively launching another wave of Endgames growth, mergers, and consolidation.

Do Your Due Diligence

From following the regulatory environment to tracking economic cycles, constant research is critical. A solid Endgames strategy depends on having the right information at the right time—and there is no substitute for the due diligence companies must go through to gain it:

Research the regulatory environment. The regulatory environment can be a complicated maze; how well a company navigates it can help make or break a merger. It is a good idea to be aware of public attitudes and assess the sentiment among government regulators, as they may override any potentially attractive financial combinations. In the Canadian banking industry, for example, a number of banking mergers were doomed before they started. A parade of the country's leading players—led by the Royal Bank of Canada and followed by the Bank of Montreal, CIBC, and Toronto-Dominion—all announced intentions to merge, but their plans were dashed when the Finance Minister ruled criteria had to be in place to evaluate the deals properly.

> A solid Endgames strategy depends on having the right information at the right time—and there is no substitute for the due diligence companies must go through to gain it.

When Jack Welch stretched his retirement date, he did it just to close his proposed merger with Honeywell, a deal that European competition regulators ultimately squelched despite painstaking efforts on

GE's part to pare or sell off the business lines that might be considered anticompetitive.

Examine the merger success rate. Look for companies that execute the merger process well. Companies such as Teleflex and Danaher in the industrial equipment industry are renowned for identifying good acquisition candidates on a global basis, conducting uncompromising due diligence, and integrating their acquisitions quickly and effectively. On the other hand, companies that acquire without adequate screening and due diligence processes can destroy shareholder value with dizzying rapidity. United States Senator Joseph Lieberman summed it up quite simply for reporters during the Senate investigation following the Enron scandal: too many analysts failed to ask "why" before they said "buy."

Anticipate future trends. Use the Endgames model to find new industries that are being created. Look beyond the current mania to developing trends to discover future opportunities and strategic industry shifts. One such longer-term shift is the movement toward developing a sustainable environment. New industries and subindustries that improve the quality of the environment are emerging rapidly as the spotlight on the deteriorating environment and rising energy prices shines brighter.

However, just as new opportunities and industries emerge, others will naturally decline. For example, coal mining has been in a world decline since the mid-1990s. Will petroleum follow suit? And what about the effect on automobile companies? Will they decline as well, or will they develop renewable energy power sources? Disposable packaging and collateral materials consumption will give way to more intense efforts at innovation in design that makes better and less wasteful use of the earth's resources. And long before such changes work their way through the ecosystem, there will be both consumer and capital backlash against companies that have no strategy in place to cope with the future. Industries in potential jeopardy include automotive, mining, logging, fishing, petroleum, and nuclear energy. Industries on the ascent may include remanufacturing, fuel cells, mass transportation, solar and hydrogen power generation, fish farming, nanotechnology, and biotechnology, all of which leverage technology to use materials and energy more efficiently and effectively.

Follow the cycles. Finally, merger activity is cyclical. As economist Frederic Pryor explained in a recent article:

> The only difference in the current climate is that the merger boom of the late 1990s was of a much larger magnitude than any of the previous ones. So the anticompetitive effects of the greater concentration that inevitably follows as a result of the bigger boom is theoretically greater. However ... a lot of the mergers were done quickly and for defensive purposes so they have a greater chance of failure.... Some of these were mergers of competitors with weak market positions. In such cases, it is doubtful whether increased size will solve these problems. For instance, among the world's 18 largest pharmaceutical companies, 11 of the 12 companies which experienced mergers lost (combined) market share between 1990 and 1998, while all six of the companies which had not merged gained market share.[1]

MINING FOR GOLD

As we have seen throughout the book, the Endgames model sometimes produces circumstances that are particularly opportune for identifying winning and losing companies. Because the Endgames model is predictive, investors can identify and analyze industries to determine whether they are poised for a new round of consolidation and merger activity.

They can also look at how successfully they execute Endgames strategies. In the transition from the Opening Stage to the Scale Stage, for example, some companies experience huge run-ups in their share prices due to their savvy in this area. Success traits in this Opening-to-Scale transition include:

- Developing a CEO vision to identify the right time to gain first-mover advantage by being the first company in an industry to begin aggressive consolidation.

- Building a track record of successful acquisitions. Companies that successfully identify good acquisitions—and don't overpay for them—typically emerge as Endgames leaders in their industries.
- Building the best post-merger integration capabilities in the industry and enabling consolidation and acquisition activity at a more rapid pace than the competition.

The transition from late Stage 2 or early Stage 3 to late Stage 3 or early Stage 4 also presents opportunities for investors to identify superior companies. Once most of the consolidation has occurred in an industry and only a few major global players are left, investors must be certain they choose the ultimate winner of the Endgames consolidation race from the remaining players. Some of the Endgames-based success factors in this transition include:

- A solid track record in integrating mega-mergers successfully and quickly.
- The ability to develop new growth engines for the core Stage 3 or Stage 4 business.
- Success in managing the portfolio of subindustries and spin-off industries along the Endgames curve to achieve optimum growth and shareholder value.

Clearly, the Endgames model has great potential for private equity and direct investment firms. In fact, in a recent series of executive briefings we hosted across North America and Europe, private equity firms have been extremely enthusiastic about the Endgames model and its implications. Investors not only can use the key success factors we've just discussed for specific companies, but they also can look at Endgames stages. With a typical holding period of three to seven years, private equity firms value the Endgames analysis because of its ability to predict specifically which industries will consolidate capabilities and to pinpoint the duration of industry consolidation stages. Both have significant implications for which industry a private equity firm

> *Once most of the consolidation has occurred in an industry ... investors must be certain they choose the ultimate winner of the Endgames consolidation race from the remaining players.*

should invest in and for how it should execute its exit strategy.

To illustrate, an ideal investment for a private equity firm would be in an industry in the late Opening Stage or early Scale Stage. The firm would invest in several companies in this industry, or in related or adjacent industries, and integrate the acquisitions (often by way of a "roll-up"). This strategy would be executed over a window of two to five years. Once the integration was successfully completed, the private equity firm would exit its investment by selling in the early part of Stage 3, when acquisition premiums are typically at their highest. At this point in the Endgames curve, mega-mergers are taking place among the global industry giants in order to stake out leading positions in the run-up to Stage 4. By replicating this strategy over and over, with investments progressing across the Endgames spectrum, private equity firms can optimize their portfolios—and the returns for their investors.

The final Endgames special situation is a rarity indeed—an Endgames-visionary CEO. Many CEOs can successfully execute an Endgames strategy within a particular stage and some can make a successful transition from one stage to another. But there are only a handful of CEOs who can manage successfully up and down the Endgames curve.

> There are only a handful of CEOs who can manage successfully up and down the Endgames curve.

Jack Welch of General Electric was one such CEO, consolidating industries years ahead of his competitors and selling companies in Stage 4 industries to other companies that didn't realize that the growth prospects for those industries were gone.

Lou Gerstner, the recently retired CEO of IBM, was another such visionary. IBM, once the juggernaut in mainframes along with Unisys, continued to dominate the field into the 1980s, when a shift from the mainframe to the desktop computer began. After losing its way in the 1990s, IBM was thought to be in peril of extinction like so many other Dow constituents and former members of the *Fortune* 100 club. Under the steady hand of Gerstner, though, the company survived by shifting its focus from a hardware company to a provider of end-to-end solutions and services to its clients. Hardware revenues remained virtually flat during the 1990s and have shrunk since the millennium, while services have grown nearly fivefold. The acquisitions Gerstner made along the way, Lotus Development and Tivoli Systems, supported his end-to-end solution strategy with a networked software platform.

And so, the CEO who was made famous for his anti-vision statement—telling the press in 1993, "the last thing IBM needs now is a vision"—rejected the breakup strategy followed by other Goliaths like AT&T and opted instead for the integrated scale advantage. In the process, IBM's stock price increased more than sevenfold in less than a decade. Clearly, a visionary CEO who crafts strategies that harmonize with the Endgames curve can reward shareholders immensely.

A New World of Opportunity

Investors can capitalize on several opportunities to use the Endgames Stages to their advantage. Clearly, the principles and theories embedded in the Endgames analysis all point to a rising stock market. Although the future of the market can never be predicted precisely, the positive trends are there: an increasingly rapid pace of merger activity, deregulation, freer trade, improved corporate governance, and bigger merger premiums built into stock prices.

As industries progress along the Endgames curve, investors need to adjust their strategy to achieve consistently good returns. In the early stages, look for companies that have sound business models with strong growth potential and focus. In the later stages, companies that demonstrate proven track records of successful mergers and of creating spin-off subindustries are the ones to seek.

The transition from one Endgames stage to another almost always presents investors with the opportunity to identify winners and losers—including the chance to better recognize the rare CEO who is an "Endgames visionary." Finally, the opportunities for private equity firms to use Endgames to their advantage appear extremely attractive.

The Endgames model is extremely robust: beyond its predictive capabilities, it opens the imagination of business people to a host of new opportunities, scenarios, and possibilities. In the next chapter, we examine some of the possibilities Endgames dynamics may create over the next decade.

Notes

1. Pryor, Frederic L., "Dimensions of the Worldwide Merger Boom," *Journal of Economic Issues*, 12-01-2001, p. 825.

Chapter Nine | The Endgames Vision of 2010

... it takes all the running you can do, to keep in the same place. If you want to get somewhere else, you must run at least twice as fast as that!

          —The Red Queen in
          Through the Looking Glass
          by Lewis Carroll, 1871

In this final chapter we turn our attention to the future. With more than a bit of bravado and perhaps even some brazenness, we forecast what we believe the next decade holds for the both the stock market and consolidation trends. We leave statistical rigor behind and let the panorama of our thinking go well beyond trends for mergers and equity markets. We take a cosmic view of the players and we speculate who will be the winners and losers, both in terms of nations and industries.

In this chapter, then, we offer our broad predictions for change between now and 2010. We also describe what the road to that near future will be like and what challenges will face executive travelers. We look at the 2010 horizon with a view to its corporate composition before taking a scan of global competitiveness. Finally, we come to the Endgames agenda and propose a solid strategy for those who want to be winners at the end of the first decade of the 21st century.

OUR PREDICTIONS

Dow to Soar

Little did Charles Dow realize in 1885 when he first began publishing a daily average of 12 stocks (10 of them railroads) that the Dow or Dow Jones Industrial Average (DJIA) would become the most widely known and most widely quoted stock market index in the world.

The composition of the Dow has changed radically over the years, constantly being modified to reflect the composition of the real world of business. And the DJIA has grown dramatically in the last decade. Other indices also have taken on greater significance (such as the NASDAQ, the Nikkei, the S&P 500, the FTSE 100, the Hang Seng, and DJ Euro Stoxx), but the Dow—even though made up of just 30 stocks of U.S.-based corporations—still is perceived, rightly or wrongly, as *the* index to watch. It is truly the progenitor.

In mid-2002 the Dow stood at 10,000. Over the next decade, we foresee it increasing about fourfold. Today, the DJIA has a market capitalization of approximately US$3 trillion. This, coupled with the fact that the Dow comprises the largest publicly traded companies in the United States, makes it an ideal indicator for the Endgames scenario. Each of the

> With Endgames consolidation trending to higher velocity and greater scale into the future, by 2010 the first US$1 trillion merger will become a reality.

constituent companies has a leading industry position and is poised to finish among the winners in Stage 4.

This track record, plus the Dow's periodic adjustments to more closely mirror the economy make us confident that it should continue to track the long-term upward momentum we see developing in consolidation with a very high correlation.

Of course, not all companies in the Dow will survive the Endgames curve or manage to stay on top. Chevron, a Dow component in 1997, acquired oil giant Texaco in 2000 and was dropped from the index—

although it remains a very healthy company. GE tried but failed to take over Honeywell, another Dow component company (due to strong objections from the European Union competition directorate). We can imagine another one or two companies consolidating and disappearing (or losing market share or stock price panache).

Our predictions on the future of the Dow are shared by several investment experts. Authors such as David Elias in his book *Dow 40,000* and James K. Glassman and Kevin A. Hassett in *Dow 36,000* all predict a similar bullish development.[1,2]

Elias predicts the Dow to break 40,000. This is based on his projection of the past trend into the future with annual returns of 9%. He conjectures that factors sustaining this momentum are global growth, increased savings for Social Security, and higher productivity.

Glassman and Hassett also predict that the Dow will reach 36,000 because investors will finally understand the real value of stocks. Here and in his 2002 book, *The Secret Code of the Superior Investor*, Glassman's thesis is that stocks are no riskier than bonds and, in fact, they have outperformed bonds in any 20-year period. Using an equation that defines stock returns as dividend yield plus dividend increase rate and assuming that stocks should be less and less discounted for risk—since they have done so well over such a long period of time—Glassman sees tremendous upward potential ahead. We agree. The overlay of Endgames staging fits neatly with the prediction that the Dow will witness nearly 15% to 20% compounded growth through 2010.

The overall historical growth of the Dow has been a little more than 5% annually since 1896—due to the effects of economically destructive periods such as world wars and the depression of the 1930s. (In fact, from the beginning to the 1930s, the index rose by only about 3% per year.) However, starting in the 1950s, the return has been close to 8%, and over the past 10 years—even taking into consideration the recent setback—the annual return has been almost 12%. So a projection of 15% to 20% for the next several years doesn't seem so utopian in comparison.

We are keeping a long-term perspective here, whereas the typical stock market analyst is much more focused on the short term. The main factor in our projection is a new valuation of stocks driven by industry Endgames.

The US$1 Trillion Merger

The biggest merger deals each year have increased in value tremendously over time, but with a lot of volatility. In 2001, merger activity experienced a big setback, both in the number of deals and in the total value. But this is a temporary phenomenon. The upward trend will resume shortly and continue to grow at an exponential rate.

As Figure 9-1 illustrates, the maximum value of M&A transactions has increased more or less steadily over the last 14 years, despite an occasional blip such as 2001. The largest transaction that year was the smallest since 1994.

> Industry insiders believe that the full Endgames cycle will no longer take 20 to 25 years to run its course but may cycle at 16 or 17 years in the near future.

With Endgames consolidation trending to higher velocity and greater scale into the future, by 2010 the first US$1 trillion merger will become a reality. Today's highest market cap companies are well below US$0.5 trillion; however, the positive trends

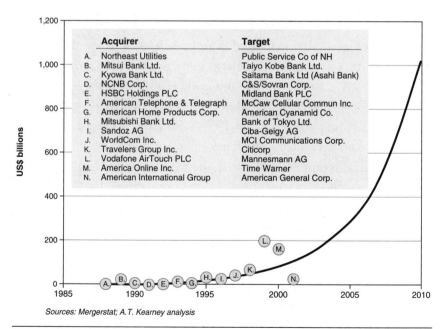

Sources: Mergerstat; A.T. Kearney analysis

Figure 9-1. Biggest mergers by year

developing in the stock market along with the globalization of the Endgames scenario are catalysts certain to bring about this mega-merger. It's only a matter of time.

THE ROAD TO 2010

In recent decades, most of the interest has centered on one or another Endgames stage. In the mid-to-late 1990s, for example, the Internet boom created a plethora of new industries and subindustries. Mergers, roll-ups, and early-stage consolidation strategies were abundant, and all the action seemed to be in the Opening Stage. By the early 2000s, though, the boom had ended and growth rates stalled. Losers in the Internet boom had been acquired or had gone out of business and winners now evolved their strategy to increasing scale and building their competitive position. The spotlight has shifted from Endgames Stage 1 to Stage 2.

What predictions can we make about the road to 2010? What role will Endgames play? What will the industrial landscape look like and where will the action be?

We see Endgames Stages 3 and 4 as the battlegrounds of the next decade. Industries that exhibited high growth rates in the 1980s and 1990s will run out of steam in what is sure to be a lower-growth global economy. Many of the traditional preferred growth engines—geographic expansion and buying up and consolidating smaller competitors—have been exhausted. In the late 1990s and early 2000s, the extreme focus placed on maximizing stock prices and quarterly results will soon take its toll as consumers become disenfranchised. This trend will implicitly commoditize companies (and industries) that neglected product innovation and customer service for so long.

As a result, companies in the major Stage 2 industries today—automotive, airlines, telecommunications, consumer products, banking, pharmaceuticals, and others—will move gradually to Stages 3 and 4 over the next decade. Merger activity and, in particular, merger size will be unprecedented as the biggest players in these industries acquire their competitors in bids for industry dominance. Spin-offs will also become rampant as companies try to assemble a winning portfolio of businesses. New industries of outsourcers designed to serve these global behemoths will be created. Finally, roll-ups will become even more popular as smaller Stage 2 companies try to grow rapidly through mergers and acquisitions so as not to "miss the window" to attain the perceived superior economic returns by transitioning into Stages 3 and 4.

What are the implications of this Endgames trend over the next decade? Is it possible to imagine headlines like these?

General Motors and Toyota merge to form global automotive powerhouse

Johnson & Johnson breaks into 50 separate businesses, unleashes growth and innovation

AT&T and Deutsche Telekom form world's largest global telecommunications company

GE Capital and Deutsche Bank merge and break the new company into separate businesses; CEO says, "We're unleashing shareholder value and refocusing into new directions"

These imaginary examples may seem far-fetched, but they are direct implications of the Endgames model. Who would have foreseen the unbelievable number and size of merger combinations in the past decade? And yet, the Endgames model would have predicted that, too.

Management Challenges

The exponential rise we see in stock prices will have a ripple effect on the whole economy. Technology innovation, product innovation, market roll-ups, and mergers, in addition to split-ups, spin-offs, and even corporate breakdowns, will happen at speeds never encountered before. Along with this will come uncharted innovation in information technology and knowledge management and an explosion of new services, new products, new industries, and new markets. The convergence of all this interconnectedness, interoperability, and value chain rationalization will turbocharge corporate developments to a speed that will make unwary executives dizzy. However, this speed has to be channeled in the direction that most benefits companies and share-holders.

This speed will also boost the velocity at which the Endgames, mergers, and consolidation trends will coalesce in the future. Industry insiders believe that the full Endgames cycle will no longer take 20 to 25 years to run its course but may cycle at 16 or 17 years in the near future. What will the cycle be in the year 2010? Will it be 10 years or even less? Perhaps as few as eight years in some industries? Even with all the technological innovations boosting productivity and making businesses more efficient, economies will not redline or overheat as productivity increases. The technology revolution has an impact on the economy that resembles that of a tax cut. Growth will continue at greater levels without the usual inflationary consequences. Information handling and control will surpass product and marketing know-how as a core competency.

Whatever it takes, management must step up to the challenge. This means learning to manage knowledge and information while staying in the driver's seat. Keeping up with the knowledge and information explosion while you're moving at Autobahn speed is no easy task.

New Global Titans

By 2005 we will almost certainly see more than a dozen companies with market capitalization of more than US$1 trillion. The largest com-pany today, GE, has a market capitalization of

> By 2005 we will almost certainly see more than a dozen companies with market capitalization of more than US$1 trillion.

US$332 billion. What will it look like—or who will surpass it—in 2010? Volume and scale bar-riers are collapsing in the face of technological and information management innovations.

Take the WorldWide Retail Exchange (WWRE). Headquartered in the United States, the WWRE is a truly global network of more than 60 retailers that conducts business that represents—in the aggregate sales of its member network—a company with more than twice the revenue of Wal-Mart. By the end of the decade, will WWRE be a global entity with US$10 trillion in revenues? Will it encompass more than 1 million employees and contractors? Will it cover more than 80 national markets? Will conglomerates be revitalized—because no single product market could nourish such a huge corporate entity? Will the speed of concentration increase so that one or two companies merge every day—not unlike the Nestlé model of an acquisition every three to four days?

> In 2010 there won't be 50 or 60 undisputed global industry leaders: there will be hundreds.

Just 10 years ago, managing a company of more than 500,000 employees and US$80 billion of revenue was unthinkable. Now the seemingly unlimited potential of information technology finds its real challenge in controlling giant complex entities online—and this trend will increase in scale as the speed of consolidation accelerates.

Coupled with this growing scale and need for complexity management are advancing technology and streamlining of the value chain. The supply chain has been tightening up for quite a while, but the value chain goes beyond supply to encompass everything from the concept to the customer. To cite the WWRE again, trading relationships have been revolutionized with open exchanges and interoperable transaction architectures offering the following benefits:

- Open exchanges and architectures allow members to form short- or long-term relationships with one or many partners.
- Electronic interfaces radically reduce transaction costs for buyers and sellers.
- Transparency has been introduced to the marketplace, eliminating the costs of maintaining hedges and being surprised by oversupplies in the value chain.
- New e-commerce business models are easily developed and adapted to the exchange, and implementing new technologies is increasingly easier.
- Transactions are conducted from end to end along the supply chain—from sourcing through settlement.
- Participants gain value through the exchange as a way to trade goods and services, and scale is no longer a barrier.

What is the future for competitors in such an industry environment? They may belong to one or more exchanges, moving in and out of them at will, to gain the benefits of a global value chain that expands their markets for goods or services on a planetwide basis, while they continue to enjoy the benefits of the low cost of doing business—thanks to the seamless pipeline developed by the public exchange. And, at the same time, these smaller businesses can continue to delight the customer on a local level, where custom services and customer relationships often matter more than the lowest transaction cost.

An analysis of roughly 150 companies along the Endgames curve also revealed that increasing consolidation is changing the economics of their business in a way that favors a division of labor between the upcoming commodity service providers and outsourcers. As businesses grow in scale and scope, the definition of core business competencies will sharpen. The consolidation trend will also usher in a tremendous increase in outsourcing, not only of traditional target activities such as MRO, but of new, complex business processes as well. Payroll, for example, will inevitably be outsourced, followed by benefits administration, facilities management, human resources, and even business processes such as assembly subsystems that are not unique to the company, but use precious processing, design, and strategic resources that could be better deployed elsewhere.

Next we'll look at how the industry titans will rise to the challenges of their dominant positions in Stage 4 of Endgames.

Keeping Success Evergreen

Maintaining momentum and managing to stay on top in Stage 4 of Endgames consolidation will require a special breed of company and management talent. Of course, some of these challenges are not new—but the penalties for missteps will be greater and swifter than in the past. There are no longer any safe havens.

In 2010 there won't be 50 or 60 undisputed global industry leaders: there will be hundreds, each in its respective industry. Companies in such dominant positions will deal with high volumes of merger transactions—perhaps 10 or more per year. They will face troublesome cultural issues in the process—not just corporate cultural issues, but national issues as well.

Executives will also confront perhaps the biggest bugaboo of all, complacency. The old watchword about fighting the lethargy that comes with contentment will be revived in the future. Throughout history, long-term market dominance has characteristically bred complacency among industry leaders. Few can stay lean, mean, and hungry once the corporate coffers are brimming with success and profits.

Today, U.S. or European companies tend to dominate the industrial scene, while many Japanese companies that were once the model of efficiency struggle with outmoded business systems. One of the areas in which the United States has enjoyed great success is in improving supply chain management. As that trend continues and extends across the entire value chain, Japanese companies will work to wring substantial costs out of their product and service delivery equation.

To compound Japan's problems, Moody's Investors Service has declared the former economic superpower a credit risk as great as Botswana, Cyprus, and Israel because of its "soaring national debt, chronic deflation and wobbly banks," according to *The Wall Street Journal*. In mid-2002, Moody's said it was slashing Japan's credit rating by two notches because government debt "will approach levels unprecedented in the postwar era in the developed world and as such Japan will be entering 'uncharted territory.'"[3]

Another key to gaining or maintaining a leading position is customer learning. With the advent of intranets and improved information sharing, companies can finally reach out and get closer to the customer. They can also get a lot closer to their employees, who possess most of the company knowledge. Companies that find ways to hear— and listen to—customers and connect their employees both to one another and to the customers stand a good chance of being industry leaders. And then they must never let up. Ever.

Even powerhouse companies that have exhibited staying power for decades must fight to maintain their hard-won competitive edge. GE, for example, has entered into uncharted—if not somewhat unstable— territory since its superstar CEO, Jack Welch, retired. It remains to be seen whether Welch's successor, Jeffrey Immelt, can continue to move the enterprise forward or whether GE will break into several viable businesses that resume rapid growth and consolidate on their own.

Companies that abandon or neglect learning and development experience the pain of losing position or market momentum. As we discussed in Chapter 6, Coca-Cola lost its position of indisputable market dominance to Pepsi and now it's fighting hard to win back market share. It is no longer a battle of the colas as each of these predatory competitors aggressively goes after the other. Pepsi was the first to understand the bigger business these companies are in—beverages—and moved into the larger market. Coke has been responding with similar purchases, such as the acquisition of the mixers business from Seagram's, in a spin-off from Diageo.

Global Culture

Global capability continues to be a critical success factor for the world dominators that will populate the corporate stage over the next few years. The Endgames masters will develop and nurture a truly global culture that can integrate nations, races, and skill sets to gain maximum productivity from stakeholders.

The new planetwide enterprise will also have expertise in resolving cultural issues. It's not just about synergy. Cultural problems and poor communication can sabotage more well-planned mergers and destroy more value than lack of due diligence.

Several cultural models have worked in the past. In the book *After the Merger*, the authors discussed cultural differences at length.[4] Our Endgames research, however, suggests several approaches work best with cross-border mergers and acquisitions.

The first approach is to expand the global platform, but keep the local flavor. This is the method favored by Masayoshi Son, the maverick globetrotting Japanese entrepreneur who founded Softbank. Son acquired Ziff-Davis in 1995 and essentially left the existing culture intact. In the same year he invested US$100 million in Yahoo! in return for a 15% interest in the company. Yahoo! employees were especially fearful he would try to change them into a Japanese-style company. But Son let the cultures remain independent. He was educated in the United States and lived there for several years afterward and feels he understands enough about American culture to trust his investments without trying to change them.

Another winning approach is to gain in international experience first—as was the case with the BP-Amoco combination. Each company had experience integrating cross-border mergers prior to BP's acquisition. BP integrated Standard Oil of Ohio, while Amoco learned valuable lessons with its purchase of Canada's Dome Petroleum.

Another approach is to try to create an entirely new culture, such as Daimler-Benz of Germany attempted when it acquired Chrysler. Daimler did its homework by conducting a study of large cross-border mergers and joint ventures to assess failures and their causes. Leaders iden-

> *In our Endgames vision, cultural integration works most easily when a more neutral and integrative Swiss-, Dutch-, or Norwegian-style culture is adopted.*

tified cultural conflict as a major problem. Consequently, DaimlerChrysler executives built a merger integration strategy around major tasks designed to minimize cultural conflict and prevent a cultural implosion. But for all its diligent preparation, the newly merged company still experienced many problems surrounding what turned out to be a strong and dominant German culture.

In our Endgames vision, cultural integration works most easily when a more neutral and integrative Swiss-, Dutch-, or Norwegian-style culture is adopted. Witness the winning method of Nestlé, which has its headquarters in Vevey, Switzerland. It takes a "United Nations" approach. The composition of its board is truly international—it has not a single Swiss national member. Nestlé acquires a company every week and finds it very easy to integrate its numerous acquisitions without any turmoil being reported in the press or trade publications. ABB, another corporate model, has successfully merged Swiss and Swedish components into a truly global culture that integrates executives and employees from many nations.

NEW PLAYERS IN THE 2010 CONSOLIDATION GAME

Consider the unprecedented size, complexity, and scale of global companies by 2010: what was once almost unimaginable becomes reality. Just to run one of these companies on a day-to-day basis, a number of new enabling industries will be created and others, mainly in professional services fields, will have to significantly change their business models. The roles of the CEO and the Board of Directors will surely change as well.

How will these trends change the world we'll be working in by 2010? Consider some potential new players and new roles for current players.

Outsourcing Companies. When Sara Lee announced a few years ago that it was outsourcing the manufacturing of many of its products, it shocked the industry. But in 2010, this will be the norm, at least for companies in Stage 3 and 4 industries. Whole new industries focused on outsourcing manufacturing, product distribution, lending or claims processes, retail branch banking, or automotive warranty administration could all be possible as Stage 3 and 4 companies focus on the true strategic differentiators and outsource their remaining processes.

As another group of A.T. Kearney authors explain in their book, *Rebuilding the Corporate Genome*, leading companies "are dissecting their companies into tiny pieces and creating new and innovative ways to make the most of their best assets." The authors liken this process to rebuilding the corporate genome because of "the similarities we see between a corporate capability (a single element of a value chain, like manufacturing, branding or purchasing) and a human gene."[5]

Taking this a step further, companies might even outsource certain parts of their line management ranks to management consulting firms to be better positioned to manage complexity, shift resources, and adjust capacity quickly and ensure continual innovation capabilities. Or they might outsource the post-merger integration of new acquisitions. As a result of an even greater volume of merger activity, they might shift the risk and burden of post-merger integration onto investment banks, rather than assuming the risk themselves—in effect, outsourcing this important business process.

New Financial "Scorekeepers." As mergers become even more predictable, commonplace, and embedded as a competitive strategy, the role of auditors and compensation consultants seems likely to change as well. Taken to an extreme, one could picture an annual report with an independent section written by a company's auditor on where the company and its industry are positioned on the Endgames curve, the five-year outlook for merger activity and consolidation in the industry, and the major strategic imperatives for the company's management to address. Or, one could imagine the role of compensation consultants changing as well. Instead of comparisons against industry groups as a key determinant of senior management compensation, one could picture a comparison versus companies in different industries but in similar Endgames stages. Management imperatives like creating superior competitiveness, realizing shareholder benefits from mega-mergers, and achieving economies of scale would become more important drivers of compensation, to the benefit of shareholders.

New Role of the CEO. Finally, the role of the CEO will change dramatically as the size and complexity of a company increases. The world's largest companies may very well have more than one million employees by 2010 or have market capitalization bigger than the gross domestic product (GDP) of some medium-sized country. Right now, GE and half a dozen other U.S. companies have market caps larger than the GDPs of all but the top 20 countries.

> The world's largest companies may very well have more than one million employees by 2010 or have market capitalization bigger than the gross domestic product (GDP) of some medium-sized country.

Strategy will have a renaissance in the CEO suite. CEOs will focus primarily on the positioning of the businesses in a company's portfolio on the Endgames curve and assess what the strategic implications and choices are for those businesses going forward. Mergers, acquisitions, spin-offs, and divestitures will become routine for CEOs, but embedding creativity, innovation, and organic growth strategies throughout all levels of a company will become more important and difficult to achieve. Organizationally, because of the size and complexity issue, CEOs may have to reorient their roles toward coaching and empowerment, just to be able to keep a business going from day to day and to have their messages reach all of their employees. Finally, particularly for CEOs in the new Stage 3 and 4 industries, keeping ahead of the technology innovation curve will be critical, so that technology does not render their company obsolete.

A Global Scan: Industry and National Competitiveness

As global culture continues to develop and technology virtually connects the continents, countries themselves will star in the galaxy of commerce. The last 10 years have seen a dramatic change in competitive positions of nations (see Figure 9-2).

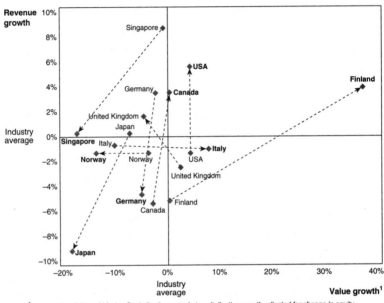

Figure 9-2. Growth portfolio (CAGR 1989–2001) of countries, benchmarked against industry average

The United States has been consistently dominant, followed by the strong performance of Canada. Canada's economy, in fact, has weathered the recent recession surprisingly well, driving it from the underperformer quadrant into the value builders section. Conversely, Japan has declined from being *the* global high performer to the declared laggard of the industrial world. Finland has been transformed from a middle player into a high-tech country, due mainly to its position in telecommunications. Nokia, the world's leading cellular phone manufacturer, accounts for

50% of the Finnish stock market capitalization. However, such reliance on a single company can be dangerous: no company is immune from the pressures of the Endgames consolidation curve.

Meanwhile, Germany has declined from the industrial European powerhouse to the bottom of the league in growth in 2001 and, to the south, Italy has transformed itself from a laggard into a veritable high performer in the European Union.

What implications does this have for the position of various industries in the Endgame? For that we created some country grids to help visualize the trends.

First we developed a global economy plot of industries according to the four Endgames stages, which resulted in a broad bell curve with roughly 15% each in the Opening and Balance stages and roughly 35% each in the Scale and Focus stages. By plotting an individual national economy against that curve, it is immediately apparent whether the economy is made up mostly of young industries and thus will have a bright future or whether it is overdominated by companies in old industries rooted in preserving the status quo.

Germany and Japan, for example, are equally strong in old industries and are substantially underrepresented in the Opening Stage where most young industries reign. In contrast, North America is equally balanced across all stages—very close to the classic S curve—while Singapore, like some other emerging markets, is front-loaded. China is weak in Stage 1 and very strong in Stage 2 companies (see Figure 9-3).

So who will be the winners and who will be the losers in the future?

Obviously, North America is well-equipped for the future and will likely strengthen its already strong position and its domination of the world economy. The same holds true for India, which is strongly front-loaded and thus has a strong position in the up-and-coming industries that will transition through the major consolidation waves. But, of course, having an abundance of companies in the young industries does not guarantee that those companies will move up the Endgames curve and become global leaders in their sectors.

Political leaders have to provide the appropriate environmental and political infrastructure to foster and nourish those industries, to

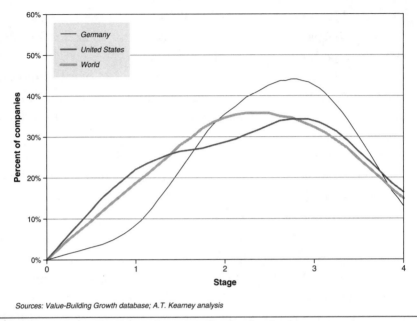

Sources: Value-Building Growth database; A.T. Kearney analysis

Figure 9-3. Distribution of companies in the Endgames stages

support their further growth, and to encourage companies to maintain
their headquarters in the native country. This opens the door to future
spin-offs and creation of industrial networks or "clusters" that form the
breeding ground for large-scale economic growth and employment. We
have seen this in the automotive and automotive supplier industry in
southwest Germany and around Turin and
Detroit. We have seen the aerospace industry
develop around Bavaria. We have seen the high-
tech industry blossom in Silicon Valley
(California), Silicon Alley (New York), and
Boston, and the biotech industry grow in Bavaria
and Berlin, Hong Kong, Singapore, and Malaysia's Multimedia Super
Corridor—all with heavy government support and encouragement.

> The state must play a proactive role by setting the right regulatory environment, along with industrial development and tax system incentives.

The authors have a message for world leaders: industrial policy is
still in vogue. It is not a vestige of the 1970s. Here is where future-ori-
ented country leaders (and leaders of states and provinces and mayors
of major cities) can make their marks. The state must play a proactive
role by setting the right regulatory environment, along with industrial

development and tax system incentives. Our recommendations for far-sighted political leaders are very clear and direct:

1. Create a growth-oriented regulatory environment.
2. Establish an infrastructure that is positive for the local economy, for industries and companies.
3. Create an educational system that stimulates people to exploit their growth potential to the utmost and ultimately induces younger industries to settle in the region and to create economic clusters that boost the national economy.
4. Understand the importance of scale and size of companies and industries at the global level and promote the formation of strong global players that are able to compete planetwide while continuing to benefit the local and national economy.

THE ENDGAMES AGENDA

Having looked at world markets, management and government challenges, new players, and suggestions for policy leaders, we will now return to our Endgames consolidation theme. For ardent pursuers of the consolidation game, we present the agenda we feel is necessary for success in the Endgames race or to be the final successful consolidator of the industry. Thus we leave you with a slate of 10 ideas you can use to improve performance as you guide your company through the cycle. We believe these are seminal thoughts that should be a part of every company's strategy platform.

10-Point Endgames Strategy

1. Diagnose where your industry stands on the Endgames curve and the short-term and long-term operational and strategic imperatives of these positions.
2. Benchmark the company's performance against its competitors in the Endgames race and plot future potential winners and losers with a long-term view.
3. Reorient your strategy, raising your growth hurdle to step or stay ahead of the growth curve of the industry.

4. Screen and evaluate potential merger candidates with regard to their value and synergy potential in the short- and long-term Endgames competition.
5. Sketch out the appropriate roll-up strategy to become the dominant and final consolidator of your industry.
6. Evaluate your current senior management team for suitability, readiness, and potential in the specific Endgames position. In addition, assess the appropriateness of the organization structure according to its Endgames requirements, its value-added depth, and the outsourcing potential appropriate to the particular Endgames stage.
7. Optimize your portfolio by evaluating the Endgames position of each individual business unit within its respective industry.
8. Screen all potential breakthrough technologies in your company for possible spin-offs to form new industries and nurture their growth.
9. Screen existing IT systems, structures, and processes for their appropriateness for further enhanced growth and integration of other acquired businesses.
10 Screen the existing culture for organic strength, openness, and diversity and take action to add any missing pieces. The culture should form a solid, yet flexible core for future global leaders who will integrate future mergers and help rolled-up companies find an emotional home.

On top of these 10 general points, we recommend specific agendas for each stage of the Endgames curve.

Opening Stage

- Stake out space in your industry and aggressively capture ground.
- Plant the seeds of a strong global culture to facilitate rapid growth.
- Get the right leadership on board to be the cadre for future growth.
- Assimilate and merge acquisitions as soon as possible to minimize disruptions and maximize the synergies.

Scale Stage

- Continue to grow rapidly, setting targets well above the average of the industry.
- Strengthen the already existing culture; continuously benchmark against the other major players in the industry.
- Target, acquire, and integrate the most attractive players in your industry.
- Create a global viewpoint and a global culture that permeate the enterprise.
- Continue to develop leadership and focus on changing skill sets. Remember: different skills are needed for different stages.
- Adjust the organization so it is capable of adapting and channeling future growth.
- Adjust the IT systems, processes, and structures to create the benchmark knowledge management practices in the industry.

Focus Stage

- Prepare for the final battle of consolidation, with solid offensive (winner take all) and defensive (exit the industry) strategies.
- Refocus the portfolio of activities to dominate the industry.
- Adjust the cost structure to achieve the most competitive value chain and outsource non-core businesses to gain flexibility and cost advantages.
- Create global coverage, a global network, and global intelligence systems necessary to achieve, of course, global dominance.

Balance and Alliance Stage

- Take necessary steps, at the appropriate time, to prepare the political and cultural environment to accept your company as the global leader in your industry.
- Consider reinvesting profits for charitable causes such as education, environmental protection, and health development.
- Fight and overcome complacency to gain a spirit of continuous competitiveness and further development to prolong industry dominance.

- Screen and benchmark other competitors and upcoming competitive technologies with regard to their potential threats to the existing business model and the impact on future development.
- Reexamine the business portfolio for potential spin-off candidates.

THE ENDGAMES FUTURE: WHAT'S NEXT?

Sometimes, taking the scenic route pays off. It's been four years since we began compiling data to study value-building growth. We wanted not only to find out how companies grow, but also to uncover what specific growth methods they use to increase shareholder value. Soon after, we extended our research to examine merger integration, scrutinizing the conundrum of combining functions and departments of widely different companies and cultures. This, in turn, led us to focus more intently on mergers, acquisitions, and the consolidation activity in industry. It's been a long journey, but the sights—and insights—we experienced along the way have been well worth our while.

But the journey is not over. The data and insights expressed in *Winning the Merger Endgame* take us to the horizon of a new age of industry titans and carefully constructed conglomerates. We believe these entities will become global corporate citizens that partner with governments and global trade organizations for the betterment of the planet and its people. We look forward to living through and writing the next chapter of this epic.

We would like to invite our readers to join us in this venture. If you agree or disagree with our views on how the Endgames model will play out over the next decade—or if you have personal experiences in consolidating industries—please share your views and experiences with us. You can write to the authors at endgames@atkearney.com.

Notes

1. David Elias, *Dow 40,000* (New York: McGraw-Hill, 1999).
2. James K. Glassman and Kevin A. Hassett, *Dow 36,000* (New York: Random House/Three Rivers Press, 2000).

3. Ken Belson, "Debt Load in Japan Brings a Downgrade," *International Herald Tribune*, 31 May 2002.
4. Max M. Habeck, Fritz Kroeger, and Michael R. Traem, *After the Merger: Seven Rules for Successful Post-Merger Integration* (London: Pearson Education Limited, 2000).
5. Johan C. Aurik, Gillis J. Jonk, and Robert E. Willen, *Rebuilding the Corporate Genome: Unlocking the Real Value of Your Business* (New York: John Wiley & Sons, 2002).

Endgames Methodology and M&A Transactions 1988 to 2001

Our life is frittered away by details. Simplify. Simplify.
—Henry David Thoreau, *Walden*

But, then again, others might argue ...

God is in the details.
—Ludwig Mies van der Rohe

The current wave of merger activity crested at the opening of the decade with a multitude of mega-deals. America Online announced it was merging with Time Warner in a strategic move to create what it called the world's first fully integrated media and communications company. The all-stock combination was valued at US$165 billion. This record U.S. deal was topped by the US$200 billion deal announced a few months earlier by Britain's Vodafone, the world's largest mobile phone provider, which declared a hostile bid for Mannesmann AG (Germany) and Orange PLC (Britain). This in turn had surpassed the earlier world record US$90 billion bid for Warner-Lambert by Pfizer. Since this flurry of deals in 2000, activity has fallen to much lower levels both in scale and number—in large part due to the meltdown of dot-coms and telecom companies. And the cratering of the stock market in 2000–2001 reduced the value of stock equities that would have contributed to the currency of most M&A activity.

In this book we have taken a much longer-term view of merger activity. In Chapter 9 we predicted that the current ebb in activity is only a pause while a new and bigger wave gathers momentum. In depleted industries—the situation in which we find telecommunications at the time of publication—assets are purchased by newly funded players, the industry reorganizes, and then consolidation begins anew. And in general downturns, stronger well-funded companies will use tough markets to look for opportunities to buy out smaller firms to maintain or improve their growth rates and capitalize on efficiencies of scale.

In looking at long-term M&A activity, we wanted to do more than simply observe the ebb and flow of global consolidation, we also wanted to:

1. Establish a sound foundation for our thesis that there is a certain predictable pattern to all the merger activity.
2. Illustrate how merger activity goes through a series of phases or stages that can be shown to form an S curve—starting with a deconsolidated industry dispersed among several hundred companies and culminating in a concentration of up to 90% or more of an industry's market share in a few large companies.
3. Define a distinct consolidation trend that is leading to an irrevocable quickening global trend toward industrial concentration.

How Is Concentration Measured?

Various audiences are interested in being able to measure concentration for a variety of reasons. Business leaders need to know the level of concentration to evaluate competitiveness (to make strategic decisions about entry into markets, for example). Government agencies monitor industry consolidation to prevent undue concentration in the hands of one company, in other words to avoid a monopoly situation. Academics and business scholars are interested in the mechanics of M&As. Therefore, not surprisingly, a number of different concentration indicators exist.

In the Endgames study, we used the two most popular metrics.

The first is a measure of the relative size of an industry's largest firms. The three-firm concentration ratio (CR_3) measures the combined share of industry sales held by the three largest firms in an industry:

$$CR_3 = s_1 + s_2 + s_3,$$

where s is market share.

Another commonly used measure is the Hirschman-Herfindahl Index (HHI), which is the sum of the squared market shares of the firms in a market:

$$HHI = s_12 + s_22 + s_32 + s_42 + s_n2,$$

where s is market share.

The HHI takes into account the relative size and distribution of the firms in a market and approaches zero when a market consists of a large number of firms of relatively equal size. For example, in a market with 20 firms each having 5% of the market, the HHI index would be 0.05. The HHI increases both as the number of firms in the market decreases and as the disparity in size among those firms increases. Markets in which the HHI is below 0.1 are considered as relatively unconcentrated, those with HHI values between 0.1 and 0.18 are considered to be moderately concentrated, and those in which the HHI is higher than 0.18 are considered to be concentrated. The maximum value is 1.0.

Transactions that increase the HHI by more than 0.01 in concentrated markets presumptively raise antitrust concerns under the Horizontal Merger Guidelines issued by the U.S. Department of Justice and the U.S. Federal Trade Commission. Occasionally, the percentage value is not normalized and the range of the HHI then goes from 0 to 10,000.

Of course, both metrics, as well as other concentration metrics, strongly correlate.

Figures A-1 and A-2 provide an overview of the most important industries in the Endgames study by the CR3 and the HHI index from 1995 to 1999.

CR3*

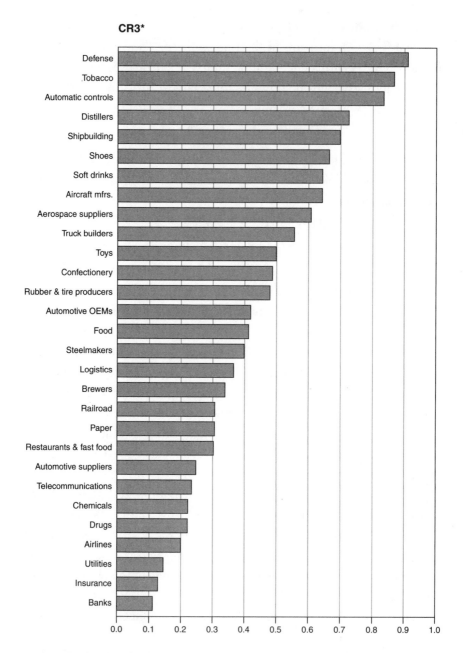

*CR3 = Market share of the three largest companies of the total market based on VBG database (25,000 companies).
Sources: Value-Building Growth database; A.T. Kearney analysis

Figure A-1. Industries ranked by consolidation level (1995–1999)

HHI*

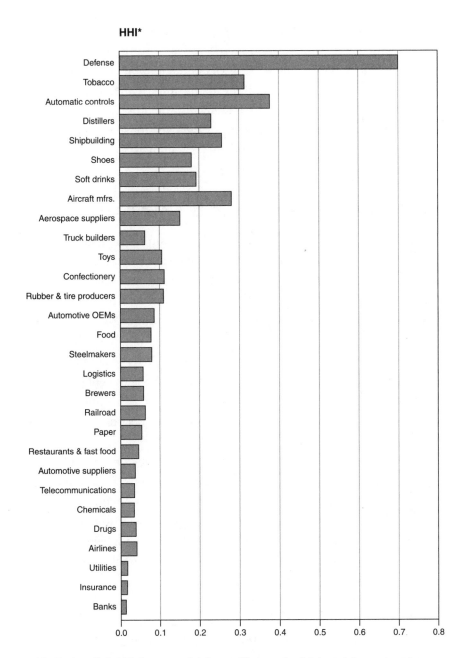

HHI = Hirschman-Herfindahl Index corresponds to the sum of the squared market shares of all companies and is greater than 90%; the axis logarithmically plotted.
Sources: Value-Building Growth database; A.T. Kearney analysis

Figure A-2. Industries ranked by consolidation level (1995–1999)

The concentration is based on the revenue figures of the included companies, which are measured in U.S. dollars. Revenue figures from countries that do not normally use U.S. dollars in their accounting have been converted into U.S. dollars using the respective year-end exchange rate. Within quantitative analyses, the official SIC (Standard Industry Classification) industry codes were used for segmentation. For deeper analyses, A.T. Kearney industry specialists were called in to fine-tune the industry picture further.

HOW THE ENDGAMES CURVE IS CALCULATED

The Endgames curve is based on two sets of values: the concentration degree on the y-axis and the dynamics or speed of concentration on the x-axis. In addition to the concentration values, information on the speed is necessary to derive the Endgames curve. As a next step therefore, we measure the dynamics—the concentration over time, for example—to understand whether an industry is consolidating or deconsolidating. This was done by defining two five-year time frames from 1990 to 1994 and 1995 to 1999, and measuring the concentration degree twice. Based on the difference between the two values one can determine whether an industry is consolidating or deconsolidating (see Figure A-3).

Furthermore, it is possible to derive an order or state of these industries based on the degree of concentration and its direction. For example, the railroad industry is modestly concentrated and deconsolidating, with the telecommunications industry following close behind. Next, look at the consolidating industries with rising degrees of concentration, such as drugs, truck and trailer manufacturers, and defense electronics. And finally a high degree of concentration exists and some industries are deconsolidating.

Based on this natural order, the time that one industry needs to reach the next level of concentration can be calculated based on its current consolidation speed. For example, airlines are not forecast many years into the future, but one can forecast the number of years the industry needs at the current consolidation speed to reach the level

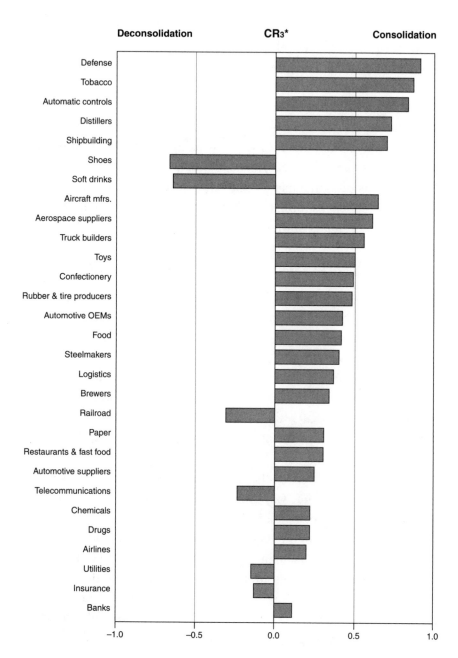

*CR₃ = Market share of the three largest companies of the total market based on VBG database (25,000 companies).
Sources: Value-Building Growth database; A.T. Kearney analysis

Figure A-3. Level of industry consolidation and deconsolidation

of concentration of the next higher concentrated industry, which is pharmaceuticals. The development of the pharmaceuticals industry is forecast to the point it reaches the same level of concentration as diversified chemicals and so forth.

By projecting the trend from one industry to the next, where the different industries reflect different points of concentration, it is possible to get a curve of more than 20 years by using only 10 years of historical data and forecasting only a couple of years into the future. The average projection from one consolidation level to the next is only 0.8 years, with the longest projection being nearly two years from the concentration of railroads down to that of telecommunications.

How Do We Define a Successful Merger?

Our analysis shows that 49.5% of all mergers fail to increase shareholder value, while 50.5% are successful. (But merger success or failure can vary by industry. See Figure 1-4 in Chapter 1 for examples of industry-specific merger success. Bubble size relates to M&A success.)

The success of a merger is defined as the change in the stock price of the company versus the industry average stock performance during the three-year period after the announcement of the merger. If the stock of the combined company outperforms the industry index, the deal is considered a success.

This analysis comprises the biggest mergers in the period 1990 to 1999 with a transaction value more than US$500 million. Both the acquirer and the target company must be publicly held companies with stock listed on a major exchange. The acquirer must hold a majority share in the acquired company of at least 51% after the transaction.

How we define a successful merger is relevant to our discussion of the implications for success rates that occur at various stages of the Endgames cycle, the type of merger that is most successful, and when external growth through acquisitions is more likely to produce favorable outcomes.

MERGERS AND ACQUISITIONS DATABASE

A.T. Kearney's mergers and acquisitions data was gathered from the SDC database with the permission of Securities Data Corporation, a subsidiary of Thomson Financial. Of the SDC database of more than 135,000 mergers and acquisitions, we selected only those with a transaction value of more than US$500 million. As we noted in Chapter 1, transactions smaller than that would not be significant in a global context.

The database that follows on pages 164 to 229 is a current list of the largest mergers from 1988 to 2001 showing when they were announced, the price of the deal, and the industries of both the acquirer and the target company.

Value of Transaction (US$ millions)	Acquirer	Target Company	Target Industry	Date Announced
ADVERTISING SERVICES				
$4,979	WPP Group PLC	Young & Rubicam Inc	Advertising Services	May-00
$2,765	Havas Advertising SA	Snyder Communications Inc	Business Services	Feb-00
$2,133	Interpublic Group of Cos Inc	True North Communications Inc	Advertising Services	Mar-01
$1,721	Publicis SA	Saatchi & Saatchi PLC	Advertising Services	Jun-00
$1,000	Outdoor Systems Inc	National Advertising Co	Advertising Services	May-97
$690	Outdoor Systems Inc	Mediacom Inc (Gannett Co Inc)	Advertising Services	Jul-96
$674	Interpublic Group of Cos Inc	NFO Worldwide Inc	Business Services	Dec-99
AEROSPACE AND AIRCRAFT				
$13,359	Boeing Co	McDonnell Douglas Corp	Aerospace and Aircraft	Dec-96
$8,762	Lockheed Martin Corp	Loral Corp	Measuring, Medical, Photo Equipment; Clocks	Jan-96
$5,204	Martin Marietta Corp	Lockheed Corp	Aerospace and Aircraft	Aug-94
$5,158	Northrop Grumman Corp	Litton Industries Inc	Measuring, Medical, Photo Equipment; Clocks	Dec-00
$3,600	Northrop Grumman Corp	Westinghouse Electric-Defense	Measuring, Medical, Photo Equipment; Clocks	Jan-96
$3,086	Boeing Co	Rockwell Intl Corp-Aerospace	Aerospace and Aircraft	Aug-96
$3,057	Northrop Grumman Corp	Newport News Shipbuilding Inc	Transportation Equipment	May-01
$3,050	Martin Marietta Corp	General Electric-Aerospace	Aerospace and Aircraft	Nov-92
$2,668	Lockheed Martin Corp	COMSAT Corp	Telecommunications	Sep-98
$2,174	Thomson-CSF	Racal Electronics PLC	Computer and Office Equipment	Jan-00
$2,104	Northrop Corp	Grumman Corp	Aerospace and Aircraft	Mar-94
$1,559	Rockwell International Corp	Reliance Electric Co	Electronics and Electrical Equipment	Oct-94
$1,525	Lockheed Corp	General Dynamics-Ft Worth Div	Aerospace and Aircraft	Dec-92
$1,270	BF Goodrich Co	Rohr Inc	Aerospace and Aircraft	Sep-97
$1,028	Northrop Grumman Corp	Logicon Inc	Business Services	May-97
$724	United Technologies Corp	Specialty Equipment Companies	Machinery	Oct-00
$600	Textron Inc	Cessna Aircraft Co	Aerospace and Aircraft	Jan-92
$598	Saab AB	Celsius AB	Measuring, Medical, Photo Equipment; Clocks	Nov-99
$517	General Dynamics Corp	Primex Technologies Inc	Measuring, Medical, Photo Equipment; Clocks	Nov-00

Value of Transaction (US$ millions)	Acquirer	Target Company	Target Industry	Date Announced
AGRICULTURE, FORESTRY AND FISHING				
$1,588	Willamette Industries Inc	Cavenham Forest Industries	Real Estate, Mortgage Bankers and Brokers	Mar-96
$740	Sime Darby Bhd	Consolidated Plantations Bhd	Agriculture, Forestry and Fishing	Nov-93
$552	Plum Creek Timber Co Inc	Riverwood Intl-US Timberlands	Agriculture, Forestry and Fishing	Aug-96
$513	Sime Darby Bhd	United Malayan Banking Corp	Commercial Banks, Bank Holding Companies	Feb-95
AIR TRANSPORTATION AND SHIPPING				
$2,471	FDX Corp	Caliber Systems Inc	Transportation and Shipping (except air)	Oct-97
$1,921	Delta Air Lines Inc	Comair Holdings Inc	Air Transportation and Shipping	Oct-99
$742	American Airlines Inc (AMR)	Trans World Airlines Inc	Air Transportation and Shipping	Jan-01
$693	Malaysian Helicopter Service	RZ Equities (Malaysian Helicop)	Investment & Commodity Firms, Dealers and Exchanges	Jun-94
$675	BAA PLC	Duty Free International Inc	Retail, General Merchandise and Apparel	Jul-97
AMUSEMENT AND RECREATION SERVICES				
$18,837	Walt Disney Co	Capital Cities/ABC Inc	Radio and Television Broadcasting Stations	Jul-95
$1,855	Premier Parks Inc	Six Flags Entertainment Corp	Amusement and Recreation Services	Feb-98
$1,148	Harrah's Entertainment Inc	Showboat Inc	Hotels and Casinos	Dec-97
BUSINESS SERVICES				
$21,101	VeriSign Inc	Network Solutions Inc	Prepackaged Software	Mar-00
$8,090	Granada Group PLC	Compass Group PLC	Retail, Restaurants	May-00
$7,047	Phone.com Inc	Software.com Inc	Prepackaged Software	Aug-00
$6,336	Sanmina Corp	SCI Systems Inc	Computer and Office Equipment	Jul-01
$6,188	Terra Networks (Telefonica SA)	Lycos Inc	Business Services	May-00
$5,946	First Data Corp	First Financial Management	Business Services	Jun-95
$5,447	Granada Group PLC	Forte PLC	Hotels and Casinos	Nov-95
$4,338	Sema Group PLC	LHS Group Inc	Business Services	Mar-00
$3,072	Rentokil Group PLC (Sophus)	BET PLC	Personal Services	Feb-96
$2,440	OpenTV Corp	Spyglass Inc	Prepackaged Software	Mar-00
$2,395	Akamai Technologies Inc	InterVU Inc	Business Services	Feb-00
$2,342	MindSpring Enterprises Inc	EarthLink Network Inc	Business Services	Sep-99

Value of Transaction (US$ millions)	Acquirer	Target Company	Target Industry	Date Announced
BUSINESS SERVICES (continued)				
$2,306	Wanadoo (France Telecom SA)	Freeserve PLC (Dixons Group)	Business Services	Dec-00
$2,212	Adia SA	ECCO	Business Services	May-96
$2,155	CMG PLC	Admiral PLC	Business Services	Apr-00
$2,103	Williams Holdings PLC	Chubb Security PLC	Communications Equipment	Feb-97
$1,948	Lucas Industries PLC	Varity Corp	Machinery	May-96
$1,835	PSINet Inc	Metamor Worldwide Inc	Business Services	Mar-00
$1,786	CMGI Inc	FlyCast Communications	Business Services	Sep-99
$1,622	Computer Sciences Corp	Continuum Co Inc	Prepackaged Software	Jun-00
$1,478	Commerce One Inc	AppNet Inc	Business Services	Jun-00
$1,475	Adecco SA	Olsten Corp	Business Services	Aug-99
$1,331	webMethods Inc	Active Software Inc	Prepackaged Software	May-00
$1,267	NOVA Corp	PMT Services Inc	Business Services	Jun-98
$1,257	VeriSign Inc	Illuminet Holdings Inc	Telecommunications	Sep-01
$1,203	WebVan Group Inc	HomeGrocer.com	Business Services	Jun-00
$1,159	First Financial Management	Western Union Finl Svcs Inc	Other Financial	Aug-94
$1,118	HBO & Co	Access Health Inc	Health Services	Sep-98
$1,052	Granada Group PLC	LWT Holdings PLC	Radio and Television Broadcasting Stations	Dec-93
$1,046	United Rentals Inc	US Rentals Inc	Business Services	Jun-98
$1,017	UEM Bhd	Projek Lebuhraya Utara-Selatan	Construction Firms	Sep-94
$1,010	AccuStaff Inc	Career Horizons Inc	Business Services	Aug-96
$1,004	Sanmina Corp	Hadco Corp	Electronics and Electrical Equipment	Apr-00
$984	Electronic Data Systems Corp	Structural Dynamics Research	Prepackaged Software	May-01
$981	Sabre Holding Corp	Getthere.Com Inc	Business Services	Aug-00
$962	Thorn EMI PLC	Virgin Music Group	Electronics and Electrical Equipment	Nov-91
$944	Pure Software Inc	Atria Software Inc	Prepackaged Software	Jun-96
$926	Infoseek Corp	Starwave Corp	Business Services	Nov-98
$914	Celltech Chiroscience PLC	Medeva PLC	Business Services	Nov-99
$900	Renters Choice Inc	THORN Americas Inc (Thorn PLC)	Business Services	Jun-98
$888	TRW Inc	BDM International Inc	Business Services	Nov-97
$878	DST Systems Inc	USCS International Inc	Business Services	Sep-98

Value of Transaction (US$ millions)	Acquirer	Target Company	Target Industry	Date Announced
BUSINESS SERVICES (continued)				
$859	Williams Holdings PLC	Yale & Valor (Williams Hldgs)	Metal and Metal Products	Jan-91
$850	Randstad Holding NV	Strategix Solutions Inc	Business Services	Aug-98
$845	Ceridian Corp	Comdata Holdings Corp	Business Services	Aug-95
$837	Arbor Software Corp	Hyperion Software Corp	Prepackaged Software	May-98
$798	Quintiles Transnational Corp	Innovex Holdings Ltd	Advertising Services	Oct-96
$793	Granada Group PLC	Yorkshire-Tyne Tees Television	Motion Picture Production and Distribution	Jun-97
$752	Anglo American Corp of SA Ltd	Anglo American Coal Corp	Mining	Oct-98
$750	Homedco Group Inc	Abbey Healthcare Group Inc	Health Services	Mar-95
$698	Equifax Inc	Telecredit Inc	Business Services	Jun-90
$670	Mandator AB	Cell Network AB	Business Services	Feb-00
$623	PerkinElmer Inc	Packard BioScience Co	Measuring, Medical, Photo Equipment; Clocks	Jul-01
$607	Olsten Corp	Lifetime Corp	Health Services	May-93
$596	First Data Corp	Card Establishment Services	Business Services	Nov-94
$576	Sanmina Corp	Segerstrom & Svensson AB	Metal and Metal Products	Jan-01
$570	Computer Sciences Corp	Policy Management Systems Corp	Prepackaged Software	Jun-00
$553	Interim Services Inc	Michael Page Group PLC	Business Services	Mar-97
$537	Tiphook PLC	Sea Containers-Cargo Container	Metal and Metal Products	Jan-90
$534	Granada Group PLC	Sutcliffe Catering, Spring	Retail, Restaurants	Mar-93
$523	CMGI Inc	Yesmail.com Inc	Advertising Services	Dec-99
$523	ServiceMaster LP	ServiceMaster Consumer Svcs LP	Agriculture, Forestry and Fishing	Nov-95
$502	Acxiom Corp	May & Speh Inc	Business Services	May-98
CHEMICALS AND ALLIED PRODUCTS				
$30,090	Sandoz AG	Ciba-Geigy AG	Drugs	Mar-96
$26,486	Monsanto Co	Pharmacia & Upjohn Inc	Business Services	Dec-99
$11,692	Dow Chemical Co	Union Carbide Corp	Chemicals and Related Products	Aug-99
$8,000	ICI PLC	Quest International, 3 Others	Chemicals and Related Products	May-97
$7,265	Hoechst AG	Marion Merrell Dow Inc	Drugs	Feb-95
$4,832	Rhone-Poulenc SA	Rhone-Poulenc Rorer Inc	Drugs	Jun-97
$3,686	Sandoz AG	Gerber Products Co	Food and Related Products	May-94

Value of Transaction (US$ millions)	Acquirer	Target Company	Target Industry	Date Announced
CHEMICALS AND ALLIED PRODUCTS (continued)				
$3,474	Hoechst AG	Roussel-Uclaf SA	Drugs	Dec-96
$3,448	Clariant AG	Hoechst AG-Specialty Chemicals	Chemicals and Related Products	Dec-96
$3,217	Mitsui Petrochemical Inds	Mitsui Toatsu Chemicals Inc	Chemicals and Related Products	Apr-92
$3,090	Hercules Inc	BetzDearborn Inc	Chemicals and Related Products	Jul-98
$3,083	Akzo Nobel NV	Courtaulds PLC	Chemicals and Related Products	Apr-98
$3,038	Akzo NV	Nobel Industrier Sweden AB	Chemicals and Related Products	Nov-93
$2,600	El du Pont de Nemours and Co	Du Pont Merck Pharmaceutical	Drugs	May-98
$2,306	Ciba Specialty Chemicals Hldgs	Allied Colloids Group PLC	Chemicals and Related Products	Jan-98
$2,263	Monsanto Co	DeKalb Genetics Corp	Business Services	May-98
$2,259	El du Pont de Nemours and Co	Imperial Chem Ind-White Pigmen	Chemicals and Related Products	Jul-97
$2,149	Praxair Inc	CBI Industries Inc	Chemicals and Related Products	Oct-95
$1,739	Clariant AG	BTP PLC	Chemicals and Related Products	Jan-00
$1,584	BASF AG	Boots Co PLC-Pharmaceutical Op	Drugs	Nov-94
$1,500	El du Pont de Nemours and Co	Protein Technologies Intl	Chemicals and Related Products	Aug-97
$1,463	Crompton & Knowles Corp	Uniroyal Chemical Co	Chemicals and Related Products	May-96
$1,400	IMC Global Inc	Harris Chemical Group	Chemicals and Related Products	Dec-97
$1,400	Monsanto Co	Cargill-International Seed Ope	Wholesale Trade, Nondurable Goods	Jun-98
$1,380	Degussa-Huels AG	SKW Trostberg AG (E.ON AG)	Chemicals and Related Products	Aug-00
$1,337	DSM NV	Koninklijke Gist-Brocades NV	Chemicals and Related Products	Feb-98
$1,219	IMC Global Inc	Vigoro Corp	Chemicals and Related Products	Nov-95
$1,210	Georgia Gulf Corp	Georgia Gulf Corp	Chemicals and Related Products	Nov-89
$1,200	Dow Chemical Co	DowElanco (Dow Chem, Eli Lilly)	Chemicals and Related Products	May-97
$1,081	SKW Trostberg AG (VIAG AG)	Master Builders Technologies	Chemicals and Related Products	Aug-96
$1,075	Monsanto Co	Kelco Biopolymers	Chemicals and Related Products	Dec-94
$1,065	Amersham International PLC	Nycomed ASA	Drugs	Jul-97
$986	Agrium Inc	Viridian Inc	Chemicals and Related Products	Oct-96
$982	Laporte PLC	Inspec Group PLC	Chemicals and Related Products	Aug-98
$964	International Flavors	Bush Boake Allen (Union Camp)	Food and Related Products	Sep-00
$955	Valspar Corp	Lilly Industries Inc	Chemicals and Related Products	Jun-00
$945	Monsanto Co	Holden's Foundation Seeds	Agriculture, Forestry and Fishing	Jan-97

Value of Transaction (US$ millions)	Acquirer	Target Company	Target Industry	Date Announced
CHEMICALS AND ALLIED PRODUCTS (continued)				
$934	Methanex Corp	Fletcher Challenge Methanol	Chemicals and Related Products	Feb-93
$832	SKW Trostberg AG (VIAG AG)	Elf Sanofi SA-Bioactivities &	Soaps, Cosmetics and Personal-Care Products	Oct-94
$830	Sherwin-Williams Co	Thompson Miniwax Holding Corp	Chemicals and Related Products	Nov-96
$824	SKW Trostberg AG (VIAG AG)	Sanofi Bio-Industries, Soprorga	Food and Related Products	Dec-94
$791	IMC Global Inc	Freeport-McMoRan Inc	Chemicals and Related Products	Jul-97
$778	BASF AG	Sandoz AG-US and Canada Corn	Chemicals and Related Products	Sep-96
$762	Witco Corp	OSi Specialties Inc	Chemicals and Related Products	Sep-95
$639	Montedison SpA	HIMONT Inc (Montedison SpA)	Chemicals and Related Products	Jul-89
$637	NOVA Corp of Alberta Ltd	Huntsman-US & Euro Styrenics	Chemicals and Related Products	Jul-98
$632	BetzDearborn Inc	WR Grace & Co-Dearborn Water	Chemicals and Related Products	Mar-96
$600	BASF AG	Daesung Corp-Lysine Unit	Chemicals and Related Products	Mar-98
$590	ICI PLC	Williams PLC-European Home	Wood Products, Furniture and Fixtures	Mar-98
$565	ARCO Chemical Co (ARCO)	Olin Corp-Isocyanates Business	Chemicals and Related Products	Oct-96
$560	ICI PLC	Acheson Industries Inc	Chemicals and Related Products	Mar-98
$541	Kalon Group PLC	Euridep	Chemicals and Related Products	Mar-95
$523	Monsanto Co	Plant Breeding Intl Cambridge	Agriculture, Forestry and Fishing	Jul-98
$510	Rhodia SA	ChiRex Inc	Chemicals and Related Products	Jul-00
COMMERCIAL BANKS, BANK HOLDING COMPANIES				
$61,633	NationsBank Corp, Charlotte, NC	BankAmerica Corp	Commercial Banks, Bank Holding Companies	Apr-98
$45,494	Sumitomo Bank Ltd	Sakura Bank Ltd	Commercial Banks, Bank Holding Companies	Oct-99
$40,097	Fuji Bank Ltd	Dai-Ichi Kangyo Bank Ltd	Commercial Banks, Bank Holding Companies	Aug-99
$38,525	Royal Bank of Scotland Group	National Westminster Bank PLC	Commercial Banks, Bank Holding Companies	Nov-99
$34,353	Norwest Corp, Minneapolis, MN	Wells Fargo Capital C	Commercial Banks, Bank Holding Companies	Jun-98
$33,788	Mitsubishi Bank Ltd	Bank of Tokyo Ltd	Commercial Banks, Bank Holding Companies	Mar-95
$33,555	Chase Manhattan Corp, NY	JP Morgan & Co Inc	Commercial Banks, Bank Holding Companies	Sep-00
$30,760	Fuji Bank Ltd	Industrial Bank of Japan Ltd	Commercial Banks, Bank Holding Companies	Aug-99
$29,616	BANC ONE Corp, Columbus, Ohio	First Chicago NBD Corp	Commercial Banks, Bank Holding Companies	Apr-98
$23,017	Mitsui Bank Ltd	Taiyo Kobe Bank Ltd	Commercial Banks, Bank Holding Companies	Aug-89
$23,009	Union Bank of Switzerland	Schweizerischer Bankverein	Commercial Banks, Bank Holding Companies	Dec-97

Value of Transaction (US$ millions)	Acquirer	Target Company	Target Industry	Date Announced
COMMERCIAL BANKS, BANK HOLDING COMPANIES (continued)				
$21,085	Firstar Corp, Milwaukee, WI	US Bancorp, Minneapolis, MN	Commercial Banks, Bank Holding Companies	Oct-00
$17,122	First Union Corp, Charlotte, NC	CoreStates Financial Corp, PA	Commercial Banks, Bank Holding Companies	Nov-97
$16,543	UBS AG	PaineWebber Group Inc	Investment & Commodity Firms, Dealers and Exchanges	Jul-00
$15,316	TSB Group PLC	Lloyds Bank PLC	Commercial Banks, Bank Holding Companies	Oct-95
$14,984	Sanwa Bank Ltd	Tokai Bank Ltd	Commercial Banks, Bank Holding Companies	Mar-00
$14,822	NationsBank Corp, Charlotte, NC	Barnett Banks, Jacksonville, FL	Commercial Banks, Bank Holding Companies	Aug-97
$13,132	First Union Corp, Charlotte, NC	Wachovia Corp, Winston-Salem, NC	Commercial Banks, Bank Holding Companies	Apr-01
$11,377	Banco Bilbao Vizcaya SA	Argentaria Caja Postal y Banco	Commercial Banks, Bank Holding Companies	Oct-99
$11,100	HSBC Holdings PLC	Credit Commercial de France	Commercial Banks, Bank Holding Companies	Apr-00
$10,959	Credito Italiano SpA	Unicredito SpA	Commercial Banks, Bank Holding Companies	Apr-98
$10,440	Chemical Banking Corp, New York	Chase Manhattan Corp	Commercial Banks, Bank Holding Companies	Aug-95
$10,373	Bank of Tokyo-Mitsubishi Ltd	Mitsubishi Trust & Banking	Commercial Banks, Bank Holding Companies	Apr-00
$9,667	NationsBank Corp, Charlotte, NC	Boatmen's Bancshares, St Louis	Commercial Banks, Bank Holding Companies	Aug-96
$9,662	Credit Suisse Group	Winterthur Schweizerische	Insurance	Aug-97
$9,603	SunTrust Banks Inc, Atlanta, GA	Crestar Finl Corp, Richmond, VA	Commercial Banks, Bank Holding Companies	Jul-98
$9,492	Istituto Bancario San Paolo di	Istituto Mobiliare Italiano	Commercial Banks, Bank Holding Companies	Apr-98
$8,929	First Bank Sys, Minneapolis, MN	US Bancorp, Portland, Oregon	Commercial Banks, Bank Holding Companies	Mar-97
$8,093	Kyowa Bank Ltd	Saitama Bank Ltd (Asahi Bank)	Commercial Banks, Bank Holding Companies	Nov-90
$7,963	Barclays PLC	Woolwich PLC	Real Estate; Mortgage Bankers and Brokers	Aug-00
$7,655	Kredietbank NV	Almanij-Banking and Insurance	Commercial Banks, Bank Holding Companies	Mar-98
$7,317	HypoVereinsbank AG	Bank Austria AG	Commercial Banks, Bank Holding Companies	Jul-00
$7,304	BANC ONE Corp, Columbus, Ohio	First USA Inc	Credit Institutions	Jan-97
$7,218	Star Banc Corp, Cincinnati, OH	Firstar Corp, Milwaukee, WI	Commercial Banks, Bank Holding Companies	Jul-98
$7,053	National City, Cleveland, Ohio	First of Amer Bk, Kalamazoo, MI	Commercial Banks, Bank Holding Companies	Dec-97
$7,012	FleetBoston Financial Corp, MA	Summit Bancorp, Princeton, NJ	Commercial Banks, Bank Holding Companies	Oct-00
$7,001	Bayerische Vereinsbank AG	Bayerische Hypotheken	Commercial Banks, Bank Holding Companies	Jul-97
$5,906	Commonwealth Bank of Australia	Colonial Ltd	Commercial Banks, Bank Holding Companies	Mar-00
$5,708	HSBC Holdings PLC	Midland Bank PLC	Commercial Banks, Bank Holding Companies	Mar-92
$5,680	DBS Group Holdings Ltd	Dao Heng Bank Group (Guoco)	Commercial Banks, Bank Holding Companies	Apr-01
$5,438	First Union Corp, Charlotte, NC	First Fidelity Bancorporation	Commercial Banks, Bank Holding Companies	Jun-95

Value of Transaction (US$ millions)	Acquirer	Target Company	Target Industry	Date Announced
COMMERCIAL BANKS, BANK HOLDING COMPANIES (continued)				
$5,415	NBD Bancorp, Detroit, Michigan	First Chicago Corp, Illinois	Commercial Banks, Bank Holding Companies	Jul-95
$5,048	Almanij NV	CERA	Commercial Banks, Bank Holding Companies	Jan-98
$4,954	Fifth Third Bancorp, Cincinnati	Old Kent Finl Corp, Michigan	Commercial Banks, Bank Holding Companies	Nov-00
$4,571	Citicorp	AT&T Universal Card Services	Credit Institutions	Dec-97
$4,372	Sanwa Bank Ltd	Toyo Trust & Banking Co Ltd	Commercial Banks, Bank Holding Companies	Jul-00
$4,259	NCNB Corp, Charlotte, NC	C&S/Sovran Corp	Commercial Banks, Bank Holding Companies	Jun-91
$4,213	BankAmerica Corp	Security Pacific,Los Angeles	Commercial Banks, Bank Holding Companies	Aug-91
$3,924	Society Corp	KeyCorp, Albany, NY (Key Corp, OH)	Commercial Banks, Bank Holding Companies	Oct-93
$3,920	Banco Ambrosiano Veneto SpA	Cassa di Risparmio delle Provi	Commercial Banks, Bank Holding Companies	May-97
$3,865	Fleet Financial Group Inc, MA	Shawmut National Corp	Commercial Banks, Bank Holding Companies	Feb-95
$3,850	Banco de Santander SA	Banesto	Commercial Banks, Bank Holding Companies	Feb-98
$3,754	Oversea-Chinese Banking Corp	Keppel Capital Holdings Ltd	Commercial Banks, Bank Holding Companies	Jun-01
$3,427	CoreStates Financial Corp, PA	Meridian Bancorp Inc	Commercial Banks, Bank Holding Companies	Oct-95
$3,344	Svenska Handelsbanken AB	Stadshypotek	Real Estate; Mortgage Bankers and Brokers	Dec-96
$3,320	First Union Corp, Charlotte, NC	Signet Bkg Corp, Richmond, VA	Commercial Banks, Bank Holding Companies	Jul-97
$3,260	Fleet Financial Group Inc, MA	National Westminster Bancorp	Commercial Banks, Bank Holding Companies	Dec-95
$3,169	BANC ONE Corp, Columbus, Ohio	First Commerce, New Orleans,LA	Commercial Banks, Bank Holding Companies	Oct-97
$3,159	Schweizerischer Bankverein	SG Warburg Grp PLC-Inv Bkg Arm	Investment & Commodity Firms, Dealers and Exchanges	May-95
$3,144	Banca Intesa SpA	Banca Commerciale Italiana SpA	Commercial Banks, Bank Holding Companies	Oct-00
$3,080	Danske Bank A/S	RealDanmark A/S	Commercial Banks, Bank Holding Companies	Oct-00
$2,872	Lloyds Bank PLC	Cheltenham & Gloucester Bldg	Real Estate; Mortgage Bankers and Brokers	Apr-94
$2,872	PNC Bank Corp, Pittsburgh, PA	Midlantic Corp	Commercial Banks, Bank Holding Companies	Jul-95
$2,810	Wells Fargo & Co, California	First Security Corp,Utah	Commercial Banks, Bank Holding Companies	Apr-00
$2,791	Grupo Financiero Bancomer SA	Bancomer SNC (Mexico)	Commercial Banks, Bank Holding Companies	Apr-91
$2,647	First American Corp, Tennessee	Deposit Guaranty, Jackson, MS	Commercial Banks, Bank Holding Companies	Dec-97
$2,589	Lloyds TSB Group PLC	Lloyds Abbey Life PLC	Commercial Banks, Bank Holding Companies	Sep-96
$2,549	Dexia Belgium	Finl Security Assurance Hldgs	Insurance	Mar-00
$2,489	Regions Financial Corp	First Commercial Corp, Arkansas	Commercial Banks, Bank Holding Companies	Jan-98
$2,460	BNP Paribas SA	BancWest Corp, Honolulu, HI	Commercial Banks, Bank Holding Companies	May-01
$2,448	Cie Financiere de Paribas SA	Cie Bancaire SA	Investment & Commodity Firms, Dealers and Exchanges	Nov-97

Value of Transaction (US$ millions)	Acquirer	Target Company	Target Industry	Date Announced
COMMERCIAL BANKS, BANK HOLDING COMPANIES (continued)				
$2,414	AMRO	ABN NV	Commercial Banks, Bank Holding Companies	Mar-90
$2,354	Credito Italiano SpA	Gruppo Bancario Credito Romagn	Commercial Banks, Bank Holding Companies	Oct-94
$2,320	Royal Bank of Canada	Centura Banks Inc, NC	Commercial Banks, Bank Holding Companies	Jan-01
$2,303	Wachovia Corp, Winston-Salem, NC	Central Fidelity Banks Inc, VA	Commercial Banks, Bank Holding Companies	Jun-97
$2,287	Banco de Santander SA	Banesto	Commercial Banks, Bank Holding Companies	Jan-94
$2,224	St George Bank Ltd	Advance Bank Australia Ltd	Commercial Banks, Bank Holding Companies	Oct-96
$2,216	Almanij NV	ABB Verzekeringen NV	Commercial Banks, Bank Holding Companies	Jan-98
$2,215	First Union Corp, Charlotte, NC	Money Store Inc	Real Estate; Mortgage Bankers and Brokers	Feb-98
$2,204	Skandinaviska Enskilda Banken	Trygg-Hansa AB	Insurance	Oct-97
$2,200	NationsBank Corp, Charlotte, NC	Chrysler First Inc (Chrysler)	Credit Institutions	Nov-92
$2,173	Kookmin Bank	H&CB	Commercial Banks, Bank Holding Companies	Dec-00
$2,162	BankAmerica Corp	Continental Bank Corp NA	Commercial Banks, Bank Holding Companies	Jan-94
$2,152	Daiwa Bank Holdings Inc	Asahi Bank Ltd	Commercial Banks, Bank Holding Companies	Sep-01
$2,151	Abbey National PLC	Natl & Provincial Bldg Society	Commercial Banks, Bank Holding Companies	Apr-95
$2,151	Union Planters Corp, Memphis, TN	Magna Group Inc, St. Louis, MO	Commercial Banks, Bank Holding Companies	Feb-98
$2,098	National City, Cleveland, Ohio	Integra Financial Corp	Commercial Banks, Bank Holding Companies	Aug-95
$2,077	Bankers Trust New York Corp	Alex Brown Inc	Investment & Commodity Firms, Dealers and Exchanges	Apr-97
$2,062	US Bancorp, Minneapolis, MN	NOVA Corp	Business Services	May-01
$2,059	Bank of Boston Corp, Boston, MA	BayBanks, Boston, Massachusetts	Commercial Banks, Bank Holding Companies	Dec-95
$2,054	Sovran Financial, Norfolk, VA	Citizens & Southern Georgia	Commercial Banks, Bank Holding Companies	Sep-89
$2,044	Chemical Banking Corp	Manufacturers Hanover Corp	Commercial Banks, Bank Holding Companies	Jul-91
$2,000	Mitsubishi Bank Ltd	Nippon Trust Bank	Commercial Banks, Bank Holding Companies	Oct-94
$1,971	ABN-AMRO Holding NV	Standard Fed Bancorp, Troy, MI	Commercial Banks, Bank Holding Companies	Nov-96
$1,961	National Commerce Bancorp	CCB Financial Corp,Durham, NC	Commercial Banks, Bank Holding Companies	Mar-00
$1,945	Chuo Trust & Banking Co Ltd	Mitsui Trust & Banking Co Ltd	Commercial Banks, Bank Holding Companies	Jan-99
$1,898	Cie Financiere de Paribas SA	Cetelem SA	Credit Institutions	Nov-97
$1,848	Mellon Bank Corp, Pittsburgh, PA	Dreyfus Corp	Commercial Banks, Bank Holding Companies	Dec-93
$1,731	Credito Agrario Bresciano SpA	Banca San Paolo di Brescia	Commercial Banks, Bank Holding Companies	Sep-98
$1,713	National Australia Bank Ltd	Michigan National Corp	Commercial Banks, Bank Holding Companies	Feb-95
$1,619	NationsBank Corp, Charlotte, NC	Bank South Corp, Atlanta, GA	Commercial Banks, Bank Holding Companies	Sep-95

Value of Transaction (US$ millions)	Acquirer	Target Company	Target Industry	Date Announced
COMMERCIAL BANKS, BANK HOLDING COMPANIES (continued)				
$1,605	National Australia Bank Ltd	Yorkshire Bank PLC	Commercial Banks, Bank Holding Companies	Jan-90
$1,600	Daiwa Bank Ltd	Lloyds Bank-US Coml Banking	Commercial Banks, Bank Holding Companies	Sep-89
$1,596	EFG Eurobank SA	Ergobank SA	Commercial Banks, Bank Holding Companies	Jan-00
$1,554	Dresdner Bank AG	Kleinwort Benson Group PLC	Commercial Banks, Bank Holding Companies	Jun-95
$1,537	Bank Austria AG	Creditanstalt-Bankverein AG	Commercial Banks, Bank Holding Companies	Jan-97
$1,525	Fleet Financial Group Inc, MA	Quick & Reilly Group Inc	Investment & Commodity Firms, Dealers and Exchanges	Sep-97
$1,482	Deutsche Bank AG	Morgan Grenfell Group PLC	Commercial Banks, Bank Holding Companies	Nov-89
$1,476	US Bancorp, Portland, Oregon	West One Bancorp, Boise, Idaho	Investment & Commodity Firms, Dealers and Exchanges	May-95
$1,453	Mellon Bank Corp, Pittsburgh, PA	Boston Co	Investment & Commodity Firms, Dealers and Exchanges	Sep-92
$1,400	Norwest Corp, Minneapolis, MN	Island Finance (ITT Corp)	Credit Institutions	Dec-94
$1,397	BNP Paribas SA	Cie Benelux Paribas SA	Credit Institutions	Jun-00
$1,387	Comerica Inc, Detroit, Michigan	Imperial Bancorp, Inglewood, CA	Commercial Banks, Bank Holding Companies	Nov-00
$1,354	Royal Bank of Canada	Dain Rauscher Corp	Investment & Commodity Firms, Dealers and Exchanges	Sep-00
$1,348	BB&T Financial Corp	Southern Natl, Winston-Salem, NC	Commercial Banks, Bank Holding Companies	Aug-94
$1,348	Sparbanken Sverige AB	Foreningsbanken	Commercial Banks, Bank Holding Companies	Feb-97
$1,333	NationsBank Corp, Charlotte, NC	MNC Financial Inc	Commercial Banks, Bank Holding Companies	Jul-92
$1,328	Royal Bank of Canada	Gentra Inc-Canadian, Intl Asset	Commercial Banks, Bank Holding Companies	Feb-93
$1,305	Abbey National PLC	CIBC Mortgages PLC	Real Estate; Mortgage Bankers and Brokers	Feb-94
$1,300	ABN-AMRO Holding NV	Bouwfonds Nederlandse	Real Estate; Mortgage Bankers and Brokers	Aug-99
$1,235	Fleet Financial Group Inc, MA	ADVANTA Corp-Credit Card	Business Services	Oct-97
$1,230	National Australia Bank Ltd	HomeSide Inc	Real Estate; Mortgage Bankers and Brokers	Oct-97
$1,229	Unicredito Italiano	Pioneer Group Inc	Investment & Commodity Firms, Dealers and Exchanges	May-00
$1,216	Bank of Philippine Islands	Far East Bank & Trust Co	Commercial Banks, Bank Holding Companies	Oct-99
$1,208	Den Danske Bank AS	Danica (Baltica Holding A/S)	Insurance	May-95
$1,200	NationsBank Corp, Charlotte, NC	Montgomery Securities, CA	Investment & Commodity Firms, Dealers and Exchanges	Jun-97
$1,190	BB&T Corp, Winston-Salem, NC	One Valley Bancorp Inc, WV	Commercial Banks, Bank Holding Companies	Feb-00
$1,187	Mercantile Bancorp, St Louis, MO	Roosevelt Finl Group, Missouri	Savings and Loans, Mutual Savings Banks	Dec-96
$1,186	Society Corp	AmeriTrust Corp, Cleveland, OH	Commercial Banks, Bank Holding Companies	May-91
$1,186	BANC ONE Corp, Columbus, Ohio	Valley National Corp, Phoenix	Commercial Banks, Bank Holding Companies	Apr-92
$1,182	Cie Financiere de Paribas SA	Cie de Navigation Mixte	Investment & Commodity Firms, Dealers and Exchanges	Feb-96

Value of Transaction (US$ millions)	Acquirer	Target Company	Target Industry	Date Announced
COMMERCIAL BANKS, BANK HOLDING COMPANIES (continued)				
$1,180	Boatmen's Bancshares, St Louis	Fourth Financial Corp	Commercial Banks, Bank Holding Companies	Aug-95
$1,162	Banco Santander Central Hispan	Banco do Estado de Sao Paulo	Commercial Banks, Bank Holding Companies	Dec-00
$1,143	UJB Financial Corp	Summit Bancorporation	Commercial Banks, Bank Holding Companies	Sep-95
$1,131	Huntington Bancshares Inc, OH	First Michigan Bank Corp, MI	Commercial Banks, Bank Holding Companies	May-97
$1,130	Westpac Banking Corp	Bank of Melbourne Ltd	Commercial Banks, Bank Holding Companies	Apr-97
$1,127	Daiwa Bank Ltd	Kinki Osaka Bank Ltd	Commercial Banks, Bank Holding Companies	Aug-01
$1,116	Marshall & Ilsley, Milwaukee, WI	Security Capital, Milwaukee, WI	Commercial Banks, Bank Holding Companies	Mar-97
$1,098	Metway Bank Ltd	Queensland Inds Dvlp, Suncorp I	Construction Firms	May-96
$1,087	Comerica Inc, Detroit, Michigan	Manufacturers National Corp	Commercial Banks, Bank Holding Companies	Oct-91
$1,075	Associated Banc, Green Bay, WI	First Finl, Stevens Point, WI	Savings and Loans, Mutual Savings Banks	May-97
$1,050	Bipop-Carire	Entrium Direct Bankers AG	Business Services	Jun-00
$1,050	Wells Fargo & Co, California	Natl Bancorp Of Alaska Inc	Commercial Banks, Bank Holding Companies	Dec-99
$1,040	Uniao de Bancos Brasileiros SA	Banco Nacional SA	Commercial Banks, Bank Holding Companies	Nov-95
$1,028	M&T Bank Corp, Buffalo, New York	Keystone Finl, Harrisburg, PA	Commercial Banks, Bank Holding Companies	May-00
$1,009	BB&T Corp, Winston-Salem, NC	F&M National, Winchester, VA	Commercial Banks, Bank Holding Companies	Jan-01
$977	Southern Natl, Winston-Salem, NC	United Carolina Bancshares	Commercial Banks, Bank Holding Companies	Nov-96
$973	Banco Santiago	Banco O'Higgins	Commercial Banks, Bank Holding Companies	Sep-95
$952	First Hawaiian Inc, Honolulu, HI	BancWest Corp, San Francisco, CA	Commercial Banks, Bank Holding Companies	May-98
$934	First Union Corp, Charlotte, NC	Dominion Bankshares, Roanoke, VA	Commercial Banks, Bank Holding Companies	Sep-92
$933	DBS Bank	Post Office Savings Bank	Commercial Banks, Bank Holding Companies	Jul-98
$916	Summit Bancorp, Princeton, NJ	Collective Bancorp Inc, NJ	Savings and Loans, Mutual Savings Banks	Feb-97
$909	Bank of Philippine Islands	CityTrust Banking Corp	Commercial Banks, Bank Holding Companies	Jun-96
$905	Bank of Ireland	Bristol & West Bldg Society	Real Estate; Mortgage Bankers and Brokers	Apr-96
$899	Deutsche Bank AG	National Discount Brokers	Investment & Commodity Firms, Dealers and Exchanges	Oct-00
$897	Fifth Third Bancorp, Cincinnati	State Savings Co, Columbus, OH	Commercial Banks, Bank Holding Companies	Jan-98
$893	First Empire State Corp, NY	ONBANCorp Inc, Syracuse, NY	Commercial Banks, Bank Holding Companies	Oct-97
$890	KeyCorp, Albany, NY (Key Corp, OH)	Puget Sound Bancorp, Tacoma, WA	Commercial Banks, Bank Holding Companies	Mar-92
$888	PNC Bank Corp, Pittsburgh, PA	Mellon Bank-50 Amer Auto Assn	Credit Institutions	Nov-96
$885	Bank of Nova Scotia	National Trustco Inc	Commercial Banks, Bank Holding Companies	Jun-97
$883	NBD Bancorp, Detroit, Michigan	INB Financial Corp	Commercial Banks, Bank Holding Companies	Mar-92

Value of Transaction (US$ millions)	Acquirer	Target Company	Target Industry	Date Announced
COMMERCIAL BANKS, BANK HOLDING COMPANIES (continued)				
$883	Barnett Banks, Jacksonville, FL	First Florida Banks Inc	Commercial Banks, Bank Holding Companies	May-92
$881	Banco Osorno y la Union	Banco Santander Chile	Commercial Banks, Bank Holding Companies	Apr-96
$878	Banco Bilbao Vizcaya SA	Banco Excel Economico SA	Commercial Banks, Bank Holding Companies	Apr-98
$875	Bank Hapoalim BM	Ampal-Amer Israel-Indl Loan	Credit Institutions	Jun-90
$875	Westpac Banking Corp	Trust Bank New Zealand Ltd	Commercial Banks, Bank Holding Companies	Apr-96
$867	Dexia Belgium	Labouchere NV (Aegon NV)	Insurance	Mar-00
$853	BANC ONE Corp, Columbus, Ohio	Liberty National Bancorp	Commercial Banks, Bank Holding Companies	Nov-93
$852	First Union Corp, Charlotte, NC	Florida Nat Bks of Florida Inc	Commercial Banks, Bank Holding Companies	Mar-89
$848	Eurafrance (Lazard Frères)	Azeo (Eurafrance)	Investment & Commodity Firms, Dealers and Exchanges	Nov-00
$828	Citicorp	Bank New England-Credit Card	Credit Institutions	Jan-90
$827	Unitas Oy	KOP	Commercial Banks, Bank Holding Companies	Feb-95
$822	North Fork Bancorp, Melville, NY	New York Bancorp,Douglaston, NY	Savings and Loans, Mutual Savings Banks	Oct-97
$820	Marshall & Ilsley, Milwaukee, WI	Valley Bancorp, Appleton, WI	Commercial Banks, Bank Holding Companies	Sep-93
$817	Mercantile Bancorp, St Louis, MO	Mark Twain Bancshares, MO	Commercial Banks, Bank Holding Companies	Oct-96
$811	Svenska Handelsbanken AB	Skopbank-Selected Assets	Real Estate; Mortgage Bankers and Brokers	May-95
$805	Union Bank, San Francisco, CA	Bank of California	Commercial Banks, Bank Holding Companies	Sep-95
$800	BankBoston Corp, Boston, MA	Robertson Stephens & Co	Investment & Commodity Firms, Dealers and Exchanges	May-98
$799	Colonial Ltd	Prudential Corp PLC-AU/NZ Ops	Insurance	Aug-98
$794	Crestar Finl Corp, Richmond, VA	Citizens Bancorp,Laurel, MD	Commercial Banks, Bank Holding Companies	Sep-96
$790	First Bank Sys, Minneapolis, MN	Metropolitan Financial Corp	Commercial Banks, Bank Holding Companies	Jul-94
$782	New York Community Bancorp Inc	Richmond County Financial Corp	Savings and Loans, Mutual Savings Banks	Mar-01
$779	Peoples Heritage Finl Group, ME	Banknorth Group Inc	Commercial Banks, Bank Holding Companies	Jun-99
$774	Regions Financial Corp	Morgan Keegan Inc	Investment & Commodity Firms, Dealers and Exchanges	Dec-00
$771	Daiwa Bank Ltd	Cosmo Securities Co Ltd	Investment & Commodity Firms, Dealers and Exchanges	Aug-93
$768	US Bancorp, Minneapolis, MN	Piper Jaffray Cos	Investment & Commodity Firms, Dealers and Exchanges	Dec-97
$768	National City, Cleveland, Ohio	Fort Wayne Natl Corp, Indiana	Commercial Banks, Bank Holding Companies	Jan-98
$763	Royal Bank of Scotland Group	Citizens Financial Group, RI	Savings and Loans, Mutual Savings Banks	Aug-98
$756	Banco de Credito Nacional SA	Banco Pontual	Commercial Banks, Bank Holding Companies	Nov-98
$750	Schweizerischer Bankverein	Brinson Partners Inc	Investment & Commodity Firms, Dealers and Exchanges	Aug-94
$747	Banca Intesa SpA	Banca Popolare Friuladria	Commercial Banks, Bank Holding Companies	Jun-98

Value of Transaction (US$ millions)	Acquirer	Target Company	Target Industry	Date Announced
COMMERCIAL BANKS, BANK HOLDING COMPANIES (continued)				
$731	Generale de Banque SA	Credit Lyonnais Bank Nederland	Commercial Banks, Bank Holding Companies	Apr-95
$726	BANC ONE Corp, Columbus, Ohio	Team Bancshares Inc	Commercial Banks, Bank Holding Companies	Mar-92
$721	Alpha Credit Bank	Ionian Bank	Commercial Banks, Bank Holding Companies	Nov-99
$713	CoreStates Financial Corp, PA	First Pennsylvania Corp	Commercial Banks, Bank Holding Companies	Sep-89
$711	First Bank Sys, Minneapolis, MN	FirsTier Financial Inc	Commercial Banks, Bank Holding Companies	Aug-95
$705	Peoples Heritage Finl Group, ME	CFX Corp,Keene, New Hampshire	Savings and Loans, Mutual Savings Banks	Oct-97
$703	GreenPoint Financial Corp, NY	Bank of America-BankAmerica	Real Estate; Mortgage Bankers and Brokers	Apr-98
$701	Star Banc Corp, Cincinnati, OH	Trans Finl, Bowling Green,KY	Commercial Banks, Bank Holding Companies	Apr-98
$701	Credit Lyonnais SA	UAF (Credit Lyonnais SA)	Insurance	Mar-00
$696	BNP	Paribas SA (BNP)	Commercial Banks, Bank Holding Companies	Nov-99
$695	BANC ONE Corp, Columbus, Ohio	Premier Bancorp, Baton Rouge, LA	Commercial Banks, Bank Holding Companies	Jul-95
$694	Banca Popolare di Verona	Credito Bergamasco	Commercial Banks, Bank Holding Companies	Jul-97
$692	Bipop-Carire	Entrium Direct Bankers AG	Business Services	Jun-00
$692	Fifth Third Bancorp, Cincinnati	CitFed Bancorp Inc,Dayton, OH	Savings and Loans, Mutual Savings Banks	Jan-98
$691	Erste Oesterreichische	GiroCredit Bank AG	Commercial Banks, Bank Holding Companies	Mar-97
$688	HSBC Holdings PLC	Roberts SA de Inversiones	Commercial Banks, Bank Holding Companies	May-97
$686	Tokyo Securities Co Ltd	Tokai Maruman Securities Co	Investment & Commodity Firms, Dealers and Exchanges	Feb-00
$685	Setouchi Bank	Hiroshima Sogo Bank	Commercial Banks, Bank Holding Companies	Oct-00
$680	Bank of Scotland PLC	Bank of Western Australia	Commercial Banks, Bank Holding Companies	Sep-95
$676	Bank of New York, New York, NY	First City Bancorp-Credit Card	Credit Institutions	Mar-90
$675	Banco Santander Central Hispano	Banco Rio de la Plata SA	Commercial Banks, Bank Holding Companies	Feb-00
$674	Royal Bank of Scotland Group	GRS Holding Co Ltd	Business Services	Dec-97
$669	Mercantile Bancorp, St Louis, MO	Firstbank of IL, Springfield, IL	Investment & Commodity Firms, Dealers and Exchanges	Feb-98
$663	Star Banc Corp, Cincinnati, OH	Great Financial Corp, Kentucky	Savings and Loans, Mutual Savings Banks	Sep-97
$655	National City, Cleveland, Ohio	Merchants National Corp	Commercial Banks, Bank Holding Companies	Oct-91
$654	Canadian Imperial Bank of Commerce	Norex Leasing Ltd (Onex Corp)	Credit Institutions	Dec-90
$653	Regions Financial Corp	First National Bancorp, Georgia	Commercial Banks, Bank Holding Companies	Oct-95
$652	Royal Bank of Canada	Tucker Anthony Sutro	Investment & Commodity Firms, Dealers and Exchanges	Aug-01
$620	Citizens Bancshares Inc, OH	Mid Am Inc, Bowling Green, Ohio	Commercial Banks, Bank Holding Companies	May-98
$615	Texas Commerce Bancshares, TX	First City Bancorp of Texas	Commercial Banks, Bank Holding Companies	Oct-92

Value of Transaction (US$ millions)	Acquirer	Target Company	Target Industry	Date Announced
COMMERCIAL BANKS, BANK HOLDING COMPANIES (continued)				
$608	Centura Banks Inc, NC	Triangle Bancorp, Raleigh, NC	Commercial Banks, Bank Holding Companies	Aug-99
$601	Banca Popolare di Milano	Banca di Legnano (Banca Comm)	Commercial Banks, Bank Holding Companies	Dec-00
$600	Lloyds TSB Group PLC	Banco Multiplic-Consumer & Cor	Commercial Banks, Bank Holding Companies	Feb-97
$594	Banco Frances del Rio de la	Banco de Credito Argentino SA	Commercial Banks, Bank Holding Companies	May-97
$594	North Fork Bancorp, Melville, NY	JSB Financial Inc, Lynbrook, NY	Commercial Banks, Bank Holding Companies	Aug-99
$592	Bank of New York, New York, NY	National Community Banks Inc	Commercial Banks, Bank Holding Companies	Jan-93
$590	National Westminster Bank PLC	Greenwich Capital Markets Inc	Investment & Commodity Firms, Dealers and Exchanges	Jun-96
$586	Boatmen's Bancshares, St Louis	Worthen Banking, Little Rock, AR	Commercial Banks, Bank Holding Companies	Aug-94
$584	BANC ONE Corp, Columbus, Ohio	Key Centurion Bancshares, WV	Commercial Banks, Bank Holding Companies	Jun-92
$579	Abbey National PLC	LMF, LTF, LBEL	Credit Institutions	Nov-98
$577	KeyCorp, Cleveland, Ohio	McDonald & Co Investments Inc	Investment & Commodity Firms, Dealers and Exchanges	Jun-98
$577	CNB Bancshares Inc, Indiana	Pinnacle Financial Svcs Inc, MI	Commercial Banks, Bank Holding Companies	Oct-97
$575	Sanwa Bank Ltd	Senshu Bank Ltd	Commercial Banks, Bank Holding Companies	Dec-00
$575	Guoco Group Ltd	Overseas Trust Bank Ltd	Commercial Banks, Bank Holding Companies	Jul-93
$575	Bankers Trust New York Corp	USL Capital-RE Financing Op	Investment & Commodity Firms, Dealers and Exchanges	Aug-96
$575	Piraeus Bank Group	Xiosbank	Commercial Banks, Bank Holding Companies	Dec-99
$568	Norwest Corp, Minneapolis, MN	Shawmut Natl Corp-Credit Card	Credit Institutions	Jan-91
$566	Old Kent Finl Corp, Michigan	First Evergreen Corp, IL	Commercial Banks, Bank Holding Companies	Apr-98
$561	Barnett Banks, Jacksonville, FL	Oxford Resources Corp	Repair Services	Jan-97
$561	MNC Financial Inc	Equitable Bancorp, Baltimore, MD	Commercial Banks, Bank Holding Companies	Jul-89
$561	First of Amer Bk, Kalamazoo, MI	Security Bancorp, Southgate, MI	Commercial Banks, Bank Holding Companies	Sep-91
$560	Bank of East Asia Ltd	FPB Bank Holding Co Ltd	Commercial Banks, Bank Holding Companies	Nov-00
$554	Colonial Ltd	Legal & General Australia Ltd	Insurance	May-98
$548	Toronto-Dominion Bank	Waterhouse Investor Services	Investment & Commodity Firms, Dealers and Exchanges	Apr-96
$545	Wachovia Corp, Winston-Salem, NC	Jefferson Bankshares Inc, VA	Commercial Banks, Bank Holding Companies	Jun-97
$544	Zions Bancorp, Utah	Sumitomo Bank of California	Commercial Banks, Bank Holding Companies	Mar-98
$541	Bank Austria AG	Creditanstalt-Bankverein AG	Commercial Banks, Bank Holding Companies	Aug-97
$541	United Building Society Hldgs	Allied, Volkskas	Commercial Banks, Bank Holding Companies	Jan-91
$539	Industri og Skipsbanken	Finansbanken ASA (Sparebanken)	Commercial Banks, Bank Holding Companies	Mar-96
$534	Bank of Osaka, Ltd	Bank of Kinki Ltd	Commercial Banks, Bank Holding Companies	May-99

Value of Transaction (US$ millions)	Acquirer	Target Company	Target Industry	Date Announced
COMMERCIAL BANKS, BANK HOLDING COMPANIES (continued)				
$530	BANC ONE Corp, Columbus, Ohio	Liberty Bancorp Inc, Oklahoma	Commercial Banks, Bank Holding Companies	Dec-96
$528	National Westminster Bank PLC	Indosuez UK Asset Management	Investment & Commodity Firms, Dealers and Exchanges	Feb-96
$522	Advance Bank Australia Ltd	State Bank of South Australia	Savings and Loans, Mutual Savings Banks	Jun-95
$514	Bank of Melbourne Ltd	Challenge Bank Ltd-Victorian	Commercial Banks, Bank Holding Companies	May-96
$513	First Bank Sys, Minneapolis, MN	Colorado National Bankshares	Commercial Banks, Bank Holding Companies	Nov-92
$509	Republic New York Corp, NY, NY	Brooklyn Bancorp Inc	Commercial Banks, Bank Holding Companies	Sep-95
$504	Union Planters Corp, Memphis, TN	Leader Financial, Memphis, TN	Savings and Loans, Mutual Savings Banks	Mar-96
$503	Westpac Banking Corp	Challenge Bank Ltd	Commercial Banks, Bank Holding Companies	Jul-95
$502	ABN-AMRO Holding NV	Cragin Financial Corp	Savings and Loans, Mutual Savings Banks	Jul-93
$502	Societe Generale SA	Hambros PLC-Banking Group	Investment & Commodity Firms, Dealers and Exchanges	Dec-97
$501	Society Corp	Trustcorp Inc, Toledo, Ohio	Commercial Banks, Bank Holding Companies	Jun-89
$500	Shawmut National Corp	Barclays Business Credit Inc	Credit Institutions	Nov-94
COMMUNICATIONS EQUIPMENT				
$10,936	Motorola Inc	General Instrument Corp	Communications Equipment	Sep-99
$7,058	Alcatel SA	Newbridge Networks Corp	Communications Equipment	Feb-00
$7,057	Nortel Networks Corp	Alteon Websystems Inc	Electronics and Electrical Equipment	Jul-00
$4,685	Alcatel Alsthom CGE	DSC Communications Corp	Communications Equipment	Jun-98
$3,580	Alcatel Alsthom CGE	Alcatel NV(Alcatel Alsthom)	Electronics and Electrical Equipment	Mar-92
$3,529	Ascend Communications Inc	Cascade Communications Corp	Communications Equipment	Mar-97
$2,798	Lucent Technologies Inc	Ortel Corp	Communications Equipment	Feb-00
$2,163	Alcatel Alsthom CGE	Telettra SpA (Fiat SpA)	Communications Equipment	Oct-90
$1,901	Alcatel Alsthom CGE	Generale Occidentale SA	Wholesale Trade, Nondurable Goods	Apr-91
$1,863	Nortel Networks Corp	Clarify Inc	Prepackaged Software	Oct-99
$1,850	Corning Inc	NetOptix Corp	Metal and Metal Products	Feb-00
$1,825	Lucent Technologies Inc	Octel Communications Corp	Communications Equipment	Jul-97
$1,772	Alcatel SA	Genesys Telecommun Labs	Prepackaged Software	Sep-99
$1,659	Corning Inc	Oak Industries Inc	Electronics and Electrical Equipment	Nov-99
$1,612	ADC Telecommunications Inc	PairGain Technologies Inc	Communications Equipment	Feb-00
$1,323	GEC PLC	Tracor Inc	Measuring, Medical, Photo Equipment; Clocks	Apr-98

Value of Transaction (US$ millions)	Acquirer	Target Company	Target Industry	Date Announced
COMMUNICATIONS EQUIPMENT (continued)				
$1,270	GEC PLC	VSEL Consortium PLC	Transportation Equipment	Oct-94
$1,044	Lucent Technologies Inc	Yurie Systems Inc	Communications Equipment	Apr-98
$1,018	GEC PLC	GPT Holdings Ltd	Communications Equipment	Jun-98
$970	Ascend Communications Inc	Stratus Computer Inc	Computer and Office Equipment	Aug-98
$874	Comverse Technology Inc	Boston Technology Inc	Electronics and Electrical Equipment	Aug-97
$664	Tellabs Inc	Coherent Communications Sys	Communications Equipment	Feb-98
$650	Lucent Technologies Inc	Livingston Enterprises	Communications Equipment	Oct-97
$565	Corning Inc	Damon Corp	Health Services	Jun-93
$500	Polycom Inc	Accord Networks Ltd	Electronics and Electrical Equipment	Dec-00
COMPUTER AND OFFICE EQUIPMENT				
$9,124	Compaq Computer Corp	Digital Equipment Corp	Computer and Office Equipment	Jan-98
$5,658	Cisco Systems Inc	ArrowPoint Communications Inc	Computer and Office Equipment	May-00
$4,834	Cisco Systems Inc	StrataCom Inc	Communications Equipment	Apr-96
$3,264	IBM Corp	Lotus Development Corp	Prepackaged Software	Jun-95
$2,780	Compaq Computer Corp	Tandem Computers Inc	Computer and Office Equipment	Jun-97
$1,925	Sun Microsystems Inc	Cobalt Networks Inc	Communications Equipment	Sep-00
$1,632	Xerox Corp	Rank Xerox (Xerox, Rank Organis)	Machinery	Jun-97
$1,375	Maxtor Corp	Quantum HDD (Quantum Corp)	Computer and Office Equipment	Oct-00
$1,245	Hewlett-Packard Co	VeriFone Inc	Computer and Office Equipment	Apr-97
$1,174	Wellfleet Communications	SynOptics Communications Inc	Business Services	Jul-94
$1,165	Seagate Technology Inc	Conner Peripherals Inc	Computer and Office Equipment	Sep-95
$1,106	Cybex Computer Products Corp	Apex Inc	Computer and Office Equipment	Mar-00
$779	FORE Systems Inc	Alantec Corp	Business Services	Dec-95
$770	Silicon Graphics Inc	Cray Research Inc	Computer and Office Equipment	Feb-96
$710	IBM Corp	Tivoli Systems Inc	Prepackaged Software	Jan-96
$678	Cisco Systems Inc	Aironet Wireless Communication	Communications Equipment	Nov-99
$571	Symbol Technologies Inc	Telxon Corp	Computer and Office Equipment	Jul-00
$529	Hewlett-Packard Co	Bluestone Software Inc	Prepackaged Software	Oct-00

Value of Transaction (US$ millions)	Acquirer	Target Company	Target Industry	Date Announced
CONSTRUCTION FIRMS				
$7,783	Halliburton Co	Dresser Industries Inc	Machinery	Feb-98
$1,695	Vinci SA	Groupe GTM	Construction Firms	Jul-00
$1,516	DR Horton Inc	Schuler Homes Inc	Construction Firms	Oct-01
$1,505	Lennar Corp	US Home Corp	Construction Firms	Feb-00
$845	Group Maintenance America	Building One Services Corp	Business Services	Nov-99
$814	Taylor Woodrow PLC	Bryant Group PLC	Construction Firms	Jan-01
$809	Bouygues SA	Colas SA (CFTR/Bouygues SA)	Construction Firms	Jul-00
$702	NBM-Amstelland NV	Wilma Nederland BV	Construction Firms	May-98
$590	DR Horton Inc	Continental Homes Holding	Construction Firms	Dec-97
$587	Halliburton Co	Landmark Graphics Corp	Business Services	Jul-96
CREDIT INSTITUTIONS				
$8,704	Household International Inc	Beneficial Corp	Credit Institutions	Apr-98
$3,975	Household International Inc	Bank of New York-AFL-CIO Union	Credit Institutions	Jun-96
$3,960	Household International Inc	Transamerica-Consumer Finance	Credit Institutions	May-97
$1,693	Newcourt Credit Group Inc	AT&T Capital Corp	Credit Institutions	Nov-97
$1,350	Commercial Credit Group Inc	BarclaysAmer/Finl-Br, Portfolio	Credit Institutions	Nov-89
$995	Associates First Capital Corp	DIC Finance (Daiei Inc)	Real Estate; Mortgage Bankers and Brokers	Mar-98
$959	Providian Financial Corp	First Union, NC-CC Receivables	Credit Institutions	Dec-97
$901	Associates First Capital Corp	USL Capital Corp-Vehicle Fleet	Repair Services	Jun-96
$896	Associates First Capital Corp	SPS Transaction Svcs-Assets	Credit Institutions	Apr-98
$620	Green Tree Financial Corp	Manufacturer and Dealer Svcs	Prepackaged Software	Oct-96
$560	First USA Inc (BANC ONE Corp)	Chevy Chase Bank FSB-Credit	Credit Institutions	Sep-98
$527	Sanyo Shinpan Finance Co Ltd	Mycal Card Inc	Credit Institutions	Mar-01
DRUGS				
$89,168	Pfizer Inc	Warner-Lambert Co	Drugs	Nov-99
$75,961	Glaxo Wellcome PLC	SmithKline Beecham PLC	Drugs	Jan-00
$14,285	Glaxo Holdings PLC	Wellcome PLC	Drugs	Jan-95
$11,070	Johnson & Johnson	ALZA Corp	Drugs	Mar-01

Value of Transaction (US$ millions)	Acquirer	Target Company	Target Industry	Date Announced
DRUGS (continued)				
$10,200	Roche Holding AG	Corange Ltd	Drugs	May-97
$9,561	American Home Products Corp	American Cyanamid Co	Drugs	Aug-94
$6,989	Upjohn Co	Pharmacia AB	Drugs	Aug-95
$6,226	Merck & Co Inc	Medco Containment Services Inc	Wholesale Trade, Nondurable Goods	Jul-93
$6,090	Astra AB	Astra Merck Inc (Merck & Co)	Wholesale Trade, Nondurable Goods	Jun-98
$5,307	Roche Holding AG	Syntex Corp	Drugs	May-94
$4,236	Fresenius AG	National Medical Care Inc	Wholesale Trade, Durable Goods	Feb-96
$4,000	Eli Lilly & Co	PCS Health Systems (McKesson)	Business Services	Jul-94
$3,748	Shire Pharmaceuticals Group	BioChem Pharma Inc	Drugs	Dec-00
$3,523	King Pharmaceuticals Inc	Jones Pharmaceutical Inc	Drugs	Jul-00
$3,488	Johnson & Johnson	Depuy Inc (Corange Ltd)	Measuring, Medical, Photo Equipment; Clocks	Jul-98
$2,925	SmithKline Beecham PLC	Sterling Winthrop Inc	Drugs	Aug-94
$2,888	Rhone-Poulenc Rorer Inc	Fisons PLC	Drugs	Aug-95
$2,417	Millennium Pharmaceuticals Inc	COR Therapeutics Inc	Drugs	Dec-01
$1,878	Johnson & Johnson	Cordis Corp	Measuring, Medical, Photo Equipment; Clocks	Oct-95
$1,858	Mallinckrodt Inc	Nellcor Puritan-Bennett	Measuring, Medical, Photo Equipment; Clocks	Jul-97
$1,825	Elf Sanofi SA	Sterling Winthrop-Prescription	Wholesale Trade, Nondurable Goods	Jun-94
$1,708	Elan Corp PLC	Dura Pharmaceuticals Inc	Drugs	Sep-00
$1,665	MedImmune Inc	Aviron	Drugs	Dec-01
$1,550	Reckitt & Colman PLC	L&F Products Group-Worldwide	Soaps, Cosmetics and Personal-Care Products	Sep-94
$1,530	Roche Holding AG	Genentech Inc	Drugs	Feb-90
$1,468	Invitrogen Corp	Dexter Corp	Chemicals and Related Products	Jul-00
$1,450	Pfizer Inc	SmithKline Beecham Animal Hlth	Wholesale Trade, Nondurable Goods	Nov-94
$1,257	Bayer AG	Nova Corp-Polysar Rubber Div	Chemicals and Related Products	May-90
$1,250	Reckitt & Colman PLC	Boyle-Midway Household Prods	Food and Related Products	Mar-90
$1,235	SmithKline Beecham PLC	Block Drug Co	Measuring, Medical, Photo Equipment; Clocks	Oct-00
$1,100	Roche Holding AG	Tastemaker	Chemicals and Related Products	Feb-97
$1,100	Bayer AG	Chiron Diagnostics Corp	Drugs	Sep-98
$1,052	Genzyme Corp	GelTex Pharmaceuticals Inc	Drugs	Sep-00
$1,050	Warner-Lambert Co	Warner Wellcome Consumer Hlth	Wholesale Trade, Nondurable Goods	Dec-95

Value of Transaction (US$ millions)	Acquirer	Target Company	Target Industry	Date Announced
DRUGS (continued)				
$1,008	Johnson & Johnson	Eastman Kodak-Clinical	Drugs	Sep-94
$1,006	American Home Products Corp	Genetics Institute Inc	Business Services	Dec-96
$933	Johnson & Johnson	Neutrogena Corp	Soaps, Cosmetics and Personal-Care Products	Aug-94
$916	Watson Pharmaceuticals Inc	Schein Pharmaceutical Inc	Drugs	May-00
$914	Yoshitomi Pharmaceutical Inds	Green Cross Corp	Drugs	Feb-97
$910	Novartis AG	Merck-Crop Protection Business	Chemicals and Related Products	May-97
$854	Corixa Corp	Coulter Pharmaceuticals Inc	Drugs	Oct-00
$825	Elan Corp PLC	Neurex Corp	Drugs	Apr-98
$822	Abbott Laboratories	MediSense Inc	Drugs	Mar-96
$821	Roche Holding AG	Nicholas (Nicholas Kiwi AU)	Drugs	Jun-91
$805	Chiron Corp	Cetus Corp	Business Services	Jul-91
$700	Chiron Corp	PathoGenesis Corp	Drugs	Aug-00
$668	Elan Corp PLC	Liposome Co Inc	Drugs	Mar-00
$667	American Home Products Corp	Genetics Institute Inc	Drugs	Sep-91
$621	Watson Pharmaceuticals Inc	Circa Pharmaceuticals Inc	Drugs	Mar-95
$616	Chiron Corp	Ciba-Corning Diag, Biocine	Drugs	Nov-94
$616	Merck & Co Inc	Rosetta Inpharmatics Inc	Business Services	May-01
$614	Merck E (Merck AG)	Merck AG	Drugs	Apr-95
$612	IVAX Corp	Zenith Laboratories Inc	Drugs	Aug-94
$605	Glaxo Wellcome PLC	Nippon Glaxo (Glaxo-Wellcome)	Drugs	Jan-95
$601	Elan Corp PLC	Athena Neurosciences Inc	Drugs	Mar-96
$594	Barr Laboratories Inc	Duramed Pharmaceuticals Inc	Drugs	Jun-01
$587	Revco DS Inc	Hook-SupeRx Inc	Miscellaneous Retail Trade	Apr-94
$580	Bayer AG	Monsanto Co-Styrenics Plastics	Rubber and Miscellaneous Plastic Products	Nov-95
$561	Galen Holdings PLC	Warner Chilcott PLC	Drugs	May-00
$554	Vertex Pharmaceuticals Inc	Aurora Biosciences Corp	Measuring, Medical, Photo Equipment; Clocks	Apr-01

Value of Transaction (US$ millions)	Acquirer	Target Company	Target Industry	Date Announced
ELECTRIC, GAS AND WATER DISTRIBUTION				
$40,428	Vivendi SA	Seagram Co Ltd	Motion Picture Production and Distribution	Jun-00
$16,006	El Paso Energy Corp	Coastal Corp	Electric, Gas and Water Distribution	Jan-00
$13,153	VEBA AG	VIAG AG	Electric, Gas and Water Distribution	Sep-99
$11,866	Vivendi SA	Canal Plus SA	Radio and Television Broadcasting Stations	Jun-00
$11,827	FirstEnergy Corp	GPU Inc	Electric, Gas and Water Distribution	Aug-00
$8,501	NiSource Inc	Columbia Energy Group	Electric, Gas and Water Distribution	Feb-00
$8,048	National Grid Group PLC	Niagara Mohawk Holdings Inc	Electric, Gas and Water Distribution	Sep-00
$7,984	Carolina Power & Light Co	Florida Progress Corp	Electric, Gas and Water Distribution	Aug-99
$7,667	Duke Power Co	PanEnergy Corp	Oil and Gas; Petroleum Refining	Nov-96
$7,386	PECO Energy Co	Unicom Corp	Electric, Gas and Water Distribution	Sep-99
$6,662	American Electric Power Co	Central & South West Corp	Electric, Gas and Water Distribution	Dec-97
$6,482	Dominion Resources Inc	Consolidated Natural Gas Co	Electric, Gas and Water Distribution	Feb-99
$6,256	RWE AG	Thames Water PLC	Electric, Gas and Water Distribution	Sep-00
$5,939	Suez Lyonnaise des Eaux SA	Societe Generale de Belgique	Holding Companies, Except Banks	Apr-98
$5,426	PowerGen PLC	LG&E Energy Corp	Electric, Gas and Water Distribution	Feb-00
$4,906	TransCanada Pipelines Ltd	NOVA Corp of Alberta Ltd	Chemicals and Related Products	Jan-98
$4,830	Northern States Power Co	New Century Energies Inc	Electric, Gas and Water Distribution	Mar-99
$4,772	Cie Generale des Eaux SA (CGE)	Havas SA	Advertising Services	Mar-98
$4,726	Brooklyn Union Gas Co	LILCO	Electric, Gas and Water Distribution	Dec-96
$4,473	Scottish Hydro-Electric PLC	Southern Electric PLC	Electric, Gas and Water Distribution	Sep-98
$4,217	National Grid Group PLC	New England Electric System	Electric, Gas and Water Distribution	Dec-98
$4,185	DTE Energy Co	MCN Energy Group Inc	Electric, Gas and Water Distribution	Oct-99
$3,879	El Paso Natural Gas Co	Tenneco Energy Resources Corp	Electric, Gas and Water Distribution	Jun-96
$3,649	Houston Industries Inc	NorAm Energy Corp	Oil and Gas; Petroleum Refining	Aug-96
$3,432	RWE AG	VEW AG	Electric, Gas and Water Distribution	Oct-99
$3,157	PowerGen PLC	East Midlands Electricity (DR)	Construction Firms	Jun-98
$3,125	VIAG AG	Bayernwerk AG	Electric, Gas and Water Distribution	Oct-92
$3,115	Cia di Partecipazioni Assicura	Montedison (Cie de Partecipazi)	Chemicals and Related Products	Feb-00
$2,870	Enova Corp	Pacific Enterprises Inc	Electric, Gas and Water Distribution	Oct-96
$2,862	North West Water Group PLC	Norweb PLC	Electric, Gas and Water Distribution	Sep-95

Value of Transaction (US$ millions)	Acquirer	Target Company	Target Industry	Date Announced
ELECTRIC, GAS AND WATER DISTRIBUTION (continued)				
$2,852	Illinova Corp	Dynegy Inc	Oil and Gas; Petroleum Refining	Jun-99
$2,757	AES Corp	IPALCO Enterprises Inc	Electric, Gas and Water Distribution	Jul-00
$2,757	Williams Cos Inc	Barrett Resources Corp	Oil and Gas; Petroleum Refining	May-01
$2,706	Williams Cos Inc	Transco Energy Co	Electric, Gas and Water Distribution	Dec-94
$2,634	Williams Cos Inc	MAPCO Inc	Oil and Gas; Petroleum Refining	Nov-97
$2,561	KeySpan Corp	Eastern Enterprises	Electric, Gas and Water Distribution	Nov-99
$2,554	Scottish Power PLC	Southern Water PLC	Electric, Gas and Water Distribution	May-96
$2,543	Central & South West Corp	Seeboard PLC	Retail Trade-Home Furnishings	Nov-95
$2,352	Hidroelectrica Iberica	Hidroelectrica Iberica Iberdue	Electric, Gas and Water Distribution	Apr-91
$2,300	Northeast Utilities	Public Service Co of NH	Electric, Gas and Water Distribution	Mar-88
$2,281	Entergy Corp	Gulf States Utilities Co	Electric, Gas and Water Distribution	Jun-92
$2,264	Dominion Resources Inc	Louis Dreyfus Natural Gas	Oil and Gas; Petroleum Refining	Sep-01
$2,166	Catalana de Gas SA	Gas Madrid, Repsol Burtano SA	Oil and Gas; Petroleum Refining	Feb-91
$2,006	GPU Inc	PowerNet Victoria (GPU Inc)	Electric, Gas and Water Distribution	Oct-97
$1,900	Sydkraft AB	Bakab Energi	Electric, Gas and Water Distribution	Mar-92
$1,855	Lyonnaise des Eaux SA	Dumez SA	Construction Firms	Jul-90
$1,845	Suez Lyonnaise des Eaux SA	United Water Resources Inc	Electric, Gas and Water Distribution	Aug-99
$1,829	Scottish Power PLC	Manweb PLC	Electric, Gas and Water Distribution	Jul-95
$1,731	VEBA AG	GFC Gmbh fuer	Chemicals and Related Products	May-97
$1,687	Texas Utilities Co	ENSERCH Corp	Electric, Gas and Water Distribution	Apr-96
$1,658	AES Corp	CA La Electricidad de Caracas	Electric, Gas and Water Distribution	Apr-00
$1,638	Energy Group PLC	Peabody Holding Co (Hanson Ind)	Mining	Mar-97
$1,631	Southern Co Inc	South Western Electricity PLC	Electric, Gas and Water Distribution	Jul-95
$1,613	Texas Utilities Co	Eastern Energy Ltd (Australia)	Electric, Gas and Water Distribution	Nov-95
$1,613	Ohio Edison Co	Centerior Energy Corp	Electric, Gas and Water Distribution	Sep-96
$1,590	PG&E Corp	New England Elec Sys-Power Gen	Electric, Gas and Water Distribution	Aug-97
$1,548	Cincinnati Gas & Electric Co	PSI Resources Inc	Electric, Gas and Water Distribution	Dec-92
$1,539	LG&E Energy Corp	KU Energy Corp	Electric, Gas and Water Distribution	May-97
$1,522	Elektrowatt AG	Landis & Gyr AG	Holding Companies, Except Banks	Dec-95
$1,473	Kinder Morgan Energy Partners	Santa Fe Pacific Pipeline	Oil and Gas; Petroleum Refining	Oct-97

Value of Transaction (US$ millions)	Acquirer	Target Company	Target Industry	Date Announced
ELECTRIC, GAS AND WATER DISTRIBUTION (continued)				
$1,445	Wisconsin Energy Corp	WICOR Inc	Electric, Gas and Water Distribution	Jun-99
$1,408	PG&E Corp	Valero Energy Corp-Natural Gas	Oil and Gas; Petroleum Refining	Jan-97
$1,404	Sonat Inc	Zilkha Energy Co	Oil and Gas; Petroleum Refining	Nov-97
$1,373	AES Corp	Cie Centro Oeste	Electric, Gas and Water Distribution	Sep-97
$1,343	Welsh Water PLC	South Wales Electricity PLC	Electric, Gas and Water Distribution	Dec-95
$1,333	VEBA AG	Vebacom GmbH	Telecommunications	Feb-97
$1,319	AES Corp	Gener SA	Electric, Gas and Water Distribution	Nov-00
$1,296	Entergy Corp	Citipower Ltd (Entergy Corp)	Electric, Gas and Water Distribution	Nov-95
$1,268	Lyonnaise des Eaux SA	Northumbrian Water Group PLC	Electric, Gas and Water Distribution	Nov-95
$1,242	Union Electric Co	CIPSCO Inc	Electric, Gas and Water Distribution	Aug-95
$1,231	Energy East Corp	CMP Group Inc	Electric, Gas and Water Distribution	Jun-99
$1,224	Public Service Co of Colorado	Southwestern Public Service Co	Electric, Gas and Water Distribution	Aug-95
$1,214	Indiana Energy Inc	SIGCORP Inc	Electric, Gas and Water Distribution	Jun-99
$1,121	WPL Holdings Inc	IES Industries Inc	Electric, Gas and Water Distribution	Nov-95
$1,099	Kansas Power & Light Co	Kansas Gas & Electric Co	Electric, Gas and Water Distribution	Sep-90
$1,096	Calpine Corp	Encal Energy Ltd	Oil and Gas; Petroleum Refining	Feb-01
$1,077	Thames Water PLC	E'town Corp	Electric, Gas and Water Distribution	Nov-99
$999	VIAG AG	Continental Can Europe	Metal and Metal Products	Apr-91
$951	Delmarva Power & Light	Atlantic Energy (Conoco)	Electric, Gas and Water Distribution	Aug-96
$941	SCANA Corp	PSNC	Electric, Gas and Water Distribution	Feb-99
$938	California Energy Co Inc	Magma Power Co	Electric, Gas and Water Distribution	Sep-94
$933	British Gas PLC	Consumers Gas Co Ltd	Electric, Gas and Water Distribution	Mar-90
$913	White Martins SA (Praxair Inc)	Liquid Carbonic Ind-South Amer	Chemicals and Related Products	May-96
$900	Western Resources Inc	Protection One Inc	Business Services	Jul-97
$890	Tejas Gas Corp	Transok Inc	Electric, Gas and Water Distribution	May-96
$868	Interprovincial Pipe Line	Consumers Gas Co Ltd	Electric, Gas and Water Distribution	Nov-93
$781	AES Corp	Southern CA Edison-Plants (12)	Electric, Gas and Water Distribution	Nov-97
$702	Westcoast Energy Inc	Inter-City Gas-Utils, Propane	Electric, Gas and Water Distribution	Dec-89
$690	Electricity Generating PLC	Khanom Electricity Generating	Electric, Gas and Water Distribution	Jun-95
$682	Northeast Utilities	Yankee Energy System Inc	Electric, Gas and Water Distribution	Jun-99

Value of Transaction (US$ millions)	Acquirer	Target Company	Target Industry	Date Announced
ELECTRIC, GAS AND WATER DISTRIBUTION (continued)				
$657	Sithe Energies (Cie Generale)	Boston Edison-Power Plants (12)	Electric, Gas and Water Distribution	Dec-97
$642	Midwest Resources Inc	Iowa-Illinois Gas & Electric	Electric, Gas and Water Distribution	Jul-94
$642	New England Electric System	Eastern Utilities Associates	Electric, Gas and Water Distribution	Jan-99
$622	Energy East Corp	Connecticut Energy	Electric, Gas and Water Distribution	Apr-99
$596	Enbridge Inc	Midcoast Energy Resources Inc	Electric, Gas and Water Distribution	Mar-01
$591	ONEOK Inc	Western Res-Ok & KS Natural	Electric, Gas and Water Distribution	Dec-96
$575	Energy East Corp	CTG Resources Inc	Electric, Gas and Water Distribution	Jun-99
$526	Seagull Energy Corp	Global Natural Resources Inc	Oil and Gas; Petroleum Refining	Jul-96
$520	Cia Forca e Luz Cataguazes	Empresa Energetica de Sergipe	Electric, Gas and Water Distribution	Dec-97
$516	Midwest Energy Co	Iowa Resources	Electric, Gas and Water Distribution	Mar-90
$501	Duke Energy Corp	PG&E-CA Generating Plants (3)	Electric, Gas and Water Distribution	Nov-97
ELECTRONIC AND ELECTRICAL EQUIPMENT				
$41,144	JDS Uniphase Corp	SDL Inc	Electronics and Electrical Equipment	Jul-00
$15,394	JDS Uniphase Corp	E-Tek Dynamics Inc	Electronics and Electrical Equipment	Jan-00
$7,406	Matsushita Electric Industrial	MCA Inc	Motion Picture Production and Distribution	Sep-90
$6,956	Texas Instruments Inc	Burr-Brown Corp	Electronics and Electrical Equipment	Jun-00
$5,502	Schneider Electric SA	Legrand SA	Electronics and Electrical Equipment	Jan-01
$5,122	Westinghouse Electric Corp	CBS Inc	Radio and Television Broadcasting Stations	Aug-95
$4,738	Westinghouse Electric Corp	Infinity Broadcasting Corp	Radio and Television Broadcasting Stations	Jun-96
$4,465	Applied Micro Circuits Corp	MMC Networks Inc	Electronics and Electrical Equipment	Aug-00
$2,766	JDS Uniphase Corp	Optical Coating Laboratory Inc	Measuring, Medical, Photo Equipment; Clocks	Nov-99
$2,723	Farnell Electronics PLC	Premier Industrial Corp	Wholesale Trade, Durable Goods	Jan-96
$2,700	Smiths Industries PLC	TI Group PLC	Metal and Metal Products	Sep-00
$2,636	Solectron Corp	C-Mac Industries Inc	Business Services	Aug-01
$2,628	Marvell Technology Group Ltd	Galileo Technology Ltd	Electronics and Electrical Equipment	Oct-00
$2,591	Flextronics International Ltd	DII Group	Electronics and Electrical Equipment	Nov-99
$2,406	Solectron Corp	NatSteel Electronics Pte Ltd	Computer and Office Equipment	Oct-00
$2,167	Sony Corp	Sony Music Entertainment (JP)	Electronics and Electrical Equipment	Mar-99
$2,165	Schneider SA	Square D Co	Electronics and Electrical Equipment	Feb-91

Value of Transaction (US$ millions)	Acquirer	Target Company	Target Industry	Date Announced
ELECTRONIC AND ELECTRICAL EQUIPMENT (continued)				
$2,017	PMC-Sierra Inc	Quantum Effect Devices Inc	Electronics and Electrical Equipment	Jul-00
$1,780	QLogic Corp	Ancor Communication Inc	Computer and Office Equipment	May-00
$1,666	Matsushita Electric Industrial	Matsushita Electronics Corp	Electronics and Electrical Equipment	Apr-93
$1,621	Maxim Integrated Products Inc	Dallas-Semiconductor Corp	Electronics and Electrical Equipment	Jan-01
$1,561	ASM Lithography Holding NV	Silicon Valley Group Inc	Electronics and Electrical Equipment	Sep-00
$1,550	Westinghouse Electric Corp	Nashville Network, Country	Radio and Television Broadcasting Stations	Feb-97
$1,525	Siemens AG	Westinghouse-Conven Power Gen	Machinery	Nov-97
$1,407	Fujitsu Ltd	International Computers Ltd	Prepackaged Software	Jul-90
$1,320	Sunbeam Corp	Coleman Co Inc	Electronics and Electrical Equipment	Mar-98
$1,312	TriQuint Semiconductor Inc	Sawtek Inc	Communications Equipment	May-01
$1,286	Micron Technology Inc	Texas Instruments-MMP Bus	Electronics and Electrical Equipment	Jun-98
$1,030	Koninklijke Philips Electronic	MedQuist Inc	Business Services	May-00
$985	Siemens AG	Siemens Nixdorf Info AG	Electronics and Electrical Equipment	Oct-91
$962	Acer Display Technology Inc	Unipac Optoelectronics Corp	Computer and Office Equipment	Mar-01
$926	Celestica Inc	Omni Industries Ltd	Electronics and Electrical Equipment	Jun-01
$925	Fujitsu Ltd	Amdahl Corp	Computer and Office Equipment	Jul-97
$890	Vishay Intertechnology Inc	General Semiconductor Inc	Electronics and Electrical Equipment	Apr-01
$866	LSI Logic Corp	C-Cube Microsystems Inc	Electronics and Electrical Equipment	Mar-01
$848	Semi-Tech Microelectronics Ltd	Singer Co NV	Wholesale Trade, Durable Goods	Jun-93
$847	Conexant Systems Inc	Maker Communications Inc	Electronics and Electrical Equipment	Dec-99
$816	Siemens AG	Elektrowatt AG-Industrial	Electric, Gas and Water Distribution	Jan-97
$786	Koninklijke Philips Electronic	ATL Ultrasound Inc	Measuring, Medical, Photo Equipment; Clocks	Jul-98
$760	LSI Logic Corp	Symbios Inc	Computer and Office Equipment	Jun-98
$756	Advanced Micro Devices Inc	NexGen Inc	Electronics and Electrical Equipment	Oct-95
$702	Intel Corp	Xircom Inc	Business Services	Jan-01
$700	ASEA AB	Incentive AB	Measuring, Medical, Photo Equipment; Clocks	Apr-90
$700	Intel Corp	Digital Equip-Semiconductor	Electronics and Electrical Equipment	Oct-97
$683	Electrolux AB	AEG Hausgeraete	Electronics and Electrical Equipment	Dec-93
$661	General Electric Co	Nuovo Pignone	Measuring, Medical, Photo Equipment; Clocks	Dec-93
$632	Flextronics International Ltd	JIT Holdings Ltd	Electronics and Electrical Equipment	Aug-00

Value of Transaction (US$ millions)	Acquirer	Target Company	Target Industry	Date Announced
ELECTRONIC AND ELECTRICAL EQUIPMENT (continued)				
$632	Whirlpool Corp	Whirlpool International BV	Electronics and Electrical Equipment	Jan-90
$630	GlobeSpan Inc	Virata Corp	Electronics and Electrical Equipment	Oct-01
$625	Texas Instruments Inc	Silicon Systems Inc (TDK USA)	Electronics and Electrical Equipment	Jun-96
$570	Thomas & Betts Corp	Augat Inc	Electronics and Electrical Equipment	Oct-96
$566	National Semiconductor Corp	Cyrix Corp	Electronics and Electrical Equipment	Jul-97
$563	Kyocera Corp	AVX Corp (Kyocera)	Electronics and Electrical Equipment	Sep-89
$557	Allegheny Teledyne Inc	Oregon Metallurgical Corp	Metal and Metal Products	Nov-97
$550	Exide Corp	CEAC (Magneti Marelli/Fiat SpA)	Electronics and Electrical Equipment	Oct-94
$537	Schneider SA	Merlin Gerlin SA (Schneider)	Electronics and Electrical Equipment	Apr-92
$527	Sansui Electric Co (Polly Peck)	Capetronics, Imperial	Electronics and Electrical Equipment	May-90
$519	General Electric Co	Greenwich Air Services Inc	Aerospace and Aircraft	Mar-97
FOOD AND RELATED PRODUCTS				
$25,065	Unilever PLC	Bestfoods	Food and Related Products	May-00
$15,968	Grand Metropolitan PLC	Guinness PLC	Food and Related Products	May-97
$14,392	PepsiCo Inc	Quaker Oats Co	Food and Related Products	Dec-00
$5,704	Seagram Co Ltd	MCA Inc (Matsushita Electric)	Motion Picture Production and Distribution	Apr-95
$4,652	Kellogg Co	Keebler Foods Co	Food and Related Products	Oct-00
$4,233	Tyson Foods Inc	IBP Inc	Food and Related Products	Dec-00
$3,300	PepsiCo Inc	Tropicana Products Inc	Food and Related Products	Jul-98
$3,294	ConAgra Inc	Beatrice Co	Machinery	Jun-90
$3,036	ConAgra Inc	International Home Foods Inc	Food and Related Products	Jun-00
$2,950	Bass PLC	Saison Holdings BV	Hotels and Casinos	Feb-98
$2,906	Sara Lee Corp	Earthgrains Co	Food and Related Products	Jul-01
$2,893	Hellenic Bottling Co SA	Coca-Cola Beverages PLC	Food and Related Products	Aug-99
$2,739	Coca-Cola Amatil Ltd	Coca-Cola Bottlers Philippines	Food and Related Products	Apr-97
$2,440	Procordia AB	Pharmacia AB (Pharmacia SpA)	Drugs	Dec-89
$2,367	Cadbury Schweppes PLC	Dr Pepper/Seven-Up Cos Inc	Food and Related Products	Mar-94
$2,225	Bass PLC	Holiday Inns Inc (Holiday Corp)	Hotels and Casinos	Aug-89
$1,999	Hellenic Bottling Co SA	Molino Beverages Holding SA	Food and Related Products	Sep-97

Value of Transaction (US$ millions)	Acquirer	Target Company	Target Industry	Date Announced
FOOD AND KINDRED PRODUCTS (continued)				
$1,935	Bacardi Corp	Diageo PLC	Wholesale Trade, Nondurable Goods	Mar-98
$1,768	Koninklijke Numico NV	Rexall Sundown Inc	Drugs	May-00
$1,703	Quaker Oats Co	Snapple Beverage Corp	Food and Related Products	Nov-94
$1,700	Seagram Co Ltd	USA Network (Viacom, Seagram)	Radio and Television Broadcasting Stations	Sep-97
$1,500	Bacardi Corp	Martini & Rossi SpA	Food and Related Products	Sep-92
$1,493	Jacobs Suchard AG	Freia Marabou AS	Food and Related Products	Sep-92
$1,372	Coca-Cola Enterprises Inc	Johnston Coca-Cola Btlg Group	Food and Related Products	Aug-91
$1,356	Procordia AB	Provendor AB (Volvo AB)	Agriculture, Forestry and Fishing	Dec-89
$1,349	PepsiCo Inc	Walkers Crisps, Smith Crisps	Food and Related Products	Jul-89
$1,310	Beghin-Say SA	Eridania Zuccherifici	Food and Related Products	Nov-91
$1,298	Loblaw Cos (George Weston Ltd)	Provigo Inc	Retail Trade, Food Stores	Oct-98
$1,185	Nestle SA	Spillers Petfoods (Dalgety PLC)	Food and Related Products	Feb-98
$1,120	Coca-Cola Enterprises Inc	Coca-Cola Bottling, Texas Bottl	Food and Related Products	Apr-98
$1,115	Campbell Soup Co	Pace Foods	Food and Related Products	Nov-94
$1,112	Panamerican Beverages Inc	Coca-Cola Hitt de Venezuela	Food and Related Products	May-97
$1,072	Scottish & Newcastle Breweries	Grand Met-Chef, Brewer Chains	Retail, Restaurants	Sep-93
$995	Suedzucker AG	Raffinerie Tirlemontoise SA	Food and Related Products	Nov-89
$991	Scottish & Newcastle Breweries	Courage Ltd	Food and Related Products	Mar-95
$972	Suiza Foods Corp	Morningstar Group Inc	Food and Related Products	Sep-97
$971	Coca-Cola Amatil Ltd	Coca-Cola Co-Italian Assets	Food and Related Products	Feb-98
$961	Coca-Cola Enterprises Inc	Coca-Cola & Schweppes Beverage	Food and Related Products	Jun-96
$955	Coca-Cola Enterprises Inc	Coca-Cola & Schweppes Beverage	Food and Related Products	Jun-96
$941	Whitbread PLC	Swallow Group PLC	Food and Related Products	Nov-99
$915	Coca-Cola Enterprises Inc	Coca-Cola Beverages SA, Coca-Co	Food and Related Products	May-96
$906	Coca-Cola Enterprises Inc	Coca-Cola Beverages Ltd	Food and Related Products	May-97
$885	Allied-Lyons PLC	Whitbread & Co-Spirits Div	Food and Related Products	Dec-89
$865	CPC International Inc	Kraft General Foods-Baking Div	Food and Related Products	Aug-95
$813	Koninklijke Wessanen NV	Koninklijke Distilleerderijen	Food and Related Products	Jan-93
$755	Nestle SA	Nestle Philippines Inc	Food and Related Products	Aug-98
$749	Saint Louis SA	Arjomari-Prioux SA	Paper and Related Products	Nov-91

Value of Transaction (US$ millions)	Acquirer	Target Company	Target Industry	Date Announced
FOOD AND KINDRED PRODUCTS (continued)				
$737	Unilever NV	Helene Curtis Industries Inc	Soaps, Cosmetics and Personal-Care Products	Feb-96
$725	HJ Heinz Co	Quaker Oats-US & CA Pet Food	Food and Related Products	Feb-95
$680	Molson Companies Ltd	Molson Breweries of CA (Molson)	Food and Related Products	Jun-98
$657	IBP Inc	Foodbrands America Inc	Food and Related Products	Mar-97
$648	Tyson Foods Inc	Hudson Foods Inc	Food and Related Products	Sep-97
$645	Northern Foods PLC	Express Dairy Ltd, Eden Vale	Wholesale Trade, Nondurable Goods	Nov-91
$583	Imperial Sugar Co	Savannah Foods & Industries	Food and Related Products	Aug-97
$570	Unilever NV	Diversey Corp (Molson Cos Ltd)	Soaps, Cosmetics and Personal-Care Products	Jan-96
$557	Verenigde Bedrijven Nutricia	Milupa AG	Food and Related Products	Aug-95
$554	Danone Group	Panzalim	Food and Related Products	Jun-94
$549	Eridania Beghin-Say	Cie Francaise de Sucrerie	Food and Related Products	Jun-96
$524	Cervecerias Backus y Johnston	Cia Nacional de Cerveza	Food and Related Products	Oct-96
$511	Coca-Cola Amatil Ltd	Coca-Cola Korea Bottling Co	Food and Related Products	Feb-98
$507	General Mills Inc	Ralcorp Hldgs-Branded Cereal	Food and Related Products	Aug-96
$507	Azucarera Ebro Agricolas SA	Puleva	Food and Related Products	Oct-00
$500	HJ Heinz Co	JL Foods Inc (John Labatt Ltd)	Food and Related Products	Jul-91
HEALTH SERVICES				
$5,605	Columbia Healthcare Corp	HCA-Hospital Corp of America	Health Services	Oct-93
$5,219	Columbia/HCA Healthcare Corp	HealthTrust Inc-The Hospital	Health Services	Oct-94
$4,188	Columbia Hospital Corp	Galen Health Care Inc	Health Services	Jun-93
$3,300	National Medical Enterprises	American Medical Holdings Inc	Health Services	Sep-94
$3,123	Tenet Healthcare Corp	OrNda HealthCorp	Health Services	Oct-96
$2,708	MedPartners/Mullikin Inc	Caremark International Inc	Health Services	May-96
$2,474	Health Care and Retirement	Manor Care Inc	Health Services	Jun-98
$2,290	United HealthCare Corp	MetraHealth Cos (Travelers, Met)	Health Services	Jun-95
$2,000	PacifiCare Health Systems Inc	FHP International Corp	Health Services	Aug-96
$1,896	Vencor Inc	Hillhaven Corp	Health Services	Jan-95
$1,651	HealthSouth Corp	Horizon/CMS Healthcare Corp	Health Services	Feb-97
$1,459	HealthSouth Corp	Surgical Care Affiliates Inc	Health Services	Oct-95

Value of Transaction (US$ millions)	Acquirer	Target Company	Target Industry	Date Announced
HEALTH SERVICES (continued)				
$1,363	Total Renal Care Holdings Inc	Renal Treatment Centers Inc	Health Services	Nov-97
$1,250	Integrated Health Services Inc	HealthSouth-Long Term Care	Health Services	Nov-97
$1,218	Mayne Nickless Ltd	FH Faulding & Co Ltd	Drugs	May-01
$1,132	Columbia/HCA Healthcare Corp	Value Health Inc	Insurance	Jan-97
$1,033	FHP International Corp	TakeCare Inc	Health Services	Jan-94
$1,004	HealthTrust Inc-The Hospital	EPIC Healthcare Group Inc	Health Services	Jan-94
$919	Integrated Health Services Inc	RoTech Medical Corp	Health Services	Jul-97
$876	Columbia Healthcare Corp	Medical Care America Inc	Health Services	May-94
$846	Medical Care International Inc	Critical Care America Inc	Health Services	Jun-92
$703	HealthSouth Corp	National Surgery Centers Inc	Health Services	May-98
$684	Qual-Med Inc	Health Net Inc	Health Services	Aug-93
$678	Genesis Health Ventures Inc	Vitalink Pharmacy Services Inc	Health Services	Apr-98
$628	Vencor Inc	Transitional Hospitals Corp	Health Services	May-97
$622	Paragon Health Network Inc	Mariner Health Group Inc	Health Services	Apr-98
$594	Horizon Healthcare Corp	Continental Medical Systems	Health Services	Mar-95
$588	Sun Healthcare Group Inc	Regency Health Services Inc	Health Services	Jul-97
$565	United HealthCare Corp	Ramsay-HMO	Health Services	Feb-94
$549	T2 Medical Inc	Medisys, HealthInfusion, 1 Other	Health Services	Feb-94
$512	United HealthCare Corp	Gencare Health Systems	Insurance	Sep-94
$500	HealthSouth Corp	Columbia/HCA Healthcare-34 Amb	Health Services	Apr-98
HOLDING COMPANIES, EXCEPT BANKS				
$48,174	British Petroleum Co PLC	Amoco Corp	Oil and Gas; Petroleum Refining	Aug-98
$11,858	CGU PLC	Norwich Union PLC	Insurance	Feb-00
$7,445	Lyonnaise des Eaux-Dumez SA	Cie de Suez SA	Electric, Gas and Water Distribution	Mar-97
$2,373	Repola Oy	Kymmene Oy (UPM-Kymmene)	Paper and Related Products	Sep-95
$1,797	GFC Financial Corp	TriCon Capita (Bell Atlantic)	Credit Institutions	Mar-94
$1,650	Knight-Ridder Inc	Walt Disney-Kansas City Star,	Printing, Publishing and Related Services	Apr-97
$1,572	Societe Generale de Belgique	TRACTEBEL SA	Holding Companies, Except Banks	Sep-96
$1,074	Internationale Nederlanden	Barings PLC-Assets	Commercial Banks, Bank Holding Companies	Mar-95

Value of Transaction (US$ millions)	Acquirer	Target Company	Target Industry	Date Announced
HOLDING COMPANIES, EXCEPT BANKS (continued)				
$962	Havas SA	Generale Occidentale-Publishin	Printing, Publishing and Related Services	Oct-95
$875	Jefferson-Pilot Corp	Chubb Life Ins Co of America	Insurance	Feb-97
$670	American Brands Inc	Cobra Golf Inc	Miscellaneous Manufacturing	Dec-95
$636	Financiere Agache SA	Au Bon Marche (Financiere)	Retail, General Merchandise and Apparel	Oct-94
$583	Yorkshire Water PLC	Aquarion Co	Electric, Gas and Water Distribution	Jun-99
$575	Jefferson-Pilot Corp	Alexander Hamilton Life Ins	Insurance	Aug-95
HOTELS AND CASINOS				
$3,138	Hilton Hotels Corp	Bally Entertainment Corp	Hotels and Casinos	Jun-96
$2,300	Accor SA	Motel 6 LP	Hotels and Casinos	Jul-90
$1,810	HFS Inc	PHH Corp	Business Services	Nov-96
$1,704	Promus Hotel Corp	Doubletree Corp	Hotels and Casinos	Sep-97
$1,696	ITT Corp	Caesars World Inc	Hotels and Casinos	Dec-94
$1,212	CapStar Hotel Co	American General Hospitality	Investment & Commodity Firms, Dealers and Exchanges	Mar-98
$1,174	Doubletree Corp	Red Lions Hotels (Red Lion Inn)	Hotels and Casinos	Aug-96
$908	Marriott International Inc	Renaissance Hotel Group NV	Hotels and Casinos	Feb-97
$903	Rank Organisation PLC	Mecca Leisure Group PLC	Retail, Restaurants	Jun-90
$832	Hilton Hotels Corp	Grand Casinos Inc	Hotels and Casinos	Jun-98
$825	HFS Inc	Resort Condominiums Intl Inc	Hotels and Casinos	Oct-96
$800	HFS Inc	Avis Inc	Repair Services	Jun-96
$750	Sterling Worldwide Corp	LY Transportation Construction	Real Estate; Mortgage Bankers and Brokers	Aug-97
$659	Bristol Hotel Co	Bass PLC-N Amer Holiday Inn	Hotels and Casinos	Dec-96
$622	Marriott International Inc	Forum Group Inc	Health Services	Feb-96
$609	Mandalay Resort Group	Gold Strike Resorts	Hotels and Casinos	Mar-95
$540	Host Marriott Corp	Forum Group Inc	Health Services	Mar-97
$532	Stakis PLC	Metropole Hotels (Holdings) Ltd	Hotels and Casinos	Oct-96
$513	Trump Hotels & Casino Resorts	Trump's Castle Casino (Trump's)	Hotels and Casinos	May-96
$502	Trusthouse Forte PLC	Bass PLC-40 Crest Hotels	Hotels and Casinos	May-90

Value of Transaction (US$ millions)	Acquirer	Target Company	Target Industry	Date Announced
INSURANCE				
$72,558	Travelers Group Inc	Citicorp	Commercial Banks, Bank Holding Companies	Apr-98
$30,957	Citigroup Inc	Associates First Capital Corp	Credit Institutions	Sep-00
$23,398	American International Group	American General Corp	Insurance	Apr-01
$22,338	Berkshire Hathaway Inc	General Re Corp	Insurance	Jun-98
$19,656	Allianz AG	Dresdner Bank AG	Commercial Banks, Bank Holding Companies	Apr-01
$19,399	Zurich Allied AG	Allied Zurich PLC	Insurance	Apr-00
$18,355	Zurich Versicherungs GmbH	BAT Industries PLC-Financial	Insurance	Oct-97
$12,821	Citigroup Inc	Banacci	Commercial Banks, Bank Holding Companies	May-01
$12,470	Fortis (B)	Fortis (NL) NV	Insurance	Sep-01
$12,299	Fortis AG	Generale de Banque SA	Commercial Banks, Bank Holding Companies	May-98
$11,153	Commercial Union PLC	General Accident PLC	Insurance	Feb-98
$10,605	Axa SA	UAP	Insurance	Nov-96
$10,180	Assicurazioni Generali SpA	INA	Insurance	Sep-99
$8,852	Travelers Group Inc	Salomon Inc	Investment & Commodity Firms, Dealers and Exchanges	Sep-97
$7,458	Nationale-Nederlanden NV	NMB Postbank Groep NV	Commercial Banks, Bank Holding Companies	Nov-90
$7,359	Conseco Inc	Green Tree Financial Corp	Credit Institutions	Apr-98
$5,974	ING Groep NV	ReliaStar Financial Corp	Insurance	Apr-00
$5,118	Allianz AG	AGF	Insurance	Nov-97
$5,075	Assicurazioni Generali SpA	Aachener und Muenchener	Insurance	Dec-97
$4,516	ING Groep NV	Banque Bruxelles Lambert SA	Commercial Banks, Bank Holding Companies	Nov-97
$4,326	Mitsui Marine & Fire Insurance	Sumitomo Marine & Fire Ins	Insurance	Mar-00
$4,000	Travelers Group Inc	Aetna Life & Casualty-Ppty	Insurance	Nov-95
$3,968	Muenchener Rueckversicherungs	American Re Corp	Insurance	Aug-96
$3,956	Primerica Corp	Travelers Corp	Insurance	Sep-93
$3,919	Prudential PLC	Scottish Amicable Life	Insurance	Mar-97
$3,807	Sun Alliance Group PLC	Royal Insurance Holdings PLC	Insurance	May-96
$3,782	St Paul Cos Inc	USF&G Corp	Insurance	Jan-98
$3,689	Fortis (NL) NV	ASR Verzekeringsgroep	Insurance	Oct-00
$3,504	Aegon NV	Providian Corp-Insurance	Insurance	Dec-96
$3,393	Muenchener Rueckversicherungs	Ergo Versicherungsgruppe AG	Insurance	Apr-01

Value of Transaction (US$ millions)	Acquirer	Target Company	Target Industry	Date Announced
INSURANCE (continued)				
$3,138	AXA-UAP	Royale Belge SA	Insurance	May-98
$3,127	SAFECO Corp	American States Financial Corp	Insurance	Jun-97
$3,100	Allianz AG Holding	Fireman's Fund Insurance Co	Insurance	Aug-90
$2,721	Swiss Reinsurance Co	Mercantile and General Reinsur	Insurance	Aug-96
$2,626	ING Groep NV	Equitable of Iowa Cos	Insurance	Jul-97
$2,449	Citigroup Inc	Travelers Property Casualty	Insurance	Mar-00
$2,374	American General Corp	USLIFE Corp	Insurance	Feb-97
$2,349	Berkshire Hathaway Inc	GEICO Corp (Berkshire Hathaway)	Insurance	Aug-95
$2,187	Allianz AG	Allianz Lebensversicherungs AG	Insurance	Apr-01
$2,130	Marsh & McLennan Cos Inc	Sedgwick Group PLC	Insurance	Aug-98
$2,122	EXEL Ltd	Mid Ocean Ltd	Insurance	Mar-98
$2,111	Great-West Lifeco (Power Finl)	London Insurance Group Inc	Insurance	Aug-97
$2,101	AGF	Athena Assurances	Insurance	Nov-97
$2,098	Commercial Union PLC	Cie Financiere Groupe Victoire	Insurance	Jun-94
$1,930	Allianz AG	PIMCO Advisors Holdings LP	Investment & Commodity Firms, Dealers and Exchanges	Oct-99
$1,800	Marsh & McLennan Cos Inc	Johnson & Higgins	Insurance	Mar-97
$1,795	Swiss Reinsurance Co	Life Re Corp	Insurance	Jul-98
$1,687	American Premier Underwriters	American Financial Corp	Insurance	Dec-94
$1,667	Zurich Versicherungs GmbH	Scudder Stevens & Clark Inc	Investment & Commodity Firms, Dealers and Exchanges	Jun-97
$1,653	CIGNA Corp	Healthsource Inc	Health Services	Feb-97
$1,629	Fortis (NL) NV	Banque Generale du Luxembourg	Commercial Banks, Bank Holding Companies	Jan-00
$1,518	Berkshire Hathaway Inc	FlightSafety International	Electronics and Electrical Equipment	Oct-96
$1,457	Old Mutual PLC	United Asset Management Corp	Investment & Commodity Firms, Dealers and Exchanges	Jun-00
$1,436	Fortis AG	MeesPierson NV (ABN-AMRO Hldg)	Commercial Banks, Bank Holding Companies	Oct-96
$1,431	American International Group	HSB Group Inc	Insurance	Aug-00
$1,400	Lincoln National Corp	CIGNA-Indiv Life Ins & Annuity	Insurance	Jul-97
$1,400	Triad Hospitals Inc	Quorum Health Group Inc	Health Services	Oct-00
$1,325	Hartford Fin Svcs Group Inc	Hartford Life (ITT Hartford)	Insurance	Mar-00
$1,323	Sanlam Ltd	Gensec	Investment & Commodity Firms, Dealers and Exchanges	May-98
$1,290	Assicurazioni Generali SpA	Banca della Svizzera Italiana	Commercial Banks, Bank Holding Companies	Jun-98

Value of Transaction (US$ millions)	Acquirer	Target Company	Target Industry	Date Announced
INSURANCE (continued)				
$1,290	Fidelity National Financial	Chicago Title Corp	Insurance	Aug-99
$1,277	Foundation Health Corp	Health Systems International	Health Services	Oct-96
$1,227	Aon Corp	Alexander & Alexander Services	Insurance	Dec-96
$1,215	American General Corp	Western National Corp	Insurance	Sep-97
$1,208	Refuge Group PLC	United Friendly Group PLC	Insurance	Aug-96
$1,171	Provident Cos	Paul Revere Corp (Textron Inc)	Insurance	Apr-96
$1,170	American General Corp	Franklin Life Insurance Co	Insurance	Nov-94
$1,169	Dai-Tokyo Fire & Marine Ins Co	Chiyoda Fire & Marine Ins Co	Insurance	Mar-00
$1,164	Riunione Adriatica di Securita	Elvia Schweizerische	Insurance	Sep-94
$1,156	Sun Life and Provincial	Axa Equity and Law Life, Axa	Insurance	Jul-97
$1,150	Primerica Corp	Shearson Lehman Brothers Inc	Investment & Commodity Firms, Dealers and Exchanges	Mar-93
$1,122	American International Group	International Lease Finance	Business Services	Jun-90
$1,110	CNA Financial Corp (Loews Corp)	Continental Corp	Insurance	Dec-94
$1,073	TransAmerica Corp	Tiphook PLC-Core Container Bus	Business Services	Nov-93
$1,050	Aetna Inc	NYLCare Health Plans Inc	Health Services	Mar-98
$1,029	PartnerRe Ltd	Societe Anonyme Francaise de	Insurance	Feb-97
$1,027	Fubon Insurance Co Ltd	Fubon Securities Co Ltd	Investment & Commodity Firms, Dealers and Exchanges	Sep-01
$1,016	Berkshire Hathaway Inc	Benjamin-Moore and Co	Chemicals and Related Products	Nov-00
$1,012	Tryg Forsikring A/S	Baltica Forsikring A/S	Insurance	May-95
$1,000	Lincoln National Corp	Aetna Inc-Domestic Individual	Insurance	May-98
$976	ACE Ltd	Tempest Reinsurance Co Ltd	Insurance	Feb-96
$967	Fubon Insurance Co Ltd	Fubon Comercial Bank Co Ltd	Commercial Banks, Bank Holding Companies	Sep-01
$935	Magellan Health Services Inc	Merit Behavioral Care Corp	Health Services	Oct-97
$923	Nippon Fire & Marine Insurance	Koa Fire & Marine Insurance	Insurance	Mar-00
$905	General Re Corp	National Re Corp	Insurance	Jun-96
$868	Conseco Inc	American Travellers Corp	Insurance	Aug-96
$856	Old Mutual PLC	Gerrard Group PLC	Commercial Banks, Bank Holding Companies	Jan-00
$840	UAP	Sun Life Hldgs (TransAtlantic)	Insurance	Jul-95
$839	Conseco Inc	Life Partners Group Inc	Holding Companies, Except Banks	Mar-96
$837	Willis Faber PLC	Corroon & Black Corp	Insurance	Jun-90

Value of Transaction (US$ millions)	Acquirer	Target Company	Target Industry	Date Announced
INSURANCE (continued)				
$831	ACE Ltd	Tarquin Ltd	Insurance	Jun-98
$817	Axa SA	National Mutual Life Assn AU	Insurance	Jan-95
$817	Allmerica Financial Corp	Allmerica Property & Casualty	Insurance	Dec-96
$808	Foersaekringsbolaget SPP	London & Edinburgh Trust PLC	Real Estate; Mortgage Bankers and Brokers	Apr-90
$780	PartnerRe Ltd	Winterthur-Active Reinsurance	Insurance	Aug-98
$778	Markel Corp	Terra Nova (Bermuda) Holdings	Insurance	Aug-99
$777	CIGNA Corp	Equicor (Equitable Life, HCA)	Health Services	Nov-89
$775	Guardian Royal Exchange PLC	Netherlands Insurance Co	Insurance	May-98
$758	AGF (Allianz AG)	Royal Nederland Verzekeringsgr	Insurance	Dec-97
$749	UAP	Vinci BV (UAP)	Insurance	Oct-93
$737	Assicurazioni Generali SpA	GPA Vie (Athena Assurances)	Insurance	Dec-97
$732	Fortis AG	Generale de Banque SA	Commercial Banks, Bank Holding Companies	Jun-98
$718	Guardian Royal Exchange PLC	PPP Healthcare Group PLC	Health Services	Dec-97
$715	Conseco Inc	Capitol American Financial	Insurance	Aug-96
$711	ACE Ltd	CAT Ltd	Insurance	Mar-98
$701	Berkshire Hathaway Inc	Executive Jet Inc	Air Transportation and Shipping	Jul-98
$700	Gerling Konzern Versicherungs	Constitution Re (Exor America)	Insurance	Jul-98
$680	Fairfax Financial Holdings Ltd	Crum & Forster Hldgs (Talegen)	Insurance	Mar-98
$665	American General Corp	Home Beneficial Corp	Insurance	Dec-96
$649	Lawyers Title Corp	Commonwealth Land, Transnation	Insurance	Aug-97
$643	Humana Inc	Emphesys Financial Group Inc	Insurance	Aug-95
$630	Winterthur Schweizerische	General Casualty Cos	Insurance	Mar-90
$611	Citigroup Inc	Bank Handlowy SA	Commercial Banks, Bank Holding Companies	May-00
$599	MBIA Inc	CapMAC Holdings Inc	Insurance	Oct-97
$597	Berkshire Hathaway Inc	International Dairy Queen Inc	Wholesale Trade, Nondurable Goods	Oct-97
$584	Berkshire Hathaway Inc	Justin Industries Inc	Stone, Clay, Glass and Concrete Products	Jun-00
$584	Berkshire Hathaway Inc	XTRA Corp	Business Services	Jul-01
$577	UNUM Corp	Colonial Cos Inc	Insurance	Dec-92
$564	Conseco Inc	Pioneer Financial Services	Insurance	Dec-96
$551	Torchmark Corp	American Income Holdings	Insurance	Sep-94

Value of Transaction (US$ millions)	Acquirer	Target Company	Target Industry	Date Announced
INSURANCE (continued)				
$550	Radian Group Inc	Enhance Financial Svcs Grp	Insurance	Nov-00
$548	QBE Insurance Group Ltd	Limit PLC	Insurance	Jun-00
$545	ReliaStar Financial Corp	Security-Connecticut Corp	Insurance	Feb-97
$540	Swiss Reinsurance Co	Societe Anonyme Francaise de	Insurance	Jan-97
$533	General Accident PLC	Canadian General Insurance Grp	Insurance	Oct-97
$532	Lincoln National Corp	Delaware Management Holdings	Investment & Commodity Firms, Dealers and Exchanges	Dec-94
$524	Norwich Union PLC	London & Edinburgh Ins	Insurance	Oct-98
$524	Prudential PLC	Peninsular and Oriental-Amdal	Real Estate; Mortgage Bankers and Brokers	Dec-97
$523	Storebrand ASA	Uni Forsikring	Insurance	Jun-90
$500	SCOR US Corp (SCOR SA)	Allstate Reinsurance (Allstate)	Insurance	Jul-96
INVESTMENT & COMMODITY FIRMS, DEALERS, EXCHANGES				
$13,748	Starwood Hotels & Resorts	ITT Corp	Hotels and Casinos	Oct-97
$10,573	Dean Witter Discover & Co	Morgan Stanley Group Inc	Investment & Commodity Firms, Dealers and Exchanges	Feb-97
$8,939	Aetna Life & Casualty Co	US Healthcare Inc	Health Services	Apr-96
$7,021	Equity Office Properties Trust	Spieker Properties Inc	Investment & Commodity Firms, Dealers and Exchanges	Feb-01
$5,781	Simon DeBartolo Group Inc	Corporate Property Investors	Investment & Commodity Firms, Dealers and Exchanges	Feb-98
$5,464	United Overseas Bank Ltd	Overseas Union Bank Ltd	Commercial Banks, Bank Holding Companies	Jun-01
$5,256	Merrill Lynch & Co Inc	Mercury Asset Management Group	Investment & Commodity Firms, Dealers and Exchanges	Nov-97
$4,550	Equity Office Properties Trust	Cornerstone Properties Inc	Investment & Commodity Firms, Dealers and Exchanges	Feb-00
$4,039	Equity Office Properties Trust	Beacon Properties Corp	Investment & Commodity Firms, Dealers and Exchanges	Sep-97
$3,358	Rodamco North America NV	Urban Shopping Centers Inc	Investment & Commodity Firms, Dealers and Exchanges	Sep-00
$3,215	Archstone Communities Trust	Charles E Smith Residential	Investment & Commodity Firms, Dealers and Exchanges	May-01
$3,187	SG Warburg Group PLC	SG Warburg Group PLC	Investment & Commodity Firms, Dealers and Exchanges	May-95
$3,070	Credit Local de France SA	Credit Communal de Belgique SA	Investment & Commodity Firms, Dealers and Exchanges	Mar-96
$2,962	Simon Property Group Inc	DeBartolo Realty Corp	Investment & Commodity Firms, Dealers and Exchanges	Mar-96
$2,907	Meditrust Acquisition Co	La Quinta Inns Inc	Hotels and Casinos	Jan-98
$2,858	PC Holdings SA	Perez Companc SA	Wood Products, Furniture and Fixtures	Nov-99
$2,660	ORIX Corp	Crown Leasing Corp-Domestic	Investment & Commodity Firms, Dealers and Exchanges	Jun-97
$2,613	Charles Schwab Corp	US Trust Corp, New York, NY	Commercial Banks, Bank Holding Companies	Jan-00

Value of Transaction (US$ millions)	Acquirer	Target Company	Target Industry	Date Announced
INVESTMENT & COMMODITY FIRMS, DEALERS, EXCHANGES (continued)				
$2,100	Softbank Corp	Ziff Davis Media Inc	Printing, Publishing and Related Services	Oct-95
$2,056	Patriot Amer Hosp/Wyndham Intl	Interstate Hotels Co	Hotels and Casinos	Dec-97
$1,986	Equity Residential Pptys Trust	Merry Land & Investment Co Inc	Investment & Commodity Firms, Dealers and Exchanges	Jul-98
$1,940	E*Trade Group Inc	TeleBanc Financial Corp, VA	Savings and Loans, Mutual Savings Banks	Jun-99
$1,850	General Growth Properties Inc	Homart Development Co	Real Estate; Mortgage Bankers and Brokers	Jun-95
$1,847	Bay Apartment Communites Inc	Avalon Properties Inc	Investment & Commodity Firms, Dealers and Exchanges	Mar-98
$1,810	Cornerstone Properties Inc	William Wilson & Associates	Investment & Commodity Firms, Dealers and Exchanges	May-98
$1,793	Felcor Lodging Trust Inc	Bristol Hotel Co	Hotels and Casinos	Mar-98
$1,751	Amvescap PLC	Trimark Financial Corp	Investment & Commodity Firms, Dealers and Exchanges	May-00
$1,729	Pulte Homes Inc	Del Webb Corp	Construction Firms	May-01
$1,715	Excel Realty Trust Inc	New Plan Realty Trust	Investment & Commodity Firms, Dealers and Exchanges	May-98
$1,681	Security Capital Pacific Trust	Security Capital Atlantic Inc	Investment & Commodity Firms, Dealers and Exchanges	Apr-98
$1,599	Invesco PLC	AIM Management Group Inc	Investment & Commodity Firms, Dealers and Exchanges	Nov-96
$1,513	Amvescap PLC	Perpetual PLC	Investment & Commodity Firms, Dealers and Exchanges	Oct-00
$1,500	Investcorp	BATUS Inc-Saks Fifth Avenue	Retail, General Merchandise and Apparel	Apr-90
$1,436	Bell Resources Ltd (Bond Corp)	Bond Australian Brewing Hldgs	Food and Related Products	Sep-89
$1,300	Amvescap PLC	Chancellor LGT Asset Mgmt	Investment & Commodity Firms, Dealers and Exchanges	Jan-98
$1,217	Edper Group Ltd	Brascan Limited	Mining	Apr-97
$1,175	Cali Realty Corporation	Mack Co, Patriot American	Investment & Commodity Firms, Dealers and Exchanges	Aug-97
$1,175	Morgan Stanley Group Inc	Van Kampen/American Capital	Investment & Commodity Firms, Dealers and Exchanges	Jun-96
$1,101	CS Holding AG	Swiss Volksbank	Commercial Banks, Bank Holding Companies	Jan-93
$1,100	Westfield America Inc	TrizecHahn-Shopping Centers (7)	Real Estate; Mortgage Bankers and Brokers	Apr-98
$1,091	Cornerstone Properties Inc	Dutch Institutional Hldg-Ppty	Real Estate; Mortgage Bankers and Brokers	Aug-97
$1,071	Softbank Corp	Kingston Technology Corp	Computer and Office Equipment	Aug-96
$1,051	Westfield America Trust	Westfield America Inc	Investment & Commodity Firms, Dealers and Exchanges	Feb-01
$995	Equity Residential Pptys Trust	Wellsford Residential Ppty	Investment & Commodity Firms, Dealers and Exchanges	Jan-97
$971	Healthcare Realty Trust Inc	Capstone Capital Corp	Investment & Commodity Firms, Dealers and Exchanges	Jun-98
$951	Grupo Financiero Galicia SA	Banco de Galicia, Buenos Aires	Commercial Banks, Bank Holding Companies	May-00
$932	Equity Residential Pptys Trust	Evans Withycombe Residential	Investment & Commodity Firms, Dealers and Exchanges	Aug-97
$931	New Africa Investments Ltd	Theta Group Ltd	Investment & Commodity Firms, Dealers and Exchanges	May-98

Value of Transaction (US$ millions)	Acquirer	Target Company	Target Industry	Date Announced
INVESTMENT & COMMODITY FIRMS, DEALERS, EXCHANGES (continued)				
$913	Franklin Resources Inc	Templeton Galbraith & Hanberge	Investment & Commodity Firms, Dealers and Exchanges	Jul-92
$900	Bear Stearns Cos Inc	HF Ahmanson & Co-Single-Family	Investment & Commodity Firms, Dealers and Exchanges	Jul-93
$900	Standard Chartered PLC	First Interstate Bank-Corp	Investment & Commodity Firms, Dealers and Exchanges	Feb-92
$872	Thomson Advisory Group LP	Cadence Capital Mgmt, 3 others	Investment & Commodity Firms, Dealers and Exchanges	Feb-94
$871	General Growth Properties Inc	MEPC PLC-US Shopping Malls (8)	Real Estate; Mortgage Bankers and Brokers	Apr-98
$871	Kimco Realty Corp	Price REIT Inc	Investment & Commodity Firms, Dealers and Exchanges	Jan-98
$867	Prime Retail Inc	Horizon Group Inc	Investment & Commodity Firms, Dealers and Exchanges	Nov-97
$854	Rashid Hussain Bhd	Kwong Yik Bank Bhd	Commercial Banks, Bank Holding Companies	Oct-96
$850	PIMCO Advisors LP	Oppenheimer Capital LP	Investment & Commodity Firms, Dealers and Exchanges	Nov-97
$849	Brierley Investments Ltd	Mount Charlotte Investments	Hotels and Casinos	Sep-90
$821	Merrill Lynch & Co Inc	Smith New Court PLC	Investment & Commodity Firms, Dealers and Exchanges	Jul-95
$816	Franklin Resources Inc	Fiduciary Trust Co Intl	Investment & Commodity Firms, Dealers and Exchanges	Oct-00
$810	Apartment Investment & Mgmt Co	Insignia Properties Trust	Investment & Commodity Firms, Dealers and Exchanges	Mar-98
$806	Merrill Lynch & Co Inc	Midland Walwyn Inc	Investment & Commodity Firms, Dealers and Exchanges	Jun-98
$806	Franklin Resources Inc	Heine Securities Corp	Investment & Commodity Firms, Dealers and Exchanges	Jun-96
$805	Grupo Sanborns (Grupo Carso)	CompUSA Inc	Retail Trade-Home Furnishings	Jan-00
$787	United Dominion Realty Tr Inc	American Apartment Communities	Investment & Commodity Firms, Dealers and Exchanges	Sep-98
$773	Patriot Amer Hosp/Wyndham Intl	Wyndham Hotel Corp	Hotels and Casinos	Apr-97
$765	Investcorp	Granada Group-Welcome Break	Retail, Restaurants	Feb-97
$725	Spieker Properties Inc	Goldman Sachs-Office, Ind Ppty	Real Estate; Mortgage Bankers and Brokers	Sep-97
$715	Investec Holdings Ltd	Hambros PLC	Commercial Banks, Bank Holding Companies	Apr-98
$711	Baltica Holding A/S	Statsanstalten	Insurance	Dec-91
$700	Simon Property Group Inc	Retail Property Trust	Investment & Commodity Firms, Dealers and Exchanges	Aug-97
$676	Walden Residential Properties	Drever Partners Inc	Real Estate; Mortgage Bankers and Brokers	May-97
$670	PaineWebber Group Inc	Kidder Peabody & Co	Investment & Commodity Firms, Dealers and Exchanges	Oct-94
$663	Apartment Investment & Mgmt Co	Ambassador Apartments Inc	Investment & Commodity Firms, Dealers and Exchanges	Dec-97
$656	Vornado Realty Trust	Mendik Company Inc	Investment & Commodity Firms, Dealers and Exchanges	Mar-97
$637	Storage Equities Inc	Public Storage Inc (OLD)	Construction Firms	Mar-95
$630	Vornado Realty Trust	Merchandise Mart, Apparel Ctr, 3	Real Estate; Mortgage Bankers and Brokers	Jan-98
$625	Equity Office Properties Trust	Wright Runstad Hldgs-Of (10)	Real Estate; Mortgage Bankers and Brokers	Dec-97

Value of Transaction (US$ millions)	Acquirer	Target Company	Target Industry	Date Announced
INVESTMENT & COMMODITY FIRMS, DEALERS, EXCHANGES (continued)				
$625	Camden Property Trust	Paragon Group Inc	Investment & Commodity Firms, Dealers and Exchanges	Dec-96
$623	Direkt Anlage Bank AG	Self Trade	Investment & Commodity Firms, Dealers and Exchanges	Sep-00
$622	Highwoods Properties Inc	Associated Capital Properties	Real Estate; Mortgage Bankers and Brokers	Sep-97
$615	Arden Realty Inc	AEW/LBA Acquisition Co-Office	Real Estate; Mortgage Bankers and Brokers	Jan-98
$612	Brandywine Realty Trust	Lazard Freres-Properteis (68)	Real Estate; Mortgage Bankers and Brokers	Aug-98
$606	New Japan Securities Co Ltd	Wako Securities Co Ltd	Investment & Commodity Firms, Dealers and Exchanges	Mar-99
$600	Post Properties Inc	Columbus Realty Trust	Investment & Commodity Firms, Dealers and Exchanges	Aug-97
$597	CS Holding AG	Bank Leu Ltd (CS Holding AG)	Commercial Banks, Bank Holding Companies	Nov-93
$584	Investcorp	Falcon Building Products Inc	Stone, Clay, Glass and Concrete Products	Mar-97
$583	Grupo Financiero Mexival	Aseguradora Mexicana (Mexico)	Insurance	Sep-93
$575	Robeco NV	Weiss Peck & Greer	Investment & Commodity Firms, Dealers and Exchanges	May-98
$569	Baltica Holding A/S	Statsanstalten Livsforsikring	Credit Institutions	Sep-90
$558	Highwoods Properties Inc	JC Nichols Co	Real Estate; Mortgage Bankers and Brokers	Dec-97
$556	VastNed Offices/Industrial NV	Stichting Pensioen-Coml Ppty	Real Estate; Mortgage Bankers and Brokers	Jul-98
$548	CS Holding AG	New Bank of Argovie	Commercial Banks, Bank Holding Companies	Sep-94
$548	United Dominion Realty Tr Inc	South West Property Trust Inc	Investment & Commodity Firms, Dealers and Exchanges	Oct-96
$538	Highwoods Properties Inc	Crocker Realty Trust Inc	Investment & Commodity Firms, Dealers and Exchanges	Apr-96
$524	Westshore Terminals Income	Westshore Terminals Ltd	Transportation and Shipping (except air)	Jan-97
$502	Developers Diversified Realty	Homart Dvlp-Cmnty Ctrs Div	Real Estate; Mortgage Bankers and Brokers	Oct-95
LEATHER AND LEATHER PRODUCTS				
$3,895	Hanson PLC	Eastern Group (Hanson Trust)	Electric, Gas and Water Distribution	Jul-95
$3,220	Hanson PLC	Quantum Chemical Corp	Chemicals and Related Products	Jun-93
$2,930	Hanson PLC	Beazer PLC (Hanson PLC)	Construction Firms	Sep-91
$1,111	Hanson PLC	General Oriental Securities Co	Business Services	Oct-90
$726	Hanson PLC	Peabody Holding Co	Mining	Feb-90
$706	Orkla A/S	Pripps Ringnes (Orkla, Volvo)	Food and Related Products	Feb-97
$693	Reebok International Ltd	Pentland Holdings	Investment & Commodity Firms, Dealers and Exchanges	Feb-91

Value of Transaction (US$ millions)	Acquirer	Target Company	Target Industry	Date Announced
LEATHER AND LEATHER PRODUCTS (continued)				
$583	Orkla Borregaard A/S	Nora Industrier A/S	Food and Related Products	Jun-91
$577	Orkla Borregaard A/S	BCP Branded Cons Prods-2 Units	Food and Related Products	Apr-95
$576	Magnant SA	Cie des Entrepots et Magasins	Transportation and Shipping (except air)	May-90
MACHINERY				
$9,341	Tyco International Ltd	CIT Group Inc	Credit Institutions	Mar-01
$5,269	Tyco International Ltd	ADT Ltd	Business Services	Mar-97
$4,564	Baker Hughes Inc	Western Atlas Inc	Oil and Gas; Petroleum Refining	May-98
$4,393	Tyco International Ltd	Mallinckrodt Inc	Drugs	Jun-00
$4,083	Linde AG	AGA AB	Chemicals and Related Products	Aug-99
$3,394	Tyco International Ltd	US Surgical Corp	Wholesale Trade, Durable Goods	May-98
$2,671	EVI Inc	EVI Weatherford Inc	Business Services	Mar-98
$2,560	Ingersoll-Rand Co	Thermo King Corp	Machinery	Sep-97
$2,203	Tyco International Ltd	Sensormatic Electronics Corp	Business Services	Aug-01
$1,846	Applied Materials Inc	Etec Systems Inc	Machinery	Jan-00
$1,837	Ingersoll-Rand Co	Hussmann International Inc	Machinery	May-00
$1,770	Tyco International Ltd	Sherwood-Davis & Geck	Measuring, Medical, Photo Equipment; Clocks	Dec-97
$1,599	Friedrich Krupp GmbH	Hoesch AG	Metal and Metal Products	Nov-91
$1,474	United States Filter Corp	Culligan Water Technologies	Machinery	Feb-98
$1,467	Ingersoll-Rand Co	Clark Equipment Co	Wholesale Trade, Durable Goods	Mar-95
$1,362	Tyco International Ltd	Keystone International Inc	Metal and Metal Products	May-97
$1,325	Caterpillar Inc	Perkins Engines Group Ltd	Machinery	Dec-97
$1,270	Tenneco Inc	Mobil Corp-Plastics Division	Rubber and Miscellaneous Plastic Products	Oct-95
$957	Kennametal Inc	Greenfield Industries Inc	Machinery	Oct-97
$856	Tyco International Ltd	TyCom Ltd (Tyco Intl Ltd)	Communications Equipment	Oct-01
$850	Tyco International Ltd	AT&T Submarine Systems Inc	Communications Equipment	Apr-97
$842	Dresser Industries Inc	Baroid Corp	Machinery	Sep-93
$724	Saurer AG	BB Industrie Holding (Bank am)	Investment & Commodity Firms, Dealers and Exchanges	Apr-97
$711	Baker Hughes Inc	Petrolite Corp	Chemicals and Related Products	Feb-97
$610	Camco International Inc	Production Operators Corp	Machinery	Feb-97

Value of Transaction (US$ millions)	Acquirer	Target Company	Target Industry	Date Announced
MACHINERY (continued)				
$591	Charter PLC	Howden Group PLC	Business Services	Mar-97
$558	Baker Hughes Inc	Eastman Christensen Co (Norton)	Machinery	Dec-89
$555	Oce-van der Grinten NV	Hochleistungsdrucke HLD	Computer and Office Equipment	Feb-96
$550	Atlas Copco AB	Milwaukee Electric Tool (Amsta)	Machinery	Jun-95
$541	Weatherford International Inc	Enterra Corp	Business Services	Jun-95
$531	Durco International Inc	BW/IP Inc	Machinery	May-97
$525	Rolls-Royce PLC	Allison Engine Co	Aerospace and Aircraft	Nov-94
$501	Persetel Holdings Ltd	Q Data Ltd	Prepackaged Software	Aug-97
MEASURING, MEDICAL, PHOTO EQUIPMENT; CLOCKS				
$9,500	Raytheon Co	Hughes Aircraft (Hughes Electn)	Measuring, Medical, Photo Equipment; Clocks	Jan-97
$3,304	Medtronic Inc	MiniMed Inc	Measuring, Medical, Photo Equipment; Clocks	May-01
$2,950	Raytheon Co	Texas Instruments-Electronics	Measuring, Medical, Photo Equipment; Clocks	Jan-97
$2,255	Raytheon Co	E-Systems Inc	Measuring, Medical, Photo Equipment; Clocks	Apr-95
$2,100	Boston Scientific Corp	Schneider Worldwide	Measuring, Medical, Photo Equipment; Clocks	Jun-98
$1,661	Incentive AB	Vivra Inc	Health Services	May-97
$1,650	Stryker Corp	Howmedica (Pfizer Inc)	Measuring, Medical, Photo Equipment; Clocks	Jul-98
$1,575	Loral Corp	IBM Federal Systems Co (IBM)	Computer and Office Equipment	Dec-93
$1,569	Incentive AB	Gambro AB (Incentive AB)	Measuring, Medical, Photo Equipment; Clocks	Jan-96
$1,350	Johnson Controls Inc	Prince Automotive	Transportation Equipment	Jul-96
$1,344	KLA Instruments Corp	Tencor Instruments Inc	Electronics and Electrical Equipment	Jan-97
$1,326	Luxottica Group SpA	US Shoe Corp	Retail, General Merchandise and Apparel	Mar-95
$1,275	Emerson Electric Co	Fisher Controls International	Measuring, Medical, Photo Equipment; Clocks	Aug-92
$1,218	Boston Scientific Corp	Target Therapeutics Inc	Measuring, Medical, Photo Equipment; Clocks	Jan-97
$1,150	Beckman Instruments Inc	Coulter Corp	Measuring, Medical, Photo Equipment; Clocks	Sep-97
$1,088	Incentive AB	Investment AB Cardo (Incentive)	Transportation Equipment	Apr-94
$925	Johnson Controls Inc	Becker Group Inc	Rubber and Miscellaneous Plastic Products	Apr-98
$897	Boston Scientific Corp	SciMed Life Systems Inc	Measuring, Medical, Photo Equipment; Clocks	Nov-94
$862	Loral Corp	Unisys Corp-Defense Electn Bus	Electronics and Electrical Equipment	Mar-95
$832	Thermo Electron Corp	Thermo Instrument Systems Inc	Measuring, Medical, Photo Equipment; Clocks	Feb-00

Value of Transaction (US$ millions)	Acquirer	Target Company	Target Industry	Date Announced
MEASURING, MEDICAL, PHOTO EQUIPMENT; CLOCKS (continued)				
$736	American Cyanamid Co	Immunex Corp	Drugs	Dec-92
$733	Agilent Technologies Inc	Objective Systems Integrators	Prepackaged Software	Nov-00
$732	Siebe PLC	Unitech PLC	Electronics and Electrical Equipment	Apr-96
$715	Luxottica Group SpA	Sunglass Hut International Inc	Miscellaneous Retail Trade	Feb-01
$702	Siebe PLC	Eurotherm PLC	Measuring, Medical, Photo Equipment; Clocks	Apr-98
$700	Thoratec Cardiosystems Inc	Thermo Cardiosystems Inc	Measuring, Medical, Photo Equipment; Clocks	Oct-00
$673	Steris Corp	AMSCO International	Measuring, Medical, Photo Equipment; Clocks	Dec-95
$621	SulzerMedica (Sulzer AG)	Spine-Tech Inc	Measuring, Medical, Photo Equipment; Clocks	Dec-97
$597	Honeywell Inc	Measurex Corp	Measuring, Medical, Photo Equipment; Clocks	Jan-97
$577	GENDEX Corp	Dentsply International Inc	Measuring, Medical, Photo Equipment; Clocks	Dec-92
$567	Seton Healthcare Group PLC	Scholl PLC	Wholesale Trade, Nondurable Goods	May-98
$550	Arterial Vascular Engineering	CR Bard Inc-Coronary Catheter	Measuring, Medical, Photo Equipment; Clocks	Jul-98
$532	Eastman Kodak Co Inc	Imation-Medical Imaging Bus	Measuring, Medical, Photo Equipment; Clocks	Aug-98
$529	Medtronic Inc	Physio-Control International	Measuring, Medical, Photo Equipment; Clocks	Jun-98
$525	St Jude Medical Inc	Siemens-Pace, Siemens-Elema	Electronics and Electrical Equipment	Jun-94
$515	Invensys PLC	BAAN Co NV	Prepackaged Software	May-00
$509	Siebe PLC	APV PLC	Holding Companies, Except Banks	May-97
METAL AND METAL PRODUCTS				
$11,511	BHP Ltd	Billiton PLC	Mining	Mar-01
$7,232	Gillette Co	Duracell International Inc	Electronics and Electrical Equipment	Sep-96
$6,077	Alcoa Inc	Reynolds Metals Co	Metal and Metal Products	Aug-99
$4,981	Crown Cork & Seal Co	CarnaudMetalbox	Metal and Metal Products	May-95
$4,789	Alcan Aluminum Ltd	Alusuisse Lonza Group Ltd	Paper and Related Products	Aug-99
$3,348	Inco Ltd	Diamond Fields Resources Inc	Mining	Mar-96
$2,778	Alcoa Inc	Cordant Technologies Inc	Aerospace and Aircraft	Mar-00
$2,432	BHP	Magma Copper Co	Mining	Nov-95
$2,097	Allegheny Ludlum Corp	Teledyne Inc	Measuring, Medical, Photo Equipment; Clocks	Apr-96
$1,960	Mitsubishi Metal Corp	Mitsubishi Mining & Cement Co	Stone, Clay, Glass and Concrete Products	Apr-90
$1,884	Usinor SA	Aceralia	Metal and Metal Products	Feb-01

Value of Transaction (US$ millions)	Acquirer	Target Company	Target Industry	Date Announced
METAL AND METAL PRODUCTS (continued)				
$1,518	Preussag AG	Hapag-Lloyd AG (Preussag AG)	Transportation and Shipping (except air)	Jun-97
$1,427	Ispat International	Inland Steel Co	Metal and Metal Products	Mar-98
$1,250	Usinor SA	Arbed SA	Metal and Metal Products	Feb-01
$1,076	Tostem Corp	INAX Corp	Stone, Clay, Glass and Concrete Products	Apr-01
$930	Sumitomo Metal Industries Ltd	Sumitomo Sitix Corp	Metal and Metal Products	Dec-97
$918	Alcatel Cable SA	STC Submarine Systems	Telecommunications	Jul-93
$829	Precision Castparts Corp	Wyman-Gordon Co	Metal and Metal Products	May-99
$795	Inland Steel Industries Inc	Inland Steel Industries Inc	Metal and Metal Products	Jul-98
$791	US Industries Inc	Zurn Industries Inc	Measuring, Medical, Photo Equipment; Clocks	Feb-98
$747	Pechiney SA	Pechiney International SA	Paper and Related Products	Nov-95
$746	Ball Corp	Reynolds Metals-Aluminum Can	Metal and Metal Products	Dec-97
$725	Tower Automotive (Hidden Creek)	Automotive Products (AO Smith)	Transportation Equipment	Jan-97
$721	Usinor-Sacilor SA	Ugine SA (Usinor-Sacilor)	Metal and Metal Products	Sep-95
$710	Sanwa Shutter Corp	Overhead Door Corp	Wood Products, Furniture and Fixtures	Jun-96
$703	Thyssen AG	Giddings & Lewis Inc	Machinery	Jun-97
$700	Bethlehem Steel Corp	Lukens Inc	Metal and Metal Products	Dec-97
$699	Danaher Corp	Fluke Corp	Measuring, Medical, Photo Equipment; Clocks	Apr-98
$650	Schmalbach-Lubeca AG (E.ON AG)	Johnson Controls-Plastic Div	Rubber and Miscellaneous Plastic Products	Dec-96
$630	GKN PLC	Westland Group PLC	Aerospace and Aircraft	Feb-94
$625	WHX Corp	Handy & Harman	Metal and Metal Products	Jan-98
$590	Gillette Co	Parker Pen Holdings Ltd	Miscellaneous Manufacturing	Sep-92
$578	NCI Building Systems Inc	Metal Building Components Inc	Metal and Metal Products	Mar-98
$551	Onex Corp	Celestica Inc (IBM Canada Ltd)	Electronics and Electrical Equipment	Oct-96
$529	Crown Cork & Seal Co	CONSTAR International Inc	Rubber and Miscellaneous Plastic Products	Sep-92
$500	Kaba Holding AG	Unican Security Systems Ltd	Metal and Metal Products	Dec-00

Value of Transaction (US$ millions)	Acquirer	Target Company	Target Industry	Date Announced
MINING				
$2,822	Newmont Mining Corp	Franco-Nevada Mining Corp Ltd	Mining	Nov-01
$2,657	Cyprus Minerals Co	AMAX Inc	Metal and Metal Products	May-93
$2,506	Newmont Mining Corp	Santa Fe Pacific Gold Corp	Mining	Dec-96
$2,295	Barrick Gold Corp	Homestake Mining Co	Mining	Jun-01
$2,091	Rio Tinto Ltd	North Ltd	Mining	Jun-00
$1,973	Anglo American PLC	Tarmac PLC	Stone, Clay, Glass and Concrete Products	Nov-99
$1,615	American Barrick Resources	Lac Minerals Ltd	Mining	Jul-94
$1,535	Battle Mountain Gold Co	Hemlo Gold Mines Inc	Mining	Mar-96
$1,428	Minorco SA	Anglo American-Selected Mining	Mining	Sep-93
$1,278	Imetal SA (Parfinance)	Parfinance SA	Commercial Banks, Bank Holding Companies	Mar-98
$1,272	RJB Mining PLC	English Coal	Mining	Dec-94
$1,200	Gencor	Cerro Matoso SA (Royal Dutch/1)	Mining	Apr-94
$1,143	Gencor	Billiton Intl-Certain Assets	Mining	May-93
$1,103	Billiton PLC	Rio Algom Ltd	Mining	Aug-00
$902	Rio Tinto Ltd	Comalco Ltd (Rio Tinto Ltd)	Metal and Metal Products	Feb-00
$819	QNI Ltd (Billiton PLC)	Gencor-Nickel Division	Mining	Jun-97
$803	Barrick Gold Corp	Arequipa Resources Ltd	Oil and Gas; Petroleum Refining	Jul-96
$794	Newmont Mining Corp	Battle Mountain Gold Co	Mining	Jun-00
$705	Minorco SA	Freeport McMoRan Gold Co	Mining	Feb-90
$660	Minmet PLC	Connary Minerals PLC	Mining	Jun-98
$650	Homestake Mining Co	Plutonic Resources Ltd	Mining	Dec-97
$644	Normandy Mining Ltd	Gold Mines of Kalgoorlie	Mining	Nov-95
$630	Normandy Mining Ltd	PosGold (Normandy Mining Ltd)	Mining	Nov-95
$610	Vaal Reefs Expl & Mining Co	Western Areas Gold Mining Co	Mining	Nov-97
$560	Vaal Reefs Expl & Mining Co	Free State Consolidated Gold	Mining	Nov-97
$560	Homestake Mining Co	International Corona Corp	Mining	Mar-92
$512	Minorco SA	Tilcon Holdings Ltd (Young)	Mining	Nov-95
$504	Western Areas Gold Mining Co	South Deep Exploration Co Ltd	Mining	Jan-94

Value of Transaction (US$ millions)	Acquirer	Target Company	Target Industry	Date Announced
MISCELLANEOUS MANUFACTURING				
$3,633	Lafarge SA	Perlmooser Zementwerke AG	Stone, Clay, Glass and Concrete Products	Aug-97
$3,012	Lafarge SA	Redland PLC	Stone, Clay, Glass and Concrete Products	Oct-97
$1,435	Tyco International Ltd	Kendall International Inc	Measuring, Medical, Photo Equipment; Clocks	Jul-94
$1,327	International Game Technology	Anchor Gaming Inc	Amusement and Recreation Services	Jul-01
$540	Hasbro Inc	Tonka Corp	Miscellaneous Manufacturing	Jan-91
MISCELLANEOUS RETAIL TRADE				
$3,912	CVS Corp	Revco DS Inc	Drugs	Jan-97
$3,082	Office Depot Inc	Viking Office Products Inc	Miscellaneous Retail Trade	May-98
$3,077	Great Universal Stores PLC	Argos PLC	Retail, General Merchandise and Apparel	Feb-98
$2,394	Rite Aid Corp	Thrifty Payless Holdings Inc	Miscellaneous Retail Trade	Oct-96
$1,844	YPF SA	Maxus Energy Corp	Oil and Gas; Petroleum Refining	Feb-95
$1,700	Great Universal Stores PLC	Experian Corp	Business Services	Nov-96
$1,475	CVS Corp	Arbor Drugs Inc	Miscellaneous Retail Trade	Feb-98
$1,007	Pinault SA	Au Printemps SA (Pinault SA)	Retail, General Merchandise and Apparel	Nov-91
$988	Pinault-Printemps SA	La Redoute (Pinault-Printemps)	Miscellaneous Retail Trade	Feb-94
$863	Capstone Pharmacy Services Inc	Pharmacy Corp of America Inc	Miscellaneous Retail Trade	Apr-97
$838	Great Universal Stores PLC	Metromail Corp	Business Services	Mar-98
$778	Pinault SA	CFAO	Transportation and Shipping (except air)	Sep-90
$759	Pinault SA	Conforama SA	Retail Trade-Home Furnishings	May-91
$666	Staples Inc	Quill Corp	Business Services	Apr-98
$533	Ratners Group PLC	Kay Jewelers Inc	Miscellaneous Retail Trade	Jul-90
MISCELLANEOUS SERVICES				
$11,343	CUC International Inc	HFS Inc	Hotels and Casinos	May-97
$1,145	CUC International Inc	Davidson & Associates Inc	Prepackaged Software	Feb-96
$911	CUC International Inc	Sierra On-Line Inc	Prepackaged Software	Feb-96

Value of Transaction (US$ millions)	Acquirer	Target Company	Target Industry	Date Announced
MOTION PICTURE PRODUCTION AND DISTRIBUTION				
$6,881	Time Warner	Turner Broadcasting System Inc	Radio and Television Broadcasting Stations	Aug-95
$2,412	Time Warner	KBLCOM Inc (Houston Industries)	Radio and Television Broadcasting Stations	Jan-95
$2,272	Vivendi Universal SA	Houghton Mifflin Co	Printing, Publishing and Related Services	Jun-01
$2,094	Time Warner	Cablevision Industries Corp	Radio and Television Broadcasting Stations	Nov-94
$1,700	Time Warner	American Television & Commun	Radio and Television Broadcasting Stations	Oct-91
$1,509	CNET Networks Inc	Ziff-Davis Inc (Softbank Corp)	Printing, Publishing and Related Services	Jul-00
$1,500	General Cinema Corp	Harcourt Brace Jovanovich Inc	Printing, Publishing and Related Services	Jan-91
$564	MCA Inc	Geffen Records	Electronics and Electrical Equipment	Mar-90
$553	Paramount Communications	Macmillan Inc	Printing, Publishing and Related Services	Nov-93
OIL AND GAS: PETROLEUM REFINING				
$50,070	Total Fina SA	Elf Aquitaine	Oil and Gas; Petroleum Refining	Jul-99
$42,872	Chevron Corp	Texaco Inc	Oil and Gas; Petroleum Refining	Oct-00
$27,224	BP Amoco PLC	ARCO	Oil and Gas; Petroleum Refining	Apr-99
$10,947	Texas Utilities Co	Energy Group PLC	Electric, Gas and Water Distribution	Mar-98
$9,388	Phillips Petroleum Co Inc	Tosco Corp	Oil and Gas; Petroleum Refining	Feb-01
$9,091	Transocean Sedco Forex Inc	R&B Falcon Corp	Oil and Gas; Petroleum Refining	Aug-00
$7,250	Anadarko Petroleum Corp	Union Pacific Resources Group	Oil and Gas; Petroleum Refining	Apr-00
$6,759	Electrafina SA	Groupe Bruxelles Lambert SA	Radio and Television Broadcasting Stations	Mar-01
$6,215	Valero Energy Corp	Ultramar Diamond Shamrock Corp	Oil and Gas; Petroleum Refining	May-01
$5,646	Lyondell Petrochemical(ARCO)	ARCO Chemical Co (ARCO)	Chemicals and Related Products	Jun-98
$4,705	BP Amoco PLC	Burmah Castrol PLC	Oil and Gas; Petroleum Refining	Mar-00
$4,562	Devon Energy Corp	Anderson Exploration Ltd	Oil and Gas; Petroleum Refining	Sep-01
$3,990	KN Energy Inc	MidCon Corp (Occidental Petro)	Electric, Gas and Water Distribution	Dec-97
$3,976	ENI SpA	LASMO PLC	Oil and Gas; Petroleum Refining	Dec-00
$3,650	Occidental Petroleum Corp	US of America-Elk Hills Petrol	Oil and Gas; Petroleum Refining	Oct-97
$3,487	Devon Energy Corp	Mitchell Energy & Development	Oil and Gas; Petroleum Refining	Aug-01
$3,448	Union Pacific Resources Group	Norcen Energy Resources Ltd	Oil and Gas; Petroleum Refining	Jan-98
$3,426	Devon Energy Corp	Sante Fe Synder Corp	Oil and Gas; Petroleum Refining	May-00
$3,229	Amerada Hess Corp	Triton Energy Ltd	Oil and Gas; Petroleum Refining	Jul-01

Value of Transaction (US$ millions)	Acquirer	Target Company	Target Industry	Date Announced
OIL AND GAS: PETROLEUM REFINING (continued)				
$2,954	Burlington Resources Inc	Louisiana Land & Exploration	Oil and Gas; Petroleum Refining	Jul-97
$2,741	ARCO	Union Texas Petroleum Holdings	Oil and Gas; Petroleum Refining	May-98
$2,587	Falcon Drilling Co	Reading & Bates Corp	Oil and Gas; Petroleum Refining	Jul-97
$2,556	General Sekiyu(Esso Eastern)	Tonen Corp (Exxon Mobil)	Oil and Gas; Petroleum Refining	Feb-00
$2,080	LASMO PLC	Ultramar PLC	Oil and Gas; Petroleum Refining	Oct-91
$2,050	Tosco Corp	76 Products Co (Unocal Corp)	Miscellaneous Retail Trade	Nov-96
$2,047	Total Fina Elf SA	Elf Aquitaine (Total Fina SA)	Oil and Gas; Petroleum Refining	May-00
$2,025	Burlington Resources Inc	Canadian Hunter Exploration	Oil and Gas; Petroleum Refining	Oct-01
$1,970	Pride International Inc	Marine Drilling Cos	Oil and Gas; Petroleum Refining	May-01
$1,722	Kerr-McGee Corp	HS Resources Inc	Oil and Gas; Petroleum Refining	May-01
$1,634	Epic Energy Inc	Australia-Dampier to Bunbury	Oil and Gas; Petroleum Refining	Mar-98
$1,576	BP Amoco PLC	Vastar Resources Inc	Oil and Gas; Petroleum Refining	Mar-00
$1,464	Gulf Canada Resources Ltd	Crestar Energy Inc	Oil and Gas; Petroleum Refining	Sep-00
$1,435	Texaco Inc	Monterey Resources Inc	Oil and Gas; Petroleum Refining	Aug-97
$1,408	Patterson Energy Inc	UTI Energy Corp	Oil and Gas; Petroleum Refining	Feb-01
$1,345	Sonat Offshore Drilling	Transocean Drilling A/S	Oil and Gas; Petroleum Refining	Apr-96
$1,257	ENI SpA	British Borneo Oil & Gas PLC	Oil and Gas; Petroleum Refining	Mar-00
$1,229	Saga Petroleum AS	Santa Fe Exploration	Oil and Gas; Petroleum Refining	Dec-96
$1,222	NGC Corp	Destec Energy Inc	Electric, Gas and Water Distribution	Feb-97
$1,200	Pioneer Natural Resources Co	Chauvco Resources Ltd	Oil and Gas; Petroleum Refining	Sep-97
$1,191	Caltex Australia (Caltex Petro)	Ampol Ltd (Pioneer Intl Ltd)	Miscellaneous Retail Trade	Nov-94
$1,170	Pennzoil Co	Chevron PBC Inc (Chevron Corp)	Oil and Gas; Petroleum Refining	Sep-92
$1,125	Schlumberger Ltd	Dowell Schlumberger	Chemicals and Related Products	Dec-92
$1,120	Oryx Energy Co	British Petro-North Sea Hldgs	Oil and Gas; Petroleum Refining	Sep-89
$1,076	Canadian Natural Resources Ltd	Ranger Oil Ltd	Oil and Gas; Petroleum Refining	Jun-00
$1,049	Teck Corp	Cominco Ltd	Mining	May-01
$1,048	Westport Resources Corp	Belco Oil & Gas Corp	Oil and Gas; Petroleum Refining	Jun-01
$1,044	USX-Marathon Group	Tarragon Oil and Gas Ltd	Oil and Gas; Petroleum Refining	May-98
$1,043	Talisman Energy Inc	Bow Valley Energy Inc	Oil and Gas; Petroleum Refining	May-94
$1,032	Ocean Energy Inc	United Meridian Corp	Oil and Gas; Petroleum Refining	Dec-97

Value of Transaction (US$ millions)	Acquirer	Target Company	Target Industry	Date Announced
OIL AND GAS: PETROLEUM REFINING (continued)				
$1,014	Anadarko Petroleum Corp	Berkley Petroleum Corp	Oil and Gas; Petroleum Refining	Feb-01
$1,013	NGC Corp	Chevron-Gas Gathering, Process	Electric, Gas and Water Distribution	Jan-96
$983	Tosco Corp	Circle K Corp	Retail Trade, Food Stores	Feb-96
$939	Parker & Parsley Petroleum Co	Mesa Inc	Oil and Gas; Petroleum Refining	Apr-97
$924	Anderson Exploration Ltd	Home Oil Co Ltd	Oil and Gas; Petroleum Refining	Aug-95
$896	Devon Energy Corp	Northstar Energy Corp	Oil and Gas; Petroleum Refining	Jun-98
$886	Petroleum Geo-Services A/S	Awilco-Floating Prodn, Storage	Transportation and Shipping (except air)	Oct-97
$861	Ultramar Corp	Diamond Shamrock Inc	Oil and Gas; Petroleum Refining	Sep-96
$849	TrizecHahn Corp	Sears Tower, Chicago, Illinois	Real Estate; Mortgage Bankers and Brokers	Dec-97
$828	Panhandle Eastern Corp	Associated Natural Gas Corp	Electric, Gas and Water Distribution	Oct-94
$828	Enerplus Resources Fund	EnerMark Income Fund	Oil and Gas; Petroleum Refining	May-01
$824	Ultramar Diamond Shamrock Corp	Total Petroleum (North Amer) Ltd	Oil and Gas; Petroleum Refining	Apr-97
$775	Alberta Energy Co Ltd	Conwest Exploration Co Ltd	Mining	Dec-95
$747	Gulf Canada Resources Ltd	Stampeder Exploration Ltd	Oil and Gas; Petroleum Refining	Jul-97
$724	Renaissance Energy Ltd	Pinnacle Resources Ltd	Oil and Gas; Petroleum Refining	Jun-98
$685	Valero Energy Corp	Basis Petroleum (Salomon Inc)	Oil and Gas; Petroleum Refining	Mar-97
$672	Canadian Oil Sands Trust	Athabasca Oil Sands Trust	Oil and Gas; Petroleum Refining	Mar-01
$670	CSR Ltd	ARC America Corp	Stone, Clay, Glass and Concrete Products	Nov-89
$646	Forest Oil Corp	Forcenergy Inc	Oil and Gas; Petroleum Refining	Jul-00
$642	ARCO	Oryx Energy-Midway-Sunset	Oil and Gas; Petroleum Refining	Nov-90
$616	Pennzoil Co	Proven Properties Inc	Oil and Gas; Petroleum Refining	Aug-89
$592	Anderson Exploration Ltd	Numac Energy Inc	Oil and Gas; Petroleum Refining	Jan-01
$581	BJ Services Co	Nowsco Well Service Ltd	Oil and Gas; Petroleum Refining	Apr-96
$571	Apache Corp	Texaco-Domestic Oil and Gas	Oil and Gas; Petroleum Refining	Nov-94
$570	Arkla Inc	Diversified Energies Inc	Electric, Gas and Water Distribution	Jul-90
$568	British-Borneo Petroleum Syndi	Hardy Oil & Gas PLC	Oil and Gas; Petroleum Refining	Sep-98
$560	TrizecHahn Corp	JBG Cos-Cert Real Estate Asts	Investment & Commodity Firms, Dealers and Exchanges	Sep-97
$543	TrizecHahn Corp	Bell Canada-Commercial RE Asts	Real Estate; Mortgage Bankers and Brokers	Jan-98
$543	Vintage Petroleum	Genesis Exploration Ltd	Oil and Gas; Petroleum Refining	Mar-01
$540	Apache Corp	MW Petroleum Corp	Oil and Gas; Petroleum Refining	May-91

Value of Transaction (US$ millions)	Acquirer	Target Company	Target Industry	Date Announced
OIL AND GAS; PETROLEUM REFINING (continued)				
$538	Petro-Canada	Amerada Hess Canada Ltd	Oil and Gas; Petroleum Refining	Apr-96
$534	Nuevo Energy Co	Unocal Corp-California Crude	Oil and Gas; Petroleum Refining	Feb-96
$518	Ranger Oil Ltd	Elan Energy Inc	Oil and Gas; Petroleum Refining	Sep-97
$517	Diamond Offshore Drilling Inc	Arethusa Offshore Ltd	Oil and Gas; Petroleum Refining	Dec-95
$516	PrimeWest Energy Trust	Cypress Energy Inc	Oil and Gas; Petroleum Refining	Feb-01
$514	Caltex Australia (Caltex Petro)	Ampol Ltd (Caltex, Pioneer)	Holding Companies, Except Banks	Oct-97
$505	Canadian Natural Resources Ltd	Sceptre Resources Ltd	Oil and Gas; Petroleum Refining	Jun-96
$502	Northstar Energy Corp	Morrison Petroleums Ltd	Oil and Gas; Petroleum Refining	Feb-97
OTHER FINANCIAL				
$671	Credit National	BFCE	Commercial Banks, Bank Holding Companies	Dec-95
PAPER AND ALLIED PRODUCTS				
$9,640	International Paper Co	Champion International Corp	Paper and Related Products	Apr-00
$6,823	Kimberly-Clark Corp	Scott Paper Co	Paper and Related Products	Jul-95
$5,683	James River Corp of Virginia	Fort Howard Corp	Paper and Related Products	May-97
$4,940	Stora Enso Oyj	Consolidated Papers Inc	Paper and Related Products	Feb-00
$4,913	Enso Oy	Stora Kopparbergs Bergslags AB	Agriculture, Forestry and Fishing	Jun-98
$4,851	Sealed Air Corp	Grace Packaging (WR Grace & Co)	Chemicals and Related Products	Aug-97
$4,818	Abitibi-Consolidated Inc	Donohue Inc	Paper and Related Products	Feb-00
$3,737	International Paper Co	Federal Paper Board Co	Paper and Related Products	Nov-95
$2,961	Mead Corp	Westvaco Corp	Paper and Related Products	Aug-01
$2,601	New Oji Paper Co	Honshu Paper Co Ltd	Paper and Related Products	Mar-96
$2,331	Bowater Inc	Avenor Inc	Paper and Related Products	Mar-98
$1,978	Rexam PLC	American National Can Group	Metal and Metal Products	Apr-00
$1,935	Svenska Cellulosa AB (SCA)	PWA Papierwerke Waldhof	Holding Companies, Except Banks	Jan-95
$1,808	Svenska Cellulosa AB (SCA)	Reedpack Ltd	Investment & Commodity Firms, Dealers and Exchanges	Jun-90
$1,399	Smurfit-Stone Container Corp	St Laurent Paperboard Inc	Paper and Related Products	Feb-00
$1,313	Sappi Ltd	KNP Leykam (KNP BT)	Paper and Related Products	Sep-97
$1,040	Jefferson Smurfit Group PLC	Cellulose du Pin-Paper & Pkg	Paper and Related Products	Aug-94

Value of Transaction (US$ millions)	Acquirer	Target Company	Target Industry	Date Announced
PAPER AND ALLIED PRODUCTS (continued)				
$1,011	Wiggins Teape Appleton PLC	Arjomari-Prioux SA-Assets	Paper and Related Products	Nov-90
$941	Nippon Paper Industries Co Ltd	Daishowa Paper Mfg Co Ltd	Paper and Related Products	Mar-00
$882	Kimberly-Clark Corp	Safeskin Corp	Rubber and Miscellaneous Plastic Products	Nov-99
$878	International Paper Co	Shorewood Packaging Corp	Paper and Related Products	Feb-00
$764	Bowater Inc	Alliance Forest Products Inc	Paper and Related Products	Apr-01
$761	Donohue Inc	QUNO Corp (Tribune Co)	Paper and Related Products	Dec-95
$708	Kimberly Clark de Mexico SA	Crisoba	Paper and Related Products	Oct-95
$704	Fletcher Challenge Canada Ltd	Crown Forest Inds-Forest Prod	Wood Products, Furniture and Fixtures	Dec-92
$660	Consolidated Papers Inc	Repap USA (Repap Enterprises)	Paper and Related Products	Jul-97
$641	Norske Skog Canada Ltd	Pacifica Papers Inc	Paper and Related Products	Mar-01
$640	Mead Corp	Boise Cascade Group-Coated	Paper and Related Products	Sep-96
$613	Enso-Gutzeit Oy	Tampella Forest Oy, 1 Other	Paper and Related Products	Apr-92
$603	Alliance Forest Products Inc	Kimberly-Clark-Coosa Pines	Paper and Related Products	Dec-96
$575	James River Corp of Virginia	Jamont Holding NV	Printing, Publishing and Related Services	Apr-94
$546	Domtar Inc	EB Eddy Forest Products Ltd	Paper and Related Products	Jun-98
$539	Koninklijke Nederlandse Papier	Buhrmann-Tetterode NV	Paper and Related Products	Nov-92
$530	Enso-Gutzeit Oy	Veitsiluoto Oy (Finland)	Paper and Related Products	May-95
$522	Trinity International Holdings	Thomson Reg Newspapers	Printing, Publishing and Related Services	Jul-95
$508	St Laurent Paperboard Inc	Chesapeake Corp-Kraft-Products	Paper and Related Products	Apr-97
$504	Avery International Corp	Dennison Manufacturing Co	Paper and Related Products	May-90
PERSONAL SERVICES				
$3,373	Cendant Corp	Galileo International Inc	Transportation and Shipping (except air)	Jun-01
$1,485	Cendant Corp	Avis Group Holdings Inc	Repair Services	Aug-00
$1,345	Cendant Corp	National Parking Corp Ltd	Holding Companies, Except Banks	Mar-98
$805	Cendant Corp	Fairfield Communities Inc	Construction Firms	Nov-00

Value of Transaction (US$ millions)	Acquirer	Target Company	Target Industry	Date Announced
PREPACKAGED SOFTWARE				
$164,746	America Online Inc	Time Warner	Motion Picture Production and Distribution	Jan-00
$18,515	Veritas Software Corp	Seagate Technology Inc	Computer and Office Equipment	Mar-00
$7,974	i2 Technologies Inc	Aspect Development Inc	Prepackaged Software	Mar-00
$6,511	3Com Corp	US Robotics Corp	Communications Equipment	Feb-97
$4,207	Kana Communications Inc	Silknet Software Inc	Business Services	Feb-00
$3,720	Computer Associates Intl Inc	Sterling Software Inc	Prepackaged Software	Feb-00
$2,466	Vignette Corp	Ondisplay Inc	Prepackaged Software	May-00
$1,924	Healtheon/WebMD Inc	Medical Manager Corp	Rubber and Miscellaneous Plastic Products	Feb-00
$1,907	Peregrine Systems Inc	Harbinger Corp	Prepackaged Software	Apr-00
$1,884	Healtheon/WebMD Inc	Careinsite Inc (Medical Mgr)	Business Services	Feb-00
$1,799	Computer Associates Intl Inc	Legent Corp	Prepackaged Software	May-95
$1,416	Novell Inc	WordPerfect Corp	Prepackaged Software	Mar-94
$1,413	NetIQ Corp	Mission Critical Software Inc	Prepackaged Software	Feb-00
$1,375	Microsoft Corp	Visio Corp	Prepackaged Software	Sep-99
$1,248	Computer Associates Intl Inc	Cheyenne Software Inc	Prepackaged Software	Oct-96
$1,218	Peregrine Systems Inc	Remedy Corp	Prepackaged Software	Jun-01
$1,142	McAfee Associates Inc	Network General Corp	Business Services	Oct-97
$1,094	FI Group PLC	Druid Group PLC	Business Services	Jan-00
$1,031	NetIQ Corp	WebTrends Corp	Prepackaged Software	Jan-01
$988	Symantec Corp	AXENT Technologies Inc	Prepackaged Software	Jul-00
$958	Rational Software Corp	Pure Atria Corp	Business Services	Apr-97
$940	Microsoft Corp	Great Plains Software Inc	Prepackaged Software	Dec-00
$916	Misys PLC	Medic Computer Systems Inc	Business Services	Sep-97
$909	Informix Corp	Ardent Software Inc	Prepackaged Software	Dec-99
$901	America Online Inc	MapQuest.com Inc	Business Services	Dec-99
$873	VA Linux Systems Inc	Andover.net Inc	Business Services	Feb-00
$858	Siebel Systems Inc	Janna Systems Inc	Business Services	Sep-00
$817	Sybase Inc	Powersoft Corp	Prepackaged Software	Nov-94
$777	BroadVision Inc	Interleaf Inc	Prepackaged Software	Jan-00
$773	Axime	Sligos (Credit Lyonnais/France)	Business Services	Oct-96

Value of Transaction (US$ millions)	Acquirer	Target Company	Target Industry	Date Announced
PREPACKAGED SOFTWARE (continued)				
$731	MedicalLogic Inc/Medscape Inc	Medscape Inc	Business Services	Feb-00
$729	Singular SA	Delta Informatics (Alpha Cr Bk)	Business Services	Oct-99
$681	3Com Corp	Chipcom Corp	Electronics and Electrical Equipment	Jul-95
$642	Network Associates Inc	Dr Solomon's Group PLC	Prepackaged Software	Jun-98
$592	Cap Gemini Sogeti SA (Sogeti)	Hoskyns Group PLC (GEC Siemens)	Prepackaged Software	Jan-90
$591	Konami Co Ltd	People Co Ltd (Mycal Finance)	Amusement and Recreation Services	Jan-01
$580	SoftKey International Inc	Learning Co	Prepackaged Software	Oct-95
$567	Adobe Systems Inc	Frame Technology Corp	Prepackaged Software	Jun-95
$548	Borland International Inc	Ashton-Tate Corp	Prepackaged Software	Jul-91
$544	BCE Emergis Inc (BCE Inc)	United Payors & United Provide	Insurance	Feb-00
$532	Micro Focus Group PLC	Intersolv Inc	Prepackaged Software	Jun-98
$531	Synopsys Inc	Viewlogic Systems Inc	Prepackaged Software	Oct-97
PRINTING, PUBLISHING AND RELATED SERVICES				
$14,110	Time Inc	Warner Communications Inc	Motion Picture Production and Distribution	Mar-89
$4,600	Pearson PLC	Simon & Schuster-Educ, Prof	Printing, Publishing and Related Services	May-98
$3,425	Thomson Corp	West Publishing Co	Printing, Publishing and Related Services	Feb-96
$2,986	News Corp Ltd	Chris-Craft Industries Inc	Radio and Television Broadcasting Stations	Aug-00
$2,521	Pearson PLC	National Computer Systems Inc	Computer and Office Equipment	Jul-00
$2,446	Gannett Co Inc	Central Newspapers Inc	Printing, Publishing and Related Services	Jun-00
$2,352	Gannett Co Inc	Multimedia Inc	Radio and Television Broadcasting Stations	Jul-95
$2,341	Verenigd Bezit VNU (VNU)	ACNielsen Corp	Business Services	Dec-00
$2,287	United News & Media PLC	MAI PLC	Business Services	Feb-96
$2,230	Jefferson Smurfit Corp	Stone Container Corp	Paper and Related Products	May-98
$2,173	News Corp Ltd	New World Commun Grp (Matco)	Radio and Television Broadcasting Stations	Jul-96
$2,100	Verenigd Bezit VNU (VNU)	ITT World Directories Inc	Printing, Publishing and Related Services	Dec-97
$1,901	Wolters Kluwer NV	Commerce Clearing House Inc	Printing, Publishing and Related Services	Nov-95
$1,508	Lagardere Group	Matra-Hachette	Printing, Publishing and Related Services	Apr-93
$1,430	Belo Corp	Providence Journal Co	Radio and Television Broadcasting Stations	Sep-96
$1,352	News Corp Ltd	Heritage Media Corp	Radio and Television Broadcasting Stations	Mar-97

Value of Transaction (US$ millions)	Acquirer	Target Company	Target Industry	Date Announced
PRINTING, PUBLISHING AND RELATED SERVICES (continued)				
$1,346	McClatchy Newspapers Inc	Cowles Media Co Inc	Printing, Publishing and Related Services	Nov-97
$1,331	Bertelsmann AG	RTL Group (Bertelsmann AG)	Radio and Television Broadcasting Stations	Dec-01
$1,300	Bertelsmann AG	Random House Inc	Printing, Publishing and Related Services	Mar-98
$1,132	Times Mirror Co	Chandis Securities (Chandler)	Investment & Commodity Firms, Dealers and Exchanges	Aug-97
$1,094	Tribune Co	Renaissance Commun Corp	Radio and Television Broadcasting Stations	Jul-96
$1,093	New York Times Co	Affiliated Publications Inc	Printing, Publishing and Related Services	Jun-93
$1,081	Thomson Corp	Primark Corp	Business Services	Jun-00
$1,064	De La Rue PLC	Portals Group PLC	Paper and Related Products	Dec-94
$991	Lagardere Group	Hachette Filipacchi Medias	Printing, Publishing and Related Services	Apr-00
$901	Hachette SA (Marlis SA)	Matra SA (Matra-Hachette)	Aerospace and Aircraft	Jan-92
$888	News Corp Ltd	BHC Communications Inc	Radio and Television Broadcasting Stations	Aug-00
$858	United News & Media PLC	Blenheim Group PLC	Amusement and Recreation Services	Oct-96
$790	News Corp Ltd	United Television Inc	Radio and Television Broadcasting Stations	Aug-00
$781	Elsevier NV (Reed Internat PLC)	Pergamon Press PLC	Printing, Publishing and Related Services	Mar-91
$776	Harcourt General Inc	National Education Corp	Educational Services	Apr-97
$726	Seat Pagine Gialle SPA	Buffetti	Wholesale Trade, Nondurable Goods	Dec-99
$710	Media General Inc	Park Acquisitions Inc	Printing, Publishing and Related Services	Jul-96
$700	PRIMEDIA Inc	About.com Inc	Business Services	Oct-00
$682	Dow Jones & Co Inc	Telerate Inc (Dow Jones & Co)	Business Services	Sep-89
$650	PRIMEDIA Inc	Murdoch Magazines (News Corp)	Printing, Publishing and Related Services	Apr-91
$580	Pearson PLC	HarperCollins Educational	Printing, Publishing and Related Services	Feb-96
$568	RR Donnelley & Sons Co	Meredith-Burda Cos	Printing, Publishing and Related Services	Dec-89
$560	Bonnier Group	Tidnings Marieberg AB	Printing, Publishing and Related Services	Mar-98
$525	News Corp Ltd	HutchVision Ltd	Radio and Television Broadcasting Stations	Jul-93
$510	Quebecor Inc	Maxwell Graphics Inc	Printing, Publishing and Related Services	Oct-89
$500	Pearson PLC	All American Communications	Motion Picture Production and Distribution	Sep-97

RADIO AND TELEVISION BROADCASTING STATIONS

Value of Transaction (US$ millions)	Acquirer	Target Company	Target Industry	Date Announced
$23,112	Clear Channel Communications	AMFM Inc	Radio and Television Broadcasting Stations	Oct-99
$11,398	US WEST Media Group	Continental Cablevision Inc	Radio and Television Broadcasting Stations	Feb-96
$5,275	HSN Inc	Universal Studios-TV assets	Motion Picture Production and Distribution	Oct-97
$4,171	Clear Channel Communications	SFX Entertainment Inc	Amusement and Recreation Services	Feb-00
$3,700	Telewest Communications PLC	Flextech PLC	Motion Picture Production and Distribution	Jan-00
$3,411	Tele-Communications Inc	Liberty Media Corp	Radio and Television Broadcasting Stations	Oct-93
$2,985	Liberty Media Group (AT&T Corp)	Associated Group Inc	Telecommunications	Jun-99
$2,536	Liberty Media Group (AT&T Corp)	UnitedGlobalCom Inc	Radio and Television Broadcasting Stations	Feb-01
$2,441	CBS Corp	American Radio Systems Corp	Radio and Television Broadcasting Stations	Sep-97
$2,050	Tele-Communications Inc	TCI Pacific Communications Inc	Radio and Television Broadcasting Stations	Jul-95
$1,998	TCI Satellite Entertainment	Primestar Inc	Radio and Television Broadcasting Stations	Jun-97
$1,628	Clear Channel Communications	Universal Outdoor Holdings Inc	Advertising Services	Oct-97
$1,574	Comcast Corp	EW Scripps Co-Cable TV Systems	Radio and Television Broadcasting Stations	Oct-95
$1,441	Canal Plus SA	NetHold BV	Radio and Television Broadcasting Stations	Sep-96
$1,411	Continental Cablevision Inc	Providence Journal-Cable Sys	Radio and Television Broadcasting Stations	Nov-94
$1,313	USA Networks Inc	Expedia Inc	Transportation and Shipping (except air)	Jul-01
$1,270	Comcast Corp	Maclean Hunter Ltd-US Cable	Radio and Television Broadcasting Stations	Jun-94
$1,261	Tele-Communications Inc	TeleCable Corp	Radio and Television Broadcasting Stations	Aug-94
$1,217	Silver King Communications Inc	Home Shopping Network (Liberty)	Miscellaneous Retail Trade	Aug-96
$1,200	Sinclair Broadcast Group Inc	River City Broadcasting LP	Radio and Television Broadcasting Stations	Apr-96
$1,189	Tele-Communications Inc	United Artists Entertainment	Motion Picture Production and Distribution	May-91
$1,150	Clear Channel Communications	Eller Media Corp	Advertising Services	Feb-97
$1,118	Telewest Communications PLC	General Cable PLC	Radio and Television Broadcasting Stations	Mar-98
$1,091	Cablevision Systems Corp	Tele-Commun-New York Area	Radio and Television Broadcasting Stations	Jun-97
$1,000	Sinclair Broadcast Group Inc	Sullivan Broadcast Holdings	Radio and Television Broadcasting Stations	Feb-98
$997	NTL Inc	Comcast UK Cable Partners Ltd	Radio and Television Broadcasting Stations	Feb-98
$930	Chancellor Media Corp	Whiteco Outdoor Advertising	Advertising Services	Aug-98
$908	NTL Inc	ComTel Ltd	Radio and Television Broadcasting Stations	Jun-98
$870	Price Communications Corp	Palmer Wireless Inc	Telecommunications	May-97
$843	Tele-Communications Inc	TKR Cable Co	Radio and Television Broadcasting Stations	Mar-96

Value of Transaction (US$ millions)	Acquirer	Target Company	Target Industry	Date Announced
RADIO AND TELEVISION BROADCASTING STATIONS (continued)				
$802	Tele-Communications Inc	Kearns-Tribune LLC	Printing, Publishing and Related Services	Apr-97
$775	Clear Channel Communications	More Group PLC	Advertising Services	Mar-98
$768	Jacor Communications Inc	Citicasters Inc	Radio and Television Broadcasting Stations	Feb-96
$759	Shaw Communications Inc	Moffat Communications Ltd	Radio and Television Broadcasting Stations	Dec-00
$749	Liberty Media Group (AT&T Corp)	Ascent Entertainment Group Inc	Motion Picture Production and Distribution	Feb-00
$688	USA Networks Inc	Precision Response Corp	Business Services	Jan-00
$687	American Radio Systems Corp	EZ Communications Inc	Radio and Television Broadcasting Stations	Aug-96
$669	Evergreen Media Corp	Chancellor Broadcasting Co	Radio and Television Broadcasting Stations	Feb-97
$638	Chancellor Media Corp	Capstar Bdcstg-Radio Statn (11)	Radio and Television Broadcasting Stations	Feb-98
$630	Sinclair Broadcast Group Inc	Heritage Media-Radio & TV	Radio and Television Broadcasting Stations	Jul-97
$629	Clear Channel Communications	Paxson Communications-Entire	Radio and Television Broadcasting Stations	Jun-97
$620	Jacor Communications Inc	Nationwide Commun-Radio (17)	Radio and Television Broadcasting Stations	Oct-97
$615	Cablevision Systems Corp	Madison Square Garden Corp	Amusement and Recreation Services	Feb-97
$610	Chancellor Media Corp	Martin Media LP	Advertising Services	Jun-98
$607	Bell Cablemedia PLC	Cable Road (UK) Ltd	Radio and Television Broadcasting Stations	Oct-96
$565	Tele-Communications Inc	Chronicle Publishing Co-Cable	Radio and Television Broadcasting Stations	Jun-95
$500	Comcast Corp	Philadelphia 76ers Basketball	Amusement and Recreation Services	Mar-96
REAL ESTATE; MORTGAGE BANKERS AND BROKERS				
$14,904	Halifax Group PLC	Bank of Scotland PLC	Commercial Banks, Bank Holding Companies	May-01
$2,200	Fund American Cos Inc	Fireman's Fund Ins-Assets	Insurance	Aug-90
$1,401	GFC	Union Immobiliere de France	Real Estate; Mortgage Bankers and Brokers	May-98
$984	Cambridge Shopping Centres Ltd	Markborough Properties Inc	Real Estate; Mortgage Bankers and Brokers	Apr-97
$978	United Industrial Corp Ltd	Singapore Land Ltd	Real Estate; Mortgage Bankers and Brokers	Apr-90
$952	Security Capital Group Inc	Security Capital US Realty	Investment & Commodity Firms, Dealers and Exchanges	Sep-00
$846	Mitsubishi Estate Co	Rockefeller Group Inc	Real Estate; Mortgage Bankers and Brokers	Oct-89
$790	Persimmon PLC	Beazer Homes PLC	Construction Firms	Jan-01
$762	Daiei Agora Corp (Daiei Inc)	Jujiya Co	Retail Trade, Food Stores	Apr-95
$736	Sefimeg (Fimalac)	Fourmi Immobiliere	Real Estate; Mortgage Bankers and Brokers	Jul-96
$714	Liberty International PLC	Capital Shopping Centres PLC	Real Estate; Mortgage Bankers and Brokers	Sep-00

Value of Transaction (US$ millions)	Acquirer	Target Company	Target Industry	Date Announced
REAL ESTATE; MORTGAGE BANKERS AND BROKERS (continued)				
$679	Wihlborgs Fastigheter AB	Klovern Foervaltnings AB	Real Estate; Mortgage Bankers and Brokers	Sep-97
$620	Ladbroke Group PLC (Hilton Grp)	Coral Group (Bass PLC)	Amusement and Recreation Services	Jan-98
$604	Brookfield Properties Corp	World Financial Properties Inc	Real Estate; Mortgage Bankers and Brokers	Apr-98
$596	WCM Beteiligungs	Kloeckner-Werke AG	Rubber and Miscellaneous Plastic Products	Nov-00
$565	Jacobs Holdings PLC	B&C Breakdown Services	Business Services	Oct-97
$555	Unibail	Cie Fonciere-Ppty Portfolio	Real Estate; Mortgage Bankers and Brokers	May-94
$527	Mitsubishi Estate Co	Rockefeller Group Inc	Real Estate; Mortgage Bankers and Brokers	Oct-89
$522	Pillar Property PLC	Wates City of London Props PLC	Real Estate; Mortgage Bankers and Brokers	Nov-00
$521	Capital Shopping Centres PLC	Church of England-MetroCentre	Construction Firms	Jun-95
$519	Boston Properties Inc	Prudential Ins-Prudential Ctr	Real Estate; Mortgage Bankers and Brokers	Jan-98
REPAIR SERVICES				
$1,681	Team Rental Group Inc	Budget Rent-A-Car Corp	Repair Services	Jan-97
$699	Budget Group Inc	Ryder TRS Inc	Repair Services	Mar-98
RETAIL TRADE - EATING AND DRINKING PLACES				
$911	Compass Group PLC	Eurest (Intl des Wagon-Lits)	Retail, Restaurants	Jun-95
$813	Greenalls Group PLC	Boddington Group PLC	Food and Related Products	Oct-95
$743	Luminar PLC	Northern Leisure PLC	Retail, Restaurants	May-00
$573	Compass Group PLC	Morrison Management Specialist	Retail, Restaurants	Feb-01
$545	Compass Group PLC	Selecta Group	Miscellaneous Retail Trade	Feb-01
RETAIL TRADE - FOOD STORES				
$15,837	Carrefour SA	Promodes	Retail Trade, Food Stores	Aug-99
$3,713	Food Lion Inc	Hannaford Bros Co	Retail Trade, Food Stores	Aug-99
$3,619	Koninklijke Ahold NV	US Foodservice Inc	Wholesale Trade, Nondurable Goods	Mar-00
$2,871	Koninklijke Ahold NV	Stop & Shop Cos	Retail Trade, Food Stores	Mar-96
$2,865	Carrefour SA	Comptoirs Modernes SA	Retail Trade, Food Stores	Aug-98
$2,634	Koninklijke Ahold NV	Giant Food Inc	Retail Trade, Food Stores	May-98
$2,252	Safeway Inc	Vons Cos Inc	Retail Trade, Food Stores	Oct-96

Value of Transaction (US$ millions)	Acquirer	Target Company	Target Industry	Date Announced
RETAIL TRADE - FOOD STORES (continued)				
$2,018	Fred Meyer Inc	Smith's Food & Drug Centers	Retail Trade, Food Stores	May-97
$1,854	Safeway Inc	Dominick's Supermarkets Inc	Retail Trade, Food Stores	Oct-98
$1,088	Koninklijke Ahold NV	Superdiplo SA	Retail Trade, Food Stores	Sep-00
$1,003	Tesco PLC	Associated British Foods-Irish	Retail Trade, Food Stores	Mar-97
$955	Iceland Group PLC	Booker PLC	Wholesale Trade, Nondurable Goods	May-00
$794	Circle K Japan Co Ltd	Sunkus & Associates Inc	Retail Trade, Food Stores	Sep-00
$780	Somerfield PLC	Kwik Save Group PLC	Retail Trade, Food Stores	Feb-98
$577	Casino Groupe	Etablissements Baud SA	Retail Trade, Food Stores	Sep-97
$572	Casino Groupe	TLC Beatrice Intl-Food Distn	Wholesale Trade, Nondurable Goods	Sep-97
$544	ASDA Group PLC	Burwood House (ASDA, British)	Real Estate; Mortgage Bankers and Brokers	Aug-95
RETAIL TRADE - GENERAL MERCHANDISE AND APPAREL				
$3,449	Federated Department Stores	RH Macy & Co Inc	Retail, General Merchandise and Apparel	Dec-93
$3,299	JC Penney Co	Eckerd Corp	Miscellaneous Retail Trade	Nov-96
$3,282	Proffitt's Inc	Saks Holdings	Retail, General Merchandise and Apparel	Jul-98
$3,096	Fred Meyer Inc	Food 4 Less Holdings Inc	Retail Trade, Food Stores	Nov-97
$2,943	Dillard's Inc	Mercantile Stores Co Inc	Retail, General Merchandise and Apparel	May-98
$2,732	CIFRA SA de CV	JV-Wal-Mart Stores Inc, CIFRA	Retail Trade, Food Stores	Jun-97
$1,825	Etablissements Delhaize Fréres	Delhaize America Inc	Retail Trade, Food Stores	Sep-00
$1,703	Fred Meyer Inc	Quality Food Centers Inc	Retail Trade, Food Stores	Nov-97
$1,666	Costco Wholesale Corp	Price Co	Retail, General Merchandise and Apparel	Jun-93
$1,614	Federated Department Stores	Broadway Stores (Federated Dep)	Retail, General Merchandise and Apparel	Aug-95
$1,506	Kingfisher PLC	Financiere Darty SA	Retail Trade-Home Furnishings	Feb-93
$1,104	Vendex International NV	Koninklijke Bijenkorf Beheer	Retail, General Merchandise and Apparel	Feb-98
$1,050	Dayton Hudson Corp	Marshall Field & Co (BATUS Inc)	Retail, General Merchandise and Apparel	Apr-90
$994	Consolidated Stores Corp	Mac Frugal's Bargains	Wholesale Trade, Nondurable Goods	Nov-97
$931	Karstadt AG	Hertie Waren und Kaufhaus GmbH	Retail, General Merchandise and Apparel	Nov-93
$868	Proffitt's Inc	Carson Pirie Scott & Co	Miscellaneous Retail Trade	Oct-97
$867	Pinault-Printemps Redoute	Gucci Group NV	Leather and Leather Products	Sep-01

Value of Transaction (US$ millions)	Acquirer	Target Company	Target Industry	Date Announced
RETAIL TRADE - GENERAL MERCHANDISE AND APPAREL (continued)				
$823	Centros Comerciales Pryca SA	Centros Comerciales Continente	Miscellaneous Retail Trade	Sep-99
$704	Pinault-Printemps Redoute	Guilbert SA	Wholesale Trade, Nondurable Goods	Jan-98
$550	TJX Co Inc	Marshall's Inc (Melville Corp)	Retail, General Merchandise and Apparel	Oct-95
RETAIL TRADE - HOME FURNISHINGS				
$715	Dixons Group PLC	Elkjop ASA	Retail Trade-Home Furnishings	Nov-99
$580	Amalgamated Retail Ltd	Beares Group (McCarthy Retail)	Retail Trade-Home Furnishings	Jun-98
RUBBER AND MISCELLANEOUS PLASTIC PRODUCTS				
$3,294	BTR PLC	BTR Nylex Ltd (BTR PLC)	Rubber and Miscellaneous Plastic Products	Jul-95
$2,731	BTR PLC	Hawker Siddeley Group PLC	Electronics and Electrical Equipment	Sep-91
$1,930	Continental AG	ITT Industries Inc-Automotive	Transportation Equipment	Jul-98
$1,500	Michelin et Cie	Uniroyal Goodrich Tire Co	Rubber and Miscellaneous Plastic Products	Sep-89
$1,124	Armstrong World Industries Inc	Triangle Pacific Corp	Wood Products, Furniture and Fixtures	Jun-98
$621	BTR Nylex Ltd (BTR PLC)	FM Holdings Inc	Paper and Related Products	Dec-94
$583	BTR PLC	Exide Electronics Group Inc	Electronics and Electrical Equipment	Oct-97
SANITARY SERVICES				
$2,350	Republic Industries Inc	National Car Rental System Inc	Repair Services	Jan-97
$1,804	Laidlaw Environmental Services	Safety-Kleen Corp	Business Services	Nov-97
$1,682	USA Waste Services Inc	United Waste Systems Inc	Sanitary Services	Apr-97
$1,651	Allied Waste Industries Inc	Laidlaw Waste Systems Inc	Sanitary Services	Sep-96
$1,450	SITA (Suez Lyonnaise des Eaux)	Browning-Ferris-Non Amer Asts	Sanitary Services	Nov-97
$1,276	Waste Management Inc	Eastern Environmental Services	Sanitary Services	Aug-98
$1,237	USA Waste Services Inc	Sanifill Inc	Sanitary Services	Jun-96
$1,067	Allied Waste Industries Inc	American Disposal Services Inc	Sanitary Services	Aug-98
$990	Rollins Environmental Services	Laidlaw Environmental Services	Sanitary Services	Jan-97
$870	Waste Management Inc	Wheelabrator Technologies Inc	Measuring, Medical, Photo Equipment; Clocks	Jun-97
$815	Republic Industries Inc	Alamo Rent-A-Car Inc	Repair Services	Nov-96
$810	USA Waste Services Inc	City Management Holdings Trust	Sanitary Services	Dec-97

Value of Transaction (US$ millions)	Acquirer	Target Company	Target Industry	Date Announced
SANITARY SERVICES (continued)				
$725	USA Waste Services Inc	Chambers Development Co Inc	Sanitary Services	Nov-94
$646	Republic Industries Inc	AutoNation USA	Miscellaneous Retail Trade	Mar-96
$528	Browning-Ferris Industries Inc	Attwoods PLC (Browning Ferris)	Sanitary Services	Sep-94
$518	USA Waste Services Inc	Allied Waste Inds-Canadian	Sanitary Services	Jan-97
$507	Philip Environmental Inc	Allwaste Inc	Sanitary Services	Mar-97
$500	Waste Management Inc	Wheelabrator Technologies Inc	Measuring, Medical, Photo Equipment; Clocks	Apr-90
SAVINGS AND LOANS, MUTUAL SAVINGS BANKS				
$14,725	Washington Mutual, Seattle, WA	HF Ahmanson & Co, Irwindale, CA	Savings and Loans, Mutual Savings Banks	Mar-98
$6,848	Washington Mutual, Seattle, WA	Great Western Finl Corp, CA	Savings and Loans, Mutual Savings Banks	Mar-97
$5,204	Washington Mutual, Seattle, WA	Dime Bancorp Inc, New York, NY	Savings and Loans, Mutual Savings Banks	Jun-01
$1,891	Washington Mutual, Seattle, WA	American Svgs Bk FA, Irvine, CA	Savings and Loans, Mutual Savings Banks	Jun-96
$1,732	Astoria Finl,Lake Success, NY	Long Island Bancorp, NY	Savings and Loans, Mutual Savings Banks	Apr-98
$1,419	Washington Mutual, Seattle, WA	Bank United Corp, Houston, TX	Savings and Loans, Mutual Savings Banks	Aug-00
$903	HF Ahmanson & Co, Irwindale, CA	Coast Savings Financial Inc, CA	Savings and Loans, Mutual Savings Banks	Oct-97
$828	Charter One Finl, Cleveland, OH	ALBANK Financial Corp, NY	Savings and Loans, Mutual Savings Banks	Jun-98
$663	Washington Mutual, Seattle, WA	Pacific First Bank FSB, Seattle, WA	Savings and Loans, Mutual Savings Banks	Oct-92
$634	Charter One Finl, Cleveland, OH	RCSB Finl Inc, Rochester, NY	Commercial Banks, Bank Holding Companies	May-97
$570	Charter One Finl, Cleveland, OH	FirstFed Michigan Corp	Savings and Loans, Mutual Savings Banks	May-95
$533	Dime Bancorp Inc	Anchor Bancorp Inc, New York, NY	Savings and Loans, Mutual Savings Banks	Jul-94
SOAPS, COSMETICS, AND PERSONAL-CARE PRODUCTS				
$2,470	LVMH Moet-Hennessy L Vuitton	DFS Group Ltd	Miscellaneous Retail Trade	Oct-96
$2,004	Procter & Gamble Co	Tambrands Inc	Paper and Related Products	Apr-97
$1,540	Tomkins PLC	Ranks Hovis McDougall PLC	Holding Companies, Except Banks	Oct-92
$1,400	Tomkins PLC	Gates Corp	Rubber and Miscellaneous Plastic Products	Dec-95
$1,289	Henkel KGaA	Loctite Corp	Chemicals and Related Products	Oct-96
$1,196	Hindustan Lever Ltd	Brooke Bond Lipton India Ltd	Agriculture, Forestry and Fishing	Apr-96
$1,060	Procter & Gamble Co	Revlon Inc-Max Factor, Betrix	Soaps, Cosmetics and Personal-Care Products	Apr-91
$1,040	Colgate-Palmolive Co	American Home Prod-Kolynos Bus	Soaps, Cosmetics and Personal-Care Products	Jan-95

Value of Transaction (US$ millions)	Acquirer	Target Company	Target Industry	Date Announced
SOAPS, COSMETICS, AND PERSONAL-CARE PRODUCTS (continued)				
$786	L'Oreal SA (Gesparal)	Maybelline Inc	Soaps, Cosmetics and Personal-Care Products	Dec-95
$670	Colgate-Palmolive Co	Mennen Co	Soaps, Cosmetics and Personal-Care Products	Nov-91
$620	LVMH Moet-Hennessy L Vuitton	BSN-Lanson, Pommery Champagne	Food and Related Products	Dec-90
$574	Tomkins PLC	Stant Corp (Bessemer Capital Partners)	Transportation Equipment	Apr-97
$552	Henkel KGaA	Barnangen (Nobel Industrier)	Soaps, Cosmetics and Personal-Care Products	Jan-92
$532	LVMH Moet-Hennessy L Vuitton	Celine(Au Bon Agache)	Wholesale Trade, Nondurable Goods	Mar-95
$529	Tomkins PLC	Phillips Industries Inc	Electronics and Electrical Equipment	Jun-90
STONE, CLAY, GLASS AND CONCRETE PRODUCTS				
$3,738	Lafarge SA	Blue Circle Industries PLC	Stone, Clay, Glass and Concrete Products	Jan-01
$3,600	Owens-Illinois Inc	BTR PLC-Global Packaging	Stone, Clay, Glass and Concrete Products	Mar-98
$2,846	Cemex	Southdown Inc	Stone, Clay, Glass and Concrete Products	Sep-00
$2,549	Hanson PLC	Pioneer International Ltd	Stone, Clay, Glass and Concrete Products	Nov-99
$2,043	Cie de Saint-Gobain SA	Meyer International PLC	Wholesale Trade, Durable Goods	Feb-00
$1,840	Cie de Saint-Gobain SA	Norton Co (Cie De Saint-Gobain)	Stone, Clay, Glass and Concrete Products	Apr-90
$1,452	RMC Group PLC	Rugby Group PLC	Stone, Clay, Glass and Concrete Products	Nov-99
$1,222	Heidelberger Zement AG	Cimenteries CBR(Heidelberger)	Stone, Clay, Glass and Concrete Products	Oct-99
$1,184	MB-Caradon PLC	RTZ Corp PLC-Pillar,Elec Divs	Metal and Metal Products	Aug-93
$1,100	Asahi Glass Co	AFG Industries Inc	Stone, Clay, Glass and Concrete Products	Jun-92
$1,087	Redland PLC	Steetley PLC	Wood Products, Furniture and Fixtures	Dec-91
$1,058	Chichibu Onoda Cement Co	Nihon Cement Co Ltd	Stone, Clay, Glass and Concrete Products	Oct-97
$1,053	Southdown Inc	Medusa Corp	Stone, Clay, Glass and Concrete Products	Mar-98
$690	Lafarge Corp (Lafarge Coppee)	Lafarge-N Amer Cnstrn Mtrl Bus	Stone, Clay, Glass and Concrete Products	Mar-98
$680	Sumitomo Cement Co Ltd	Osaka Cement	Stone, Clay, Glass and Concrete Products	Mar-94
$650	Holcim Ltd	Semen Cibinong PT	Stone, Clay, Glass and Concrete Products	Nov-01
$635	Holderbank Financiere Glarus	Cedest	Chemicals and Related Products	May-94
$631	Owens Corning	Fibreboard Corp	Wood Products, Furniture and Fixtures	May-97
$575	Newell Rubbermaid Inc	Sanford Corp	Miscellaneous Manufacturing	Nov-91
$552	RMC Group PLC	Readymix AG fuer Beteiligungen	Stone, Clay, Glass and Concrete Products	Sep-95
$548	Boral Ltd	Sagasco Holdings Ltd	Oil and Gas; Petroleum Refining	Sep-93

Value of Transaction (US$ millions)	Acquirer	Target Company	Target Industry	Date Announced
TELECOMMUNICATIONS				
$202,785	Vodafone AirTouch PLC	Mannesmann AG	Telecommunications	Nov-99
$56,307	Qwest Commun Int Inc	US WEST Inc	Telecommunications	Jun-99
$53,415	Bell Atlantic Corp	GTE Corp	Telecommunications	Jul-98
$49,279	AT&T Corp	MediaOne Group Inc	Radio and Television Broadcasting Stations	Apr-99
$41,907	WorldCom Inc	MCI Communications Corp	Telecommunications	Oct-97
$29,404	Deutsche Telekom AG	VoiceStream Wireless Corp	Telecommunications	Jul-00
$21,345	Bell Atlantic Corp	NYNEX Corp	Telecommunications	Apr-96
$16,490	SBC Communications Inc	Pacific Telesis Group	Telecommunications	Apr-96
$15,822	DDI Corp	KDD Corp	Telecommunications	Dec-99
$15,652	American Telephone & Telegraph	McCaw Cellular Commun Inc	Telecommunications	Aug-93
$13,596	WorldCom Inc	MFS Communications Co Inc	Telecommunications	Aug-96
$11,188	AT&T Corp	Teleport Communications Group	Telecommunications	Jan-98
$10,213	Telefonica SA	Telecomunicacoes de Sao Paulo	Telecommunications	Jan-00
$7,893	American Telephone & Telegraph	NCR Corp	Computer and Office Equipment	Dec-90
$6,407	Teleglobe Inc	Excel Communications Inc	Telecommunications	Jun-98
$6,321	Telecom Italia SpA	Telecom Italia SpA	Telecommunications	Nov-96
$6,243	GTE Corp	Contel Corp	Telecommunications	Jul-90
$6,153	VoiceStream Wireless Corp	Powertel Inc	Telecommunications	Aug-00
$5,949	ALLTEL Corp	360 Communications Co	Telecommunications	Mar-98
$5,828	SBC Communications Inc	Southern New England Telecomm	Telecommunications	Jan-98
$5,676	AirTouch Communications Inc	MediaOne Grp-Wireless & Cable	Telecommunications	Jan-98
$5,066	Bell Canada Enterprises Inc	Teleglobe Inc	Telecommunications	Feb-00
$4,931	Tiscali SpA	World Online International NV	Business Services	Sep-00
$4,884	TeleCorp PCS Inc	Tritel Inc	Telecommunications	Feb-00
$4,816	VoiceStream Wireless Corp	Omnipoint Corp	Telecommunications	Jun-99
$4,785	AT&T Wireless Services Inc	TeleCorp PCS Inc	Telecommunications	Oct-01
$4,750	US WEST Communications Inc	US WEST Media Grp-US WEST Dex	Printing, Publishing and Related Services	May-97
$4,612	Telefonica SA	Endemol Entertainment NV	Motion Picture Production and Distribution	Mar-00
$4,532	Telus Corp	Clearnet Communications Inc	Telecommunications	Aug-00
$4,154	WorldCom Inc	Intermedia Communications Inc	Telecommunications	Sep-00

Value of Transaction (US$ millions)	Acquirer	Target Company	Target Industry	Date Announced
TELECOMMUNICATIONS (continued)				
$3,967	Sprint Corp	Centel Corp	Telecommunications	May-92
$3,880	Telecom Italia (Ing C Olivetti)	Telecom Italia Mobile SpA	Telecommunications	Jul-00
$3,841	SBC Communications Inc	Sterling Commerce Inc	Prepackaged Software	Feb-00
$3,718	Telefonica SA	Telefonica de Argentina SA	Telecommunications	Jan-00
$2,793	Global Crossing Ltd	IPC Communications (Citicorp)	Business Services	Feb-00
$2,684	Vodafone Group PLC	Japan Telecom Co Ltd	Telecommunications	Sep-01
$2,647	Hutchison Whampoa Ltd	Cheung Kong Infrastructure	Construction Firms	Jan-97
$2,533	WorldCom Inc	Brooks Fiber Properties Inc	Telecommunications	Oct-97
$2,500	LDDS Communications Inc	Williams Telecomm Group Inc	Telecommunications	May-94
$2,478	VoiceStream Wireless Corp	Aerial Communications Inc	Telecommunications	Sep-99
$2,464	Bell Atlantic Corp	Metro Mobile CTS Inc	Telecommunications	Sep-91
$2,432	Telefonica SA	Telesudeste Celular	Telecommunications	Jan-00
$2,230	Cable & Wireless PLC	Nynex CableComms (NYNEX)	Radio and Television Broadcasting Stations	Oct-96
$2,225	Century Telephone Enterprises	Pacific Telecom (PacifiCorp)	Telecommunications	Jun-97
$2,095	Rogers Communications Inc	Maclean Hunter(Rogers Commun)	Radio and Television Broadcasting Stations	Feb-94
$2,063	NextLink Communications Inc	Concentric Network Corp	Telecommunications	Jan-00
$2,061	MFS Communications Co Inc	UUNet Technologies Inc	Business Services	Apr-96
$1,961	Resurgens Communications Group	LDDS Communications Inc	Telecommunications	May-93
$1,906	Telefonica SA	Telefonica del Peru SA	Telecommunications	Jan-00
$1,818	Telefonica de Argentina SA	Paginas Doradas (Meller SAICIC)	Printing, Publishing and Related Services	Jun-92
$1,758	McLeodUSA Inc	SplitRock Services Inc	Telecommunications	Jan-00
$1,750	Cable & Wireless PLC	MCI Communications Corp-Whl	Business Services	May-98
$1,661	Frontier Corp	ALC Communications Corp	Telecommunications	Apr-95
$1,657	AirTouch Communications Inc	Cellular Communications Inc	Telecommunications	Apr-96
$1,611	Cable & Wireless Communicati	Bell Cablemedia PLC	Radio and Television Broadcasting Stations	Oct-96
$1,524	BCE Inc	CTV Inc	Radio and Television Broadcasting Stations	Feb-00
$1,300	Contel Cellular Inc (Contel)	McCaw Cellular Commun-AL,KY, TN	Telecommunications	Oct-89
$1,283	MCI Communications Corp	SHL Systemhouse Inc	Business Services	Sep-95
$1,250	MCI Communications Corp	Telecom USA Inc	Telecommunications	Apr-90
$1,208	Call-Net Enterprises Inc	Fonorola Inc	Telecommunications	Apr-98

Value of Transaction (US$ millions)	Acquirer	Target Company	Target Industry	Date Announced
TELECOMMUNICATIONS (continued)				
$1,200	US WEST Inc	Wometco Cable Co, Georgia Cable	Radio and Television Broadcasting Stations	Jul-94
$1,186	WorldCom Inc	CompuServe Inc (H&R Block)	Business Services	Sep-97
$1,100	Citizens Communications Co	GTE Tele Op-500,000 Lines	Telecommunications	May-93
$1,084	TeleWest PLC	SBC CableComms (SBC, Cox)	Radio and Television Broadcasting Stations	Jun-95
$1,046	Excel Communications Inc	Telco Communications Group Inc	Telecommunications	Jun-97
$1,000	British Telecommunications PLC	Concert Commun (British, MCI)	Business Services	Aug-98
$922	Nextel Communications Inc	Motorola-Mobile Radio Licenses	Telecommunications	Nov-93
$907	Teleport Communications Group	ACC Corp	Telecommunications	Nov-97
$882	Telefonica de Espana SA	Telefonica Internacional SA	Telecommunications	Nov-97
$880	LDDS Communications Inc	IDB Communications Group Inc	Telecommunications	Jul-94
$877	Global Crossing Ltd	IXnet Inc (IPC Information)	Other Financial	Feb-00
$825	Telefonica de Espana SA	Telefonica Internacional SA	Telecommunications	Aug-97
$761	Hutchison Whampoa Ltd	Cavendish International Hldgs	Real Estate; Mortgage Bankers and Brokers	Feb-91
$737	Helsingin Puhelinyhdistys	Helsingin Puhelin (Helsingin)	Telecommunications	Mar-98
$726	Energis PLC	Ision Internet AG	Business Services	Dec-00
$722	AT&T Corp	Firstcom Corp	Telecommunications	Nov-99
$719	Tiscali SpA	Liberty Surf Groupe SA	Business Services	Jan-01
$718	MetroNet Communications Corp	Rogers Telecommunications Inc	Telecommunications	May-98
$718	Nextel Communications Inc	Dial Page Inc	Telecommunications	Aug-94
$714	GTE Corp	BBN Corp	Business Services	May-97
$693	Resurgens Communications Group	Metromedia Communications	Telecommunications	Oct-92
$690	Time Warner Telecom Inc	GST Telecommunications Inc	Telecommunications	Aug-00
$680	Southwestern Bell Corp	Associated Communications Corp	Telecommunications	Feb-94
$674	Nextel Communications Inc	OneComm Corp	Telecommunications	Jul-94
$650	Southwestern Bell Corp	Montgomery Cablevision,1 Other	Radio and Television Broadcasting Stations	Feb-93
$610	Ameritech Corp	Republic Security Co Holdings	Business Services	Sep-97
$586	LDDS Communications Inc	Advanced Telecommunications	Telecommunications	Jun-92
$559	Telecom Italia SpA	Finsiel SpA (IRI/Italy)	Prepackaged Software	Oct-92
$550	CoreComm Inc	OCOM Inc (NTL Inc)	Telecommunications	Jun-98
$532	McLeodUSA Inc	CapRock Communications Corp	Construction Firms	Oct-00

Value of Transaction (US$ millions)	Acquirer	Target Company	Target Industry	Date Announced
TELECOMMUNICATIONS (continued)				
$530	United Telecommunications Inc	US Sprint Communications Co	Telecommunications	Jul-88
$517	360 Communications Co	Independent Cellular Network	Telecommunications	Apr-96
$512	Ameritech Corp	CyberTel Finl, CyberTel RSA	Telecommunications	May-91
$504	Intermedia Communications Inc	Shared Technologies Fairchild	Communications Equipment	Nov-97
TEXTILE AND APPAREL PRODUCTS				
$768	Pillowtex Corp	Fieldcrest Cannon Inc	Textile and Apparel Products	Sep-97
$690	Shaw Industries Inc	Queen Carpet Corp	Textile and Apparel Products	Aug-98
$565	Jones Apparel Group Inc	McNaughton Apparel Group Inc	Textile and Apparel Products	Apr-01
$546	Tarkett Pegulan-Werke AG	Sommer Allibert SA-Floor	Textile and Apparel Products	May-97
TOBACCO PRODUCTS				
$19,275	Philip Morris Cos Inc	Nabisco Holdings Corp (Nabisco)	Food and Related Products	Jun-00
$11,065	RJ Reynolds Tobacco Holdings	Nabisco Group Holdings Corp	Food and Related Products	Jun-00
$2,607	Cie Financiere Richemont AG	Rothmans International PLC	Tobacco Products	Apr-95
$2,238	Philip Morris Cos Inc	Colima Holding AG	Investment & Commodity Firms, Dealers and Exchanges	Jun-90
$1,729	Cie Financiere Richemont AG	Vendome Luxury Group PLC	Miscellaneous Manufacturing	Nov-97
$1,086	Imperial Tobacco Group PLC	Douwe Egbert Van Nelle Tobacco	Tobacco Products	Apr-98
$1,000	BAT Industries PLC	American Tobacco (Amer Brands)	Tobacco Products	Apr-94
$941	Gallaher Group PLC	Austria Tabakwerke AG	Tobacco Products	Jun-01
$761	DIMON Inc	Intabex Holding, Tabex Private	Investment & Commodity Firms, Dealers and Exchanges	Jan-97
$602	British American Tobacco PLC	British American Australasia	Tobacco Products	Jan-01
TRANSPORTATION AND SHIPPING, EXCEPT AIR				
$4,036	Union Pacific Corp	Southern Pacific Rail Corp	Transportation and Shipping (except air)	Aug-95
$3,748	Burlington Northern Inc	Santa Fe Pacific Corp	Transportation and Shipping (except air)	Jun-94
$2,931	Canadian National Railway Co	Illinois Central Corp	Transportation and Shipping (except air)	Feb-98
$2,731	Preussag AG	Thomson Travel Group PLC	Transportation and Shipping (except air)	May-00
$2,256	Union Pacific Corp	Chicago and North Western Tran	Transportation and Shipping (except air)	Mar-95
$2,185	Ocean Group PLC	NFC PLC	Transportation and Shipping (except air)	Feb-00

Value of Transaction (US$ millions)	Acquirer	Target Company	Target Industry	Date Announced
TRANSPORTATION AND SHIPPING, EXCEPT AIR (continued)				
$1,386	Westfarmers Ltd	Franked Income Fund	Investment & Commodity Firms, Dealers and Exchanges	Feb-01
$1,355	Westfarmers Ltd	Howard Smith Ltd	Miscellaneous Retail Trade	Jun-01
$1,342	Kvaerner ASA	Trafalgar House PLC	Construction Firms	Mar-96
$1,315	Royal Caribbean International	Celebrity Cruise Lines Inc	Transportation and Shipping (except air)	Jun-97
$1,199	Canadian National Railway Co	Wisconsin Central Transport	Transportation and Shipping (except air)	Jan-01
$1,174	Iron Mountain Inc	Pierce Leahy Corp	Transportation and Shipping (except air)	Oct-99
$900	Galileo International Inc	Apollo Travel Services	Transportation and Shipping (except air)	May-97
$878	Neptune Orient Lines Ltd	APL Ltd	Real Estate; Mortgage Bankers and Brokers	Apr-97
$784	Delmas	SCAC (Bollore Technologies)	Miscellaneous Retail Trade	Jan-92
$759	Stagecoach Holdings PLC	Porterbrook Leasing Co MEBO	Transportation and Shipping (except air)	Jul-96
$750	Osprey Maritime Ltd	Gotaas-Larsen Shipping Corp	Transportation and Shipping (except air)	May-97
$693	Inchcape PLC	IEP (Automotive) Ltd	Investment & Commodity Firms, Dealers and Exchanges	Dec-91
$691	Inchcape PLC	Tozer Kemsley & Millbourn Hldg	Wholesale Trade, Durable Goods	Dec-91
$665	Inchcape PLC	TKM	Amusement and Recreation Services	Mar-92
$661	TeeKay Shipping	Ugland Nordic Shipping A/S	Transportation and Shipping (except air)	Mar-01
$591	Bergesen DY A/S	Havtor	Oil and Gas; Petroleum Refining	Nov-95
$559	EGL Inc	Circle International Group Inc	Transportation and Shipping (except air)	Jul-00
$554	Roadway Express Inc	Arnold Industries Inc	Transportation and Shipping (except air)	Aug-01
$523	Tidewater Inc	OIL Ltd (Ocean Group PLC)	Oil and Gas; Petroleum Refining	Mar-97
TRANSPORTATION EQUIPMENT				
$40,466	Daimler-Benz AG	Chrysler Corp	Transportation Equipment	May-98
$4,125	Dana Corp	Echlin Inc	Transportation Equipment	May-98
$2,575	Autoliv Sverige AB	Morton Automotive Safety Prods	Repair Services	Sep-96
$2,563	Bayerische Motoren Werke AG	Rover Group Holdings Ltd	Transportation Equipment	Nov-93
$2,319	SPX Corp	General Signal Corp	Electronics and Electrical Equipment	Jul-98
$2,250	Federal-Mogul Corp	T&N PLC	Transportation Equipment	Oct-97
$2,199	Honeywell International Inc	Pittway Corp	Miscellaneous Manufacturing	Dec-99
$1,900	Federal-Mogul Corp	Cooper Automotive	Transportation Equipment	Aug-98
$1,839	SPX Corp	United Dominion Industries Ltd	Machinery	Mar-01

Value of Transaction (US$ millions)	Acquirer	Target Company	Target Industry	Date Announced
TRANSPORTATION EQUIPMENT (continued)				
$1,700	Valeo SA	ITT Inds-Automotive Electrical	Transportation Equipment	Jun-98
$1,100	Eaton Corp	Westinghouse Elec-Distn, Crtl	Electronics and Electrical Equipment	Aug-93
$922	ITT Industries Inc	Goulds Pumps Inc	Machinery	Apr-97
$912	MascoTech Inc	TriMas Corp	Metal and Metal Products	Dec-97
$891	Toyoda Automatic Loom Works	BT Industries AB	Machinery	Apr-00
$880	Volvo AB	BCP Branded Consumer Products	Food and Related Products	Jun-93
$790	Volkswagen AG	Rolls-Royce Motor Cars Ltd	Transportation Equipment	Apr-98
$734	Ford Motor Co	Hertz Corp (Ford Motor Co)	Repair Services	Sep-00
$720	Federal-Mogul Corp	Fel-Pro Inc (Felt Products)	Rubber and Miscellaneous Plastic Products	Jan-98
$613	Lear Seating Corp	Automotive Industries Holding	Transportation Equipment	Jul-95
$600	General Dynamics Corp	Computing Devices Intl	Measuring, Medical, Photo Equipment; Clocks	Nov-97
$581	DaimlerChrysler AG	Detroit Diesel	Machinery	Jul-00
$573	Volvo AB	VME Group NV	Machinery	Mar-95
$555	Wassall PLC	TLG PLC	Electronics and Electrical Equipment	Sep-98
$543	PACCAR Inc	DAF Trucks NV	Transportation Equipment	Oct-96
$533	Volvo AB	Procordia AB-Branded Consumer	Food and Related Products	Jun-93
WHOLESALE TRADE - DURABLE GOODS				
$13,314	USA Waste Services Inc	Waste Management Inc	Sanitary Services	Mar-98
$9,269	Northern Telecom Ltd (BCE Inc)	Bay Networks Inc	Computer and Office Equipment	Jun-98
$3,944	Aluminum Co of America (Alcoa)	Alumax Inc	Metal and Metal Products	Mar-98
$3,014	Hughes Electronics Corp	PanAmSat Corp	Telecommunications	Sep-96
$2,636	Northern Telecom Ltd (BCE Inc)	STC PLC	Wholesale Trade, Durable Goods	Nov-90
$1,145	Mattel Inc	Fisher-Price Inc	Miscellaneous Manufacturing	Aug-93
$804	Tuboscope Inc	Varco International Inc	Machinery	Mar-00
$800	Softbank Corp	Interface Grp-Exhibition Unit	Business Services	Feb-95
$737	Mattel Inc	Tyco Toys Inc	Miscellaneous Manufacturing	Nov-96
$700	Mattel Inc	Pleasant Co	Miscellaneous Retail Trade	Jun-98
$695	Resource Group International	Aker A/S	Holding Companies, Except Banks	Sep-96
$689	Avnet Inc	Kent Electronics Corp	Wholesale Trade, Durable Goods	Mar-01

Value of Transaction (US$ millions)	Acquirer	Target Company	Target Industry	Date Announced
WHOLESALE TRADE - DURABLE GOODS (continued)				
$688	Danka Business Systems PLC	Eastman Kodak-Sales Marketing	Wholesale Trade, Durable Goods	Sep-96
$679	Physician Sales & Service Inc	Gulf South Medical Supply Inc	Wholesale Trade, Durable Goods	Dec-97
$673	Rexel SA (Pinault-Printemps)	Westburne Inc	Wholesale Trade, Durable Goods	Jul-00
$610	Aluminum Co of America (Alcoa)	Inespal	Metal and Metal Products	Feb-97
$589	Meritor Automotive Inc	Arvin Industries Inc	Transportation Equipment	Apr-00
$551	Posim Bhd	Sabah Forest Industries Sdn	Paper and Related Products	Jan-96
$520	Meyer International PLC	Harcros Timber & Building	Wholesale Trade, Durable Goods	Oct-97
WHOLESALE TRADE - NONDURABLE GOODS				
$4,479	AmeriSource Health Corp	Bergen Brunswig Corp	Wholesale Trade, Nondurable Goods	Mar-01
$3,312	Ferruzzi Agricola Finanziaria	Montedison SpA	Chemicals and Related Products	Jul-90
$2,902	Enron Corp	Portland General Corp	Electric, Gas and Water Distribution	Jul-96
$2,834	Metro AG (Metro GmbH/Metro AG)	Metro Holding-Wrldwd Whl	Wholesale Trade, Nondurable Goods	Sep-98
$2,631	Metro AG (Metro GmbH/Metro AG)	Makro Holdings-European	Retail Trade, Food Stores	Jul-97
$2,542	Cardinal Health Inc	RP Scherer Corp	Drugs	May-98
$2,455	Suiza Foods Corp	Dean Foods Co	Food and Related Products	Apr-01
$2,227	Enron Corp	Wessex Water PLC	Electric, Gas and Water Distribution	Jul-98
$1,973	Nippon Oil Co Ltd	Nippon Petroleum Refining Co	Oil and Gas; Petroleum Refining	Dec-95
$1,751	Cardinal Health Inc	Bindley Western Industries Inc	Wholesale Trade, Nondurable Goods	Dec-00
$1,722	Abitibi-Price Inc	Stone-Consolidated Corp	Paper and Related Products	Feb-97
$1,436	JP Foodservice Inc	Rykoff-Sexton Inc	Wholesale Trade, Nondurable Goods	Jun-97
$1,146	Gehe Invest PLC (Gehe AG)	Lloyds Chemists PLC	Miscellaneous Retail Trade	Jan-96
$1,085	Fleming Cos Inc	Scrivner Inc (Franz Haniel)	Retail Trade, Food Stores	Jun-94
$1,084	Super Valu Stores Inc	Wetterau Inc	Wholesale Trade, Nondurable Goods	Jun-92
$907	Cardinal Health Inc	Pyxis Corp	Business Services	Feb-96
$775	McKesson Corp	General Medical Corp	Wholesale Trade, Durable Goods	Jan-97
$660	Dalgety PLC	Quaker Oats-European Petfood	Food and Related Products	Feb-95
$633	Gehe AG (Franz Haniel & Cie)	AAH PLC	Wholesale Trade, Nondurable Goods	Feb-95
$598	McKesson Corp	FoxMeyer Drug Co	Wholesale Trade, Nondurable Goods	Sep-96
$561	Booker PLC	Fitch Lovell PLC	Food and Related Products	Jul-90

Value of Transaction (US$ millions)	Acquirer	Target Company	Target Industry	Date Announced
WHOLESALE TRADE - NONDURABLE GOODS (continued)				
$560	Nine West Group Inc	US Shoe Corp-Footwear Division	Leather and Leather Products	Mar-95
$544	Cardinal Health Inc	Owen Healthcare Inc	Wholesale Trade, Nondurable Goods	Nov-96
$509	UniChem PLC	Alliance Sante SA	Wholesale Trade, Nondurable Goods	Nov-97
WOOD PRODUCTS, FURNITURE, AND FIXTURES				
$11,198	Georgia-Pacific Corp	Fort James Corp	Paper and Related Products	Jul-00
$3,596	Georgia-Pacific Corp	Great Northern Nekoosa Corp	Paper and Related Products	Oct-89
$690	Weyerhaeuser Co Ltd	TJ International Inc	Wood Products, Furniture and Fixtures	Nov-99
$650	UPM-Kymmene	Blandin Paper Co	Paper and Related Products	Sep-97
$600	Weyerhaeuser Co Ltd	Procter&Gamble-Pulp Mills, Saw	Paper and Related Products	Jun-92
$520	Weyerhaeuser Co Ltd	Bowater Inc-Pulp & Paper Mill	Paper and Related Products	Aug-98
$519	John Mansfield Group PLC	Waddington PLC	Paper and Related Products	Dec-99

|Index

ABOUT THE AUTHORS

Graeme K. Deans leads A.T. Kearney's Global Strategy and Organization management consulting practice and is chairman of A.T. Kearney Canada. He formerly led A.T. Kearney's operations across Southeast Asia and India. Mr. Deans' consulting specialties include business and marketing strategy, organizational design and effectiveness, and corporate restructuring.

Dr. Fritz Kroeger is vice president of A.T. Kearney in Germany. He is a senior management consultant and specialist in growth and strategic development and has worked in Europe, the United States, and Japan since 1976. He is author or co-author of seven books on restructuring, growth strategy, and merger integration.

Dr. Stefan Zeisel is an A.T. Kearney consultant based in Germany and a member of the European strategy core team. His areas of expertise include the automotive, consumer goods, and retail industries. He has worked for major European companies in the areas of growth strategy, mergers and acquisitions, and marketing.